British Aircraft Corporation

A History

Other titles in the Crowood Aviation Series

British Aircraft Corporation

A History

Stephen Skinner

The Crowood Press

First published in 2012 by
The Crowood Press Ltd
Ramsbury, Marlborough
Wiltshire SN8 2HR

www.crowood.com

British Library Cataloguing-in-Publication Data
A catalogue record for this book is available from
the British Library.

ISBN 978 1 84797 318 4

List of Acroyms

ADV	–	Air Defence Variant (Tornado)
AFVG	–	Anglo-French Variable Geometry (aircraft project)
ASI	–	Air Speed Indicator
AT	–	Anti-Tank
BA	–	British Airways
BAC	–	British Aircraft Corporation
BAe	–	British Aerospace
BEA	–	British European Airways
BMA	–	British Midland Airways
BOAC	–	British Overseas Airways Corporation
BUA	–	British United Airways
CA	–	Controller (Air)
ECR	–	Electronic Combat and Reconnaissance
ESRO	–	European Space Research Organization
ETPS	–	Empire Test Pilots' School
FAA	–	Federal Aviation Administration
FLIR	–	Forward Looking Infra-Red
GW	–	Guided Weapons
HAL	–	Hindustan Aircraft Limited
HEOS	–	Highly Eccentric Orbiting Satellite
IAF	–	Indian Air Force
IDS	–	Interdictor/Strike (variant of Tornado)
JFK	–	John F. Kennedy airport, New York
LRMTS	–	Laser Rangefinder and Marked Target Seeker
MBB	–	Messerschmitt-Bolkow-Blohm
MoU	–	Memorandum of Understanding
MRCA	–	Multi-Role Combat Aircraft (later Tornado)
MTU	–	Motoren-Turbinen-Union
NATO	–	North Atlantic Treaty Organization
OCU	–	Operational Conversion Unit
OR	–	Operational Requirement
RAE	–	Royal Aeronautical Establishment
RAF	–	Royal Air Force
RARDE	–	Royal Armament & Research Development Establishment
RN	–	Royal Navy
RSAF	–	Royal Saudi Air Force
SNECMA	–	Société Nationale d'Étude et de Construction de Moteurs d'Aviation
SST	–	Supersonic Transport
STAR	–	Satellites for Technology Applications and Research
STOL	–	Short Take-Off and Landing
TIALD	–	Thermal Imaging Airborne Laser Designation
TSP	–	Tornado Sustainment Programme
TTTE	–	Trinational Tornado Training Establishment
UKVG	–	United Kingdom Variable Geometry (aircraft project)
USAF	–	United States Air Force
VG	–	Variable Geometry
VTOL	–	Vertical Take-Off and Landing

Typeset by Servis Filmsetting Ltd, Stockport, Cheshire
Printed and bound in India by Replika Press

Contents

Preface

The remarkable achievements of the British Aircraft Corporation in its short, seventeen-year history have not, I believe, received their due praise. Created at the insistence of the British Government, the new company had to bring together the different histories and traditions of four proud companies and quickly meld them into a cohesive and coherent totality.

BAC could not and did not sustain itself from the existing products of its founding firms. Instead it developed new projects and distributed work around the organization to avoid imminent plant closures.

Even though more than thirty years have passed since BAC became part of the nationalized British Aerospace in 1977, some of its aircraft and guided weapons still serve while Concorde has become a singularly popular museum exhibit. Notable among the BAC aircraft still in service are the Tornado and the VC10, which were both taking part in Operation *Ellamy* to support the Libyan rebels as these words were being written in 2011.

This book covers all the aircraft and missiles that fell within the aegis of the Corporation at its formation, thereby embracing older types such as the Britannia, Viscount, Canberra and Bloodhound. I have also continued the history of BAC's products beyond nationalization in 1977.

Acknowledgements

I would like to pay special thanks for the help have I received from the following individuals and organizations: Barry Guess and Trevor Friend of BAE Systems Archives at Farnborough; Peter Hardman of BAE Systems North West Heritage at Warton; Brian Riddle of the National Aerospace Library at Farnborough, who gave access to Sir Freddie Page's unpublished memoirs; Howard Betts; Mike Phipp, MR photos; Jean-Pierre Touzier; Dieter Hitchens and his mother Mrs Marianne Hitchens, who allowed me to use the photos of the late Richard Hitchens.

My special thanks are rightly reserved for the continued enthusiasm, support and editorial help that my wife Jane provided throughout the writing of this book.

CHAPTER ONE

The Formation of the British Aircraft Corporation

Consolidation of the Aircraft Industry

On 16 September 1957 the senior management of Britain's aircraft industry was called to a meeting in Whitehall at the Ministry of Supply. During these discussions the policy of the Conservative government was outlined in no uncertain terms: if the industry was to be effective and compete as a force in world markets, the large number of British aircraft manufacturers then in existence would need to consolidate to avoid wasteful competition and better manage resources. To underline this policy, the firms were informed that the contract for a new aircraft to meet Operational Requirement 339 – the replacement for the Canberra light bomber – would only be awarded to a consortium.

At the end of the Second World War

Britain had a total of twenty-seven airframe and eight aero-engine manufacturers. Although some consolidation had taken place, the majority of these enterprises were run by powerful figures – some of them founding fathers of the British aircraft industry – who were unwilling to merge and share power with those they had regarded for so many years as the competition.

Earlier in 1957 the industry had been shocked by the 1957 Defence White Paper, which stated that the age of the missile had come and that manned aircraft would no longer be required. As a result, all existing military aircraft projects, some with great potential, were cancelled except for the English Electric Lightning fighter and the Canberra replacement. Though the industry had enough existing military orders to tide it over until the early 1960s, there was

a general consensus that now was time to redirect investment toward the civil sector and expand on the 30 per cent of output that it had traditionally provided.

The rationalization policy was officially announced on 13 May 1958 and, to encourage companies to join forces with one another, the Government announced that it would only fund work from those manufacturers who agreed to merge. As the firms were heavily dependent on the Government for both military and civil projects, they had no alternative other than to comply.

English Electric, which manufactured the Canberra, was a clear favourite to win the contract to build OR339 and their impressive proposal offered a delta-winged twin-seater with a futuristic VTOL capability provided by the extraordinary means of a lifting platform (built by Short Brothers) powered by sixty lift-jets with ten additional engines for propulsion. However, Vickers-Armstrongs' submission to OR339 also interested the defence chiefs, who asked the two firms to work together on a revised proposal, OR343. In January 1959 the Government announced the award of the contract to Vickers-Armstrongs with English Electric (to their chagrin) as a sub-contractor. An uneasy relationship then developed between the two companies, with English Electric holding the view that they should have been given control of the project as they had more recent experience with major military projects – the Canberra and the Mach 2 Lightning fighter – while Vickers had never built a truly supersonic aircraft.

English Electric Canberra WH763. The Canberra was a great success for English Electric and 1,376 were built. Its replacement was to be the TSR2, but this was cancelled and the Canberra far outlived it, serving with the RAF until 2006.
BAE Systems via Warton Heritage

A Bloodhound 1 surface-to-air missile ready to leave for public display outside the Bristol factory. Bristol Aero Collection

of £7–8m. There was progress on SST studies and the Bristol 188 research aircraft, and some hope of producing a competitor to the projected Vickers VC11 and DH121 (Trident), but that would need at least 50 per cent funding from the Government, which was very unlikely. The threat of bankruptcy for Bristol was only averted by the sale of the Bloodhound 1 surface-to-air missile system to Sweden, which brought in a substantial advance payment.

Meanwhile, Vickers/English Electric talks with de Havilland foundered when it was bought by Hawker Siddeley. With this purchase Hawker Siddeley no longer had any interest in Bristol, which sought refuge with the new grouping of Vickers and English Electric.

As the OR343 contract would be the mainstay of the two firms in the years ahead it was clear that Vickers and English Electric would need to combine their aviation interests. In order to strengthen their position, they sought another major aviation firm with solid contracts for major work. Discussions ensued with de Havilland a strong candidate with its DH121 (later named Trident), which was then regarded as having great potential. But de Havilland was simultaneously talking to Hawker Siddeley about the merger of its Engine Division with Armstrong Siddeley

Engines. At the same time the Bristol Aeroplane Company was also discussing the merger of its aircraft and engine interests with Hawker Siddeley, but Hawker Siddeley had no real interest in Bristol other than its SST (later Concorde) design team.

In October 1959 Sir Matthew Slattery, chairman of Bristol, admitted that the aircraft group was virtually in liquidation. Production of the Bristol Britannia turboprop airliner was almost at an end with just one remaining unsold, and the poor sales performance of the Britannia had brought about losses to the firm

The British Aircraft Corporation

The British Aircraft Corporation (BAC) came into being in June 1960 when the Boards of Vickers-Armstrongs, English Electric and Bristol agreed to set up a joint company. Vickers and English Electric each had a 40 per cent holding and Bristol 20 per cent in the new concern. BAC was to consist solely of their collective aircraft manufacturing companies, while their non-aviation sections would remain wholly with the parent companies. As a further part of the consolidation of the aircraft industry, Bristol's Engine Division joined with Armstrong Siddeley, de Havilland Engines and Blackburn Engines to form Bristol Siddeley Engines. Bristol's Helicopter Division became part of Westland Helicopters.

The other major British aircraft manufacturer was Hawker Siddeley, which had existed as a loose grouping since 1935 when Hawker took control of Avro, Armstrong Whitworth and Gloster. Although much work sharing had taken place between these firms they had maintained considerable independence. With the need to adhere to the Government's

Ceremonial handover of the first VC10 for the RAF at the Wisley Flight Test Centre on 30 September 1966. BAC's first Chairman, Lord Portal, is addressing the audience. BAE Systems

Sir George Edwards (1908–2003). In 1948 he became Vickers' Chief Designer, leading the team that designed the Viking, Viscount and Valiant. As Chairman and Managing Director of BAC (Operating) Ltd from 1961 to 1968 and later (1968–75) of the whole organization, he was intimately involved in all aspects of its projects during BAC's short history. BAE Systems

dictum, in 1959 Hawker Siddeley acquired Folland Aircraft followed in 1960 by de Havilland Aircraft Company and Blackburn Aircraft; in 1963 the

different company names were dropped, all the aircraft and missiles in the group now being branded as Hawker Siddeley products.

Handley Page declined to join either of the two major groups, and Shorts in Belfast was a special case as it was a nationalized company. Two major aero-engine manufacturers, Bristol Siddeley and Rolls-Royce emerged from the con-solidation process and all UK helicopter work was centralized under Westland, which took over the helicopter interests of Bristol, Fairey and Saunders-Roe.

BAC's first press release in May 1960 announced its new name, the sharehold-ings, the names of the board of directors and the capital of £20m. The combined grouping had 30,000 employees. The same release announced that the first act of the new Corporation was to buy the aircraft interests of the Hunting Group for £1.3m.

Lord Portal, renowned as Chief of the Air Staff during the Second World War, became non-executive Chairman with two Deputy Chairmen from the majority partners: Sir Charles Dunphie from Vickers and Lord Nelson from English Electric. Sir George Edwards was appointed Executive Director (Aircraft)

and Lord Caldecote Executive Director (Guided Weapons). Just over a year later Sir George became Managing Director (Aircraft) with Lord Caldecote as his deputy but with sole responsibility for Guided Weapons. Edwards later became BAC's chairman, resigning in 1975.

BAC formally came into existence on 1 June 1960. It was to have a short but impressive seventeen-year life.

BAC's Companies in June 1960

Bristol Aeroplane Company

Bristol came into being in 1910 as the British & Colonial Aeroplane Co. Ltd, leasing premises from Bristol Tramways at Filton, Bristol. By the end of that year Bristol Boxkites were in production at Filton and during the First World War the company built large numbers of air-craft, most notably the Bristol Fighter. During 1918 alone Bristol constructed 2,000 aircraft, but with the Armistice in November, Bristol along with other aviation companies had to adjust to much reduced demand. In 1920 the firm was renamed the Bristol Aeroplane Company.

Rearmament began in the late 1930s and during the Second World War Bristol aircraft included the Blenheim and Beaufort bombers and the highly successful Beaufighter fighter/torpedo bomber. After the war Bristol built and flew the huge Brabazon airliner, but this proved a commercial failure – not being ordered by any airlines – and was soon scrapped. The Brabazon was replaced by the turboprop-powered Britannia; unfortunately, despite its potential, the time lost in solving its various engine

A map indicating the major sites that were used by BAC for aircraft and guided weapons manufacture from the creation of the Corporation in 1960 until nationalization in 1977. All the sites inherited from the Bristol, English Electric, Hunting and Vickers-Armstrongs remained in use during that period except for the Luton guided weapons works (formerly English Electric), closed in 1962 and the Luton aircraft factory (formerly Hunting), closed in 1966. Also in 1966, the Cardiff guided weapons factory (formerly Bristol) was disposed of to Bristol Siddeley Engines. The Wisley Flight Test Centre (formerly Vickers) closed in 1972, while the Concorde Test Centre at Fairford only functioned from 1969 to 1976. BAE Systems

The prototype Britannia Series 301, G-ANCA, which first flew on 31 July 1956, photographed together with Bristol Fighter D8096, which was restored to airworthy condition by Bristol at Filton in 1951. G-ANCA crashed near Filton on 6 November 1957 in a fatal accident that has never been fully explained. Peter Rushby Collection

Two Concordes for BOAC (later British Airways) under construction in the huge Brabazon hangar at Filton. BAE Systems

BAC's Beagle 206 G-AVHO at BAC's Hurn plant in early 1968. The Beagle 206 design owed much to the Bristol 220 proposal, with which BAC did not proceed. G-AVHO was delivered to BAC in November 1967 and often flown by Sir George Edwards. It was sold by BAC in 1976. Author

problems delayed its entry into service, by which time airlines were ordering jet airliners such as the Boeing 707. In 1960 Bristol had four sites:

Filton, Bristol (from 1923): aircraft and guided weapons manufacture and flight test. The Filton site is now owned by Airbus, BAE Systems and GKN.

Bournemouth, Dorset (closed by September 1963): drawing office.

Cardiff, Glamorgan (1956–66): guided weapons manufacture.

Fairford, Gloucestershire (1969–77): BAC flight test centre for Concorde (Concorde flight test relocated to Filton in 1977).

Bristol's aircraft and guided weapons projects were as follows:

Bristol Britannia: at the time of the formation of BAC, production of fifty-five Bristol Britannias at Filton was complete, the last Filton-built aircraft having flown in March 1960. Production of thirty Britannias at Shorts in Belfast was virtually complete, with just three aircraft for the RAF's order remaining to fly.

Britannic wings: construction of ten wings based on the Britannia wing design for the Shorts Britannic (later re-named Belfast) military airlifter.

Bristol 188: two aircraft under construction for research into structures for high-speed supersonic aircraft.

Bloodhound: anti-aircraft missile ordered for the RAF, Sweden and Australia.

Supersonic airliner: in 1959 the Supersonic Transport Aircraft Committee chose Bristol, led by Chief Engineer Archibald Russell, to develop its design for a 132-seater airliner powered by six Olympus engines. This evolved into the Type 223, a slender 100-seater delta with four Olympuses, recognizable as a progenitor of Concorde.

Bristol 216: this was a car ferry project in collaboration with Bregeut of France. It was to be powered by twin Rolls-Royce Darts with accommodation for six cars and their passengers. BAC did not proceed with it.

Bristol 220: a twin-engined, five-seater replacement for the Avro Anson, which had started life while Sir Peter Masefield was Managing Director of Bristol. BAC did not want to proceed with this. Sir Peter left Bristol when it joined BAC and took the project with him, which was later developed into the Beagle 206.

English Electric Aviation

The English Electric Company was created in 1918 by the merger of five electrical and mechanical firms that between them produced aircraft, electric motors, transformers, turbines, locomotives and consumer goods. Following amalgamation there was a hiatus in aircraft manufacture until 1923 when the first English Electric aircraft, the single-seat Wren monoplane, made its maiden flight from Preston. The Wren was succeeded by the large Kingston and Ayr flying boats, which were flown at Lytham St Anne's, just a few miles north of Warton. However, aircraft development ceased in 1926 due

to a reduction in aircraft orders from the government after the First World War.

In 1938 as part of the Government's rearmament programme English Electric re-entered the aircraft industry as a sub-contractor. Preston was chosen as the aircraft factory and an airfield was built at Samlesbury. During the Second World War it produced aircraft for other manufacturers, for example the 770 Handley Page Hampdens and 2,145 Halifaxes. After the war the firm made modifications to over 200 Avro Lincolns and between 1944 and 1952 licence-built 1,369 de Havilland Vampires.

Most significantly in the immediate post-war years, English Electric shocked the other firms in the British aircraft industry with its startlingly successful Canberra jet-engined light bomber. English Electric's Chief Engineer, Teddy Petter, had first designed a jet fighter-bomber when he worked for Westland, but had been unable to develop it. English Electric, however, was ready to take up the challenge. The project was substantially developed to become the Canberra, an outstanding design that first flew in 1949 and was sold in large numbers to the RAF and many other countries, besides being licence-built in the USA and Australia. It served with the RAF from 1951 until 2006.

Following on from the Canberra, before Petter left the firm he started the design of a supersonic fighter that was developed by his successor, Freddie Page, to become the P.1A, which first flew in 1954. This led onto the P.1B in 1957 which, with further refinement, entered service with the RAF as the Lightning in 1960. English Electric's sites were:

Warton, Lancashire (from 1947): aircraft manufacture and flight test.

Samlesbury, Lancashire (from 1940): aircraft manufacture and flight test.

Preston, Lancashire (1918–26 and 1938–90): aircraft manufacture.

Accrington, Lancashire (1952–68): passed over to GEC (Engineering) in

Between 1940 and 1942, 770 Handley Page Hampdens were licence-built at English Electric's Samlesbury site. These were succeeded on the production line by another Handley Page design – the Halifax – and, following the war, Vampires, Canberras, Lightnings and the TSR2. Author

The penultimate Development Batch Lightning, XG336, is rolled out at Warton. It first flew in August 1959 and served briefly with the Air Fighting Development Squadron.
BAE Systems via Warton Heritage

Warton was used by the USAAF as a repair and overhaul facility for aircraft and engines during 1942–45. It was then unused until 1947 when English Electric took it over for flight testing. In this photo, looking east over the 7,946ft (2,422m) runway 08/26 , the main hangers and flight test apron are on the left of the photo. Warton became the centre for final assembly and flight test under BAC and is still in use today with BAE Systems.
BAE Systems via Warton Heritage

Close-up of a TSR2 under construction at Weybridge. The rear fuselages were built at Samlesbury, the forward fuselage and wings at Weybridge; assembly of the prototypes took place at Weybridge. The fineness of the wings and all-moving tail and elevons is evident in this photo.
BAE Systems via Warton Heritage

1968, but continued with aircraft component manufacture.

Luton, Bedfordshire (1950–62): guided weapons manufacture.

Stevenage, Hertfordshire (from 1952): guided weapons manufacture.

The Samlesbury and Warton sites are now part of BAE Systems. The Stevenage site is still in existence today as part of MBDA and Astrium. English Electric' projects in hand in 1960 were:

Canberra: production of 925 Canberras manufactured in the UK – including seventy-five built by Avro, seventy-five by Handley Page and 132 by Shorts – was virtually complete, with just ten remaining to be completed by Shorts. English Electric also had fifteen new-build Canberra in stock for future orders. Australia built forty-eight Canberras and the USA (as the Martin B-57) 403, making a grand total of 1,376.

A Thunderbird air-to-air missile of the British Army, deployed in the field with a gas-masked soldier guarding it. MBDA

Hunting Jet Provost T.51 CJ701, the first of twelve delivered to the Ceylon (now Sri Lankan) Air Force in 1959, on its way to the Farnborough Air Display in September that year. Ceylon was the launch customer for this variant of the RAF's trainer. It possessed twin machine guns and underwing ordnance racks. This machine is preserved in Colombo, Sri Lanka. Author

Lightning: by June 1960, forty-two Lightnings and related development aircraft had flown, these being the two P.1As, three P.1Bs, twenty pre-production aircraft, fifteen F.1s and two T.4s. Lightning F.1s, F.1As, F.2s and T.4s were in large-scale production for the RAF.

TSR2: under development with Vickers for the RAF. The prototype was due to fly in 1963.

Blue Water: a battlefield missile with a nuclear warhead.

Thunderbird: an anti-aircraft missile in service with the British Army.

PT428: an anti-aircraft missile system.

Hunting Aircraft

Edgar Percival founded Percival Aircraft in 1933 in Gravesend, moving to Luton three years later and joining the Hunting Group in 1944. Percival Aircraft was renowned for its extensive range of light aircraft such as the Mew

Gull, in which the famous pilot Alex Henshaw made record-breaking flights during the 1930s.

Post-war, Percival produced the Prince and Pembroke family of communications aircraft and Provost piston-engined trainer for the RAF. The Jet Provost military trainer first flew in 1954 and in the same year the firm was renamed Hunting Percival, becoming simply Hunting Aircraft in 1957. That same year the RAF adopted the Jet Provost, which soon began to win export orders, enabling Hunting to set up quantity production. When Hunting was purchased by BAC in 1960 it had plenty of Jet Provost work in hand but it remained a small operation with limited facilities; indeed it had just one site:

Luton, Bedfordshire (1936–66): aircraft manufacture and flight test.

Hunting's aircraft projects in 1960 were:

Jet Provost: eighty-one Jet Provost T.3s in service with the RAF, 120 more being built. 185 Jet Provost T.4s ordered in late 1960.

Hunting H.126: a single jet-flap research aircraft under construction.

BAC 221: conversion of the first Fairey Delta 2 into a supersonic research aircraft with a slender delta wing. BAC transferred this conversion from Hunting to Bristol's factory at Filton before Hunting had actually received the aircraft.

Hunting H.107: a project for a fifty-nine seat airliner with twin Bristol Siddeley

G-AWAU was the Vickers Vimy replica constructed at Weybridge and Hurn between 1967 and 1969. It made its 30-minute maiden flight from Brooklands to Wisley on the evening of 1 June 1969 flown by BAC test pilot 'Dizzy' Addicott. It later appeared at the Paris Air Show alongside Concorde, but was damaged by fire at Manchester Airport and reconstructed at Wisley for static display at the RAF Museum, Hendon. BAE Systems

The sole Vickers Valiant B.2, WJ954 at Vickers Wisley Flight Test Centre. It was intended for the low-level 'pathfinder' role with a beefed-up structure to cope with the stresses of low-altitude flight, and was much faster than the Valiant B.1 bomber. A total of 107 B.1s was built, the last one in 1957. WJ594 had a short life, first flying in September 1953 and being scrapped in 1958. In the background is RAF Boeing B-29 Washington WW349, which was employed on missile trials by Vickers. It was written off when a Valiant collided with it on the Wisley apron on 29 July 1955.
Paul Robinson

BS75 engines of around 7,000lb thrust, a 500mph cruise speed and a range of 600 miles. By September 1960 this had become the BAC 107, and later turned into the BAC One-Eleven.

Vickers-Armstrongs (Aircraft)

The shipbuilding, engineering and armaments giant Vickers made its first foray into aviation with the construction of an airship in 1908. The next steps were the construction of aircraft and the establishment of a flying school at the Brooklands racing track in Weybridge, Surrey. During the First World War the firm was engaged in the manufacture of aircraft designed by the Royal Aircraft Factory. Vickers' own designs from the war years included the Vickers Vimy bomber made famous by the first non-stop crossing of the Atlantic, piloted by Alcock and Brown. Following the war Vickers continued in aircraft manufacture, merging with Armstrong Whitworth in 1928 to become Vickers-Armstrongs (this merger did not include Armstrong Whitworth Aircraft Ltd) and taking over Supermarine at Southampton. With this acquisition Vickers-Armstrongs, as owners of its subsidiary Vickers-Supermarine, became the parent firm of the Spitfire fighter, the most famous British aircraft of the Second World War. Vickers also built the Wellington bomber, which played an important role with the RAF in the early years of the war.

Before the end of the Second World War Vickers had started planning the Viking, a civil airliner that sold in respectable numbers. This was superseded by the much more technically advanced, turboprop-engined Viscount, which sold well worldwide and generated reasonable profits for Vickers. Simultaneously the first 'V' bomber, the Vickers Valiant, entered production while the Vickers-Supermarine division was developing a series of jet-engined fighters, starting with the rather uninspiring Attacker for the Royal Navy. Next came the Swift, which became the RAF's first swept-wing fighter but which was beset by problems and was rapidly superseded by the Hawker Hunter. These were followed by the final Supermarine aircraft, the Scimitar naval strike fighter, and in 1957 Supermarine was fully integrated into Vickers.

With the end of Valiant manufacture in 1957 and only a small order for seventy-six Scimitars for the Royal Navy, Vickers now had to rely on the more challenging civil airliner market in which, in addition to the Viscount, Vickers now had the four-turboprop Vanguard and four-jet VC10 under development. However,

Brooklands airfield, the main site of Vickers-Armstrongs at Weybridge and later the BAC Weybridge Division. The short, restricted 3,600ft (1,100m) runway is evident. The large hangers on the far left were built for VC10 construction. The two long, smaller hangers nearer to the runway were used for Viscount and TSR2 production.
BAE Systems

A Viscount Series 828 for All Nippon Airways at Hurn with the main production line hangers behind it in 1962. In the background, a Valiant is receiving modification work. The Hurn factory built the majority of the Vickers Viscounts and BAC One-Elevens. BAE Systems

The prototype VC10, G-ARTA, under construction in one of the two large hangers built for this task on the south side of the Weybridge site in 1962. The tail of a Vanguard for BEA is also just visible. BAE Systems

Vickers lobbied hard for the 'Canberra replacement' (OR339) contract and managed to become prime contractor for TSR2 with English Electric in a subordinate role.

In 1960 Vickers' sites were a follows:

Weybridge, Surrey (1915–89): aircraft and guided weapons manufacture.

Hurn, Dorset (1951–84): aircraft manufacture and production flight test.

Wisley, Surrey (1943–72): aircraft experimental flight and production flight test.

The Vickers-Armstrongs Supermarine factory at South Marston, near Swindon, Wiltshire, which was completing the last five of an order for seventy-six Scimitars for the Royal Navy, did not become part of the Corporation. It remained with Vickers and became the headquarters of Vickers-Armstrongs (Engineering). The factory at Itchen remained with the parent company but continued to produce aircraft sub-assemblies, notably for TSR2.

Vickers had the following work in hand in 1960:

Viscount: of the 444 Viscounts manufactured between 1948 and 1964 at Hurn and Weybridge, twenty-two remained to be built following the formation of BAC in mid-1960.

Vanguard: of the forty-three Vanguards on order eight had flown from Weybridge and were engaged in the test programme. None had yet entered service. The final delivery was in April 1964.

VC10: Thirty-five VC10s were on order for BOAC. The prototype VC10 first flew in June 1962 and a larger, longer-range Super VC10 was in development.

A new account programme for the Filton factory was the manufacture of wings for the Shorts Belfast military freighter, of which only ten were built. The wings and other empennage were based on the design of the Britannia. XR365 is shown landing at the 1970 Farnborough Air Show: this aircraft was the last Belfast to remain in service and was withdrawn from use in 2010. Author

TSR2: Under development with English Electric as a supersonic bomber for the RAF. The prototype was due to fly in 1963.

Vigilant: the V.891 Vigilant, a wire-guided infantry anti-tank weapon built for the British Army.

Vickers VC11: a project for a four-engined, 138-seat medium-range airliner in a configuration similar to the VC10. BAC did not eventually proceed with this.

Account Responsibilities for Existing and Future Products

The boards of the separate companies continued in existence, keeping account responsibility (profits and losses) for certain products. However, as Hunting had been purchased by the new Corporation, all of its aircraft and projects became part of BAC.

'Old' account types whose profits and losses stayed with the parent companies were as follows:

Bristol: Britannia, Bristol 188 and Bloodhound Mark 1.

English Electric: Canberra, Lightning F.1–F.3 and T.4, Thunderbird Mark 1.

Vickers: Viscount, Vanguard, VC10 and Super VC10, Scimitar and Vigilant.

'New' account types, whose profits and losses were the responsibility of BAC:

Bristol: Short Britannic (later renamed Belfast) wings, BAC 221, Bloodhound Mark 2.

English Electric: Lightning F.2a, F.5, F.6 and T.5, *Blue Water*, Thunderbird Mark 2.

Vickers: VC11 (though this was not proceeded with).

BAC: TSR2.

CHAPTER TWO

From Formation to Nationalization

Integration and Early Challenges

There was no magical process by which Bristol, English Electric, Hunting and Vickers could become BAC overnight. However, in order to promote the new entity, within a few weeks the Board of Directors decided that companies were to refer to themselves as, for example, 'Vickers-Armstrongs (Aircraft) Limited, a member company of the British Aircraft Corporation'. A huge exercise took place to educate all staff in the products of the new firm: the Bristol staff newspaper *Airframe* became the BAC company newspaper and a company road show was organized to meld together the 30,000 employees and to allay fears of redundancy.

An early challenge for the management was to find airframe work for the large Bristol factory at Filton, with its huge Brabazon hangars, which was virtually bereft of work: now that production of the Britannia had ended the factory had very little to do besides the construction of the two Bristol 188 supersonic

research aircraft. As a result, the Fairey Delta 2/BAC221 conversion was transferred there from Hunting at Luton, while some VC10 work, Canberra modification, Lightning conversion and Lightning T.5 trainer front fuselage production soon followed. It was fortunate for the Filton workforce that Bristol joined BAC, for if Hawker Siddeley had become the owners it would almost certainly have closed Filton.

Both the major partners' best sellers (English Electric's Canberra and Vickers' Viscount) were coming to the end of their production runs. However, the great advantage for English Electric was the huge demand for Canberra overhaul, refurbishment and modification work, which continued throughout the history of BAC and well beyond.

1962 and Guided Missile Cancellations

In 1962 BAC's Chairman, Viscount Portal of Hungerford, reported on excellent progress with the company's integra-

tion of its activities made during its first financial year. Total sales amounted to £75m: £28m from new projects and £47m from work started prior to BAC's formation. The value of BAC's order book at the end of 1961 was an impressive £238m: £118m for new and £120m for pre-merger projects. There was the first mention of co-operation with Sud Aviation on a supersonic transport which, less than eight years later, was to fly in the form of Concorde. This report heralded what appeared to be a positive start for the new Corporation.

Yet even as the Corporation was consolidating it became the victim of Government cuts, when in 1962 two of English Electric's guided weapons projects were cancelled. These were the PT428 cancelled in February, which was a lightweight, eighteen-round anti-aircraft missile battery, followed in August by the *Blue Water* tactical missile for the Army which had been due to enter service in 1965. The loss of these two systems was such a serious blow that it provoked the closure of English Electric's guided weapons factory at Luton, though the Stevenage works remained open.

On a brighter note, the prototype Vickers VC10, Britain's largest airliner, successfully made its first flight on 29 June 1962 from the Weybridge plant. It participated noisily and impressively at the Farnborough Air Show in September that year. With work proceeding on Concorde, the Chairman of BAC accurately predicted that Concorde would be the first supersonic airliner to enter service; at this juncture he could not have known that during its operational

A dynamic photo of pre-production Lightning XG313 during the testing of the 2-inch rocket packs in 1960. It had first flown on 2 February 1959 and was sent to Saudi Arabia as an instructional machine in 1968. It is preserved in Dhahran, Saudi Arabia.
BAE Systems via Warton Heritage

On 29 June 1962 the prototype VC10, G-ARTA, sets out on its maiden flight from the extremely short 3,600ft (1,100m) runway situated within the former Brooklands racing circuit at the Weybridge factory. Owing to the railway embankment to the north, all flights out took place from the north and landings from the south. BAE Systems

existence it would not have any serious competitors.

Meanwhile, production of the RAF's first supersonic fighter, the Lightning, was well in hand at Samlesbury and Warton, and by the end of 1962 fifty of the early F.1 and F.1A variants were in service with the RAF. The first batch of TSR2s

under construction at Samlesbury and Weybridge had advanced well, and the first flight was expected by end of 1963. In fact, the prototype missed this schedule and did not fly until late in 1964. Work was also proceeding at Luton on the company-funded pressurized version of the Jet Provost trainer, to be designated the T.5.

One-Eleven

A major event was the maiden flight on 20 August 1963 of the One-Eleven from the Hurn plant; the 'bus-stop jet', as it was then marketed, became the major airliner project of BAC. It had already accumulated sixty orders at the time of its first flight and the predictions were that it would emulate the Viscount and make 400 sales. However, despite its initial commercial success, it failed to achieve expectations. Two factors impeded progress: the problematic test programme and the difficulties in stretching an already optimized design, compounded by the lack of growth potential in the Spey engine.

Only two months after its first flight, on 22 October, the first One-Eleven was on stalling tests when it entered a 'deep stall' – at the time an insufficiently understood phenomenon – and crashed, killing all the crew. BAC had to introduce modifications to prevent this happening again,

The prototype BAC One-Eleven, G-ASHG, in the livery of launch customer British United, being towed back to one of the Hurn final assembly hangars in July 1963. Note how the sign on the other final assembly hanger behind refers to Vickers-Armstrongs (Aircraft) Ltd. It was not until the following year, when BAC established a divisional structure, that this company became BAC (Weybridge Division). BAE Systems

and the loss of the prototype cast a long shadow over the project for customers and potential customers. Despite the setback, though, the One-Eleven entered service with British United Airways on 9 April 1965.

The Creation of the BAC Divisions

From 1 January 1964, the process of integration was accelerated when the old names of the firms were superseded by the Corporation's title. Thus Bristol became BAC (Filton Division), English Electric became BAC (Preston Division), Hunting was BAC (Luton Division) and Vickers was renamed BAC (Weybridge Division). The guided weapons sections had already been united in March 1963 as the Guided Weapons Division, which combined the missile and space interests of Bristol, English Electric and Vickers. These Divisions were all subsidiaries of BAC (Operating) Ltd; this company reported to the BAC (Holdings) Board, on which sat representatives of the shareholding companies of the Corporation (Bristol, English Electric and Vickers-Armstrongs) and which retained control of broader policy.

TSR2 Cancellation and its Ramifications

1965 was to prove an exceedingly difficult year for the new Corporation. On 6 April BAC received a calamitous blow when the TSR2 low-level strike aircraft was cancelled. For a time the very existence of BAC was in doubt as a compensation settlement from the Government was not forthcoming until 1967. 5,000 BAC employees lost their jobs, primarily at Weybridge and Samlesbury. Then, as there was over-capacity, at the end of 1965 the former Hunting factory at Luton

The effect on the size of the workforce of the TSR2 cancellation. BAE Systems

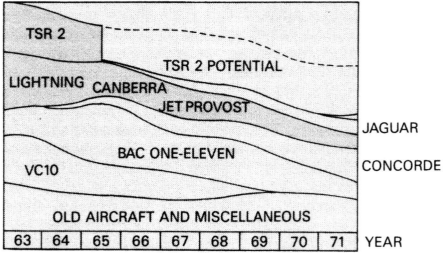

BAC PRODUCTION MANNING — AIRCRAFT

SOURCE: BAC MANNING RECORDS TO 1971

Partially-built XR226 awaiting the scrap men at Weybridge in September 1965. The forward fuselage, built at Weybridge, is in yellow primer while the rear fuselage, built at Samlesbury, is in white paint. This aircraft was intended for armament trials. Richard Hitchins

was closed with the loss of 2,000 jobs and its work redistributed.

Elsewhere, there were considerable problems with BAC's civil programmes. Sales of the VC10 and Super VC10 had been put under severe threat when Sir Giles Guthrie, Chairman of BOAC, attempted to drastically reduce the airline's order for it, which badly dented its limited sales potential. The BAC One-Eleven had just entered service and was only beginning to repay its £30m development costs, for which the Government had originally contributed launch aid of £9.75m. BAC wanted to build the larger One-Eleven 500 to stave off competition

from larger versions of the Douglas DC-9 and Boeing 737, which were outselling the One-Eleven. However, BAC could not afford to fund this development without Government aid. Meanwhile, Concorde was suffering heavy press criticism in the UK and the Labour Government wished to cancel the project; fortunately, owing to French pressure, Concorde's development was not halted.

A long tussle then ensued between BAC and the Labour Government over the settlement of financial compensation for the TSR2 cancellation. BAC threatened the Government with an eventual rundown of the business owing to

its poor financial position if it did not receive the sum it believed it was due, but the Government was eager to force a merger of BAC with Hawker Siddeley by delaying settlement of BAC's claim. The BAC Board might have accepted being bought out at a fair valuation, but had little desire to be forcibly merged with their investment locked within Hawker Siddeley.

Fortunately for the Preston Division, matters gradually improved when in May 1965 the British and French Governments signed a Memorandum of Understanding on the development of two aircraft: an advanced strike/trainer

Following the TSR2 cancellation this photo was taken of TSR2 XR219, Lightning F.6 XR755 and Canberra B.2 WD937 at Warton.
BAE Systems via Warton Heritage

BAC's display stand at the 1967 Paris Air Show boldly stating the company is the 'Most powerful aerospace company in Europe'. There are models of the Jaguar centre left and the stillborn Anglo-French Variable-Geometry on the extreme right. The BAC display also claims that the company has an order book of £340m, of which 64.5 per cent, or £242m, were for export. BAE Systems

One of the factors in BAC's recovery from the TSR2's cancellation was the Saudi Arabian contract to supply Lightnings and Strikemasters. Photographed at Warton, this is the first Lightning F.53 for the Royal Saudi Arabian Air Force, registered 53-666, with the extended belly fuel tank of the Lightning F.6, rocket pods and pylon-mounted trial bombs. Originally flown as an RAF F.6, XR722, it was modified to become the first F.53 and first flew in its new form on 19 October 1966.
BAE Systems via Warton Heritage

aircraft and the Anglo-French Variable-Geometry aircraft. Although the French withdrew from the latter at an early stage, the strike/trainer was developed into the Jaguar, which flew with the RAF and was also exported successfully. Under Lord Plowden the Government had set up a committee to examine the aviation industry, which reported at the end of 1965. Chief among its recommendations was that the aviation industry had to collaborate with Europe on all major projects, as already demonstrated by the Jaguar/AFVG collaboration with France.

1965 was to end on a high note when, in December, BAC received a real fillip by winning a huge order from Saudi Arabia for Lightnings and Strikemasters (the latter a light-attack derivative of the Jet Provost) worth £100m. In 1966 the Government finally agreed to provide £9m support for the One-Eleven 500 and in September 1967 agreed a compensation deal on TSR2 with BAC. So, with improving income from One-Eleven sales on the civil side, the future of the Preston Division was more than stabilized by the start of Jaguar work, the launch of the Saudi Arabian Lightning and Strikemaster production, and also manufacture of the tails for the RAF's new Phantoms.

1967 proved a watershed for BAC when its fortunes recovered sufficiently for it to resist a forced merger with Hawker Siddeley, and talks were abandoned. The Government continued to press BAC to merge, but as the firm was intransigent talks of merger were abandoned for the time being.

During 1968 BAC continued making a substantial contribution to the British economy with record export deliveries of £81.5m, representing 63 per cent of the £128.3m earned by the firm. New orders in the year were valued at £149.7m, of

The 200th airliner built by BAC for a North American customer, American Airlines' N5019 at BAC's Hurn factory. This figure of 200 consisted of 147 Viscounts and fifty-three One-Elevens in March 1966; more One-Elevens were to follow. BAE Systems

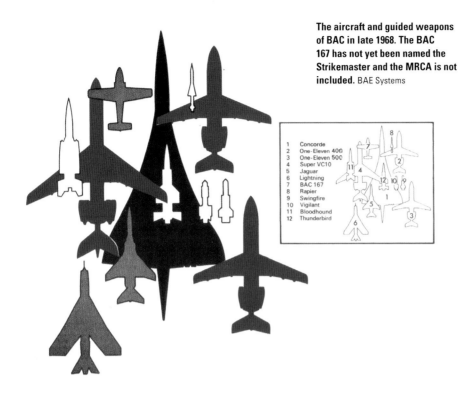

The aircraft and guided weapons of BAC in late 1968. The BAC 167 has not yet been named the Strikemaster and the MRCA is not included. BAE Systems

1 Concorde
2 One-Eleven 400
3 One-Eleven 500
4 Super VC10
5 Jaguar
6 Lightning
7 BAC 167
8 Rapier
9 Swingfire
10 Vigilant
11 Bloodhound
12 Thunderbird

BAC Organisation

Four Divisions

British Aircraft Corporation has four divisions, seven major factories, six airfields, and employs over 36,000 people. The four divisions are:—

Weybridge	Concorde, BAC One-Eleven, BAC Three-Eleven.
Filton	Concorde
Preston	Lightning, Jaguar, BAC 167, M.R.C.A.
Guided Weapons	Thunderbird, Bloodhound, Rapier, Sea Wolf, Vigilant, Swingfire, and communication satellite programmes.

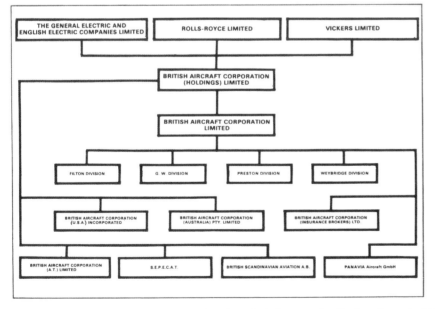

The organizational structure of BAC in late 1968. Note how the Strikemaster is still referred to as the BAC 167 and the MRCA only gained its name much later. The Corporation's workforce totals 36,000 at that date. BAE Systems

which £101.8m or 68 per cent were for export while the total value of BAC's export backlog was £103m. Many of these export deliveries were of One-Elevens to airlines worldwide, and in the face of stiff competition the lengthened One-Eleven 500 finally took to the air in the summer of 1967.

GEC Buys English Electric

Rolls-Royce had acquired Bristol in 1966 and in so doing had become a 20 per cent share holder in BAC. In mid-1968 Rolls-Royce indicated its wish to sell this holding. Under the BAC founding agreement English Electric and Vickers had first refusal, but if neither wished to bid then Rolls-Royce's holding would be offered to Hawker Siddeley Aviation. Therefore, if English Electric and Vickers wished to avoid their British competitor having direct access to their business affairs, they would need to buy the holding to keep Hawker Siddeley out of the picture.

This difficult situation was compounded when Plessey entered the fray with a bid for English Electric, indicating that if successful they would divest themselves of English Electric's 40 per cent holding in BAC. The Government shrewdly identified this as an opportunity to merge Hawker Siddeley and BAC. However, the Corporation was now on a much firmer footing and able to resist this threat, having rebounded after the trauma of TSR2 cancellation. In November 1968 a new player emerged. GEC was a major UK firm producing engineering, consumer and defence electronics. GEC bid for English Electric and succeeded against Plessey in buying it.

GEC's purchase brought a new member onto the BAC board in the shape of Sir Arnold Weinstock, a man described by the *Guardian* newspaper as 'Britain's premier post-Second-World-War industrialist'. Although he was primarily interested in guided weapons, Weinstock was content for the airframe side to continue to the extent that in 1972 both Vickers and GEC reluctantly bought out Rolls-Royce's 20 per cent share holding to become the joint owners of BAC. With a partnership of two owners, BAC benefited from a period of stability for its remaining years in private ownership.

At the end of 1968 BAC's order book stood at a value of over £350 million, of

The first British Concorde prototype, G-BSST, at the Fairford, Gloucester Flight Test Centre with the BAC staff based there. In the front centre is Brian Trubshaw, BAC's Concorde Chief Test Pilot, wearing orange trousers with his deputy, John Cochrane, on his right. G-BSST first flew from Filton to Fairford on 2 March 1969. BAE Systems

Concorde, Jaguar and MRCA

1969 proved an auspicious year for the company with the first flight of the French- and British-assembled Concorde prototypes on 2 March and 9 April, respectively. The challenging but ultimately successful seven-year test programme had just begun. A month later, on 14 May, a Memorandum of Understanding was signed by representatives of the British, West German and Italian Governments to establish a joint development and production programme for a Multi-Role Combat Aircraft (MRCA), which was later named the Tornado. This project was to provide BAC and its successor firms with work for many years, and at the time of writing still does. The first British prototype of the Anglo-French Jaguar flew on 12 October 1969, and this also proved to be a very productive and profitable programme.

which more than £225 million was for export. This was stated in the annual report for 1969 by the Chairman of BAC (Holdings), Sir Reginald Verdon-Smith, his first since taking office in January 1968 following the retirement of Viscount Portal.

By 1968 BAC and its constituent firms had, since the early 1950s, sold 243 medium and large subsonic airliners on the North American continent, to earn £200 million, compared with forty-three such aircraft sold to North America by the rest of the European and British industries combined. For future exports, the Corporation was relying primarily on further developments of the One-Eleven, Concorde, Jaguar and MRCA, and on three guided weapon systems: Rapier, Sea Wolf and Swingfire.

BAC Three-Eleven Cancellation and Increasing Profits

With the military and Guided Weapons Divisions flourishing but with no serious outlook for substantial Concorde sales, the only civil project with sales prospects was the One-Eleven, whose sales had passed their peak. Arguably the One-Eleven should have been developed more at this juncture, but instead the wholly new BAC Three-Eleven wide-body airliner was projected. There was serious airline interest in the project and BAC expended the considerable sum of £4m on these proposals and initial project work, which the Labour Government viewed

Lightning 53-686 was first flown on 11 June 1968 and was shown as G-AWON in a static display at the 1968 Farnborough Air Show. It proudly displayed the Queen's Award for Industry 1967–68. Author

The first BAC-assembled Tornado, XX946, during ground tests at Warton. BAE Systems

favourably. However, the change of government in 1970 was to bode ill for the Three-Eleven, and in the December the new Conservative administration indicated that it was not willing to provide launch aid.

In 1971, in a further reorganization of the Corporation the Weybridge and Filton Divisions became the Commercial Aircraft Division and the Preston Division became the Military Aircraft Division. The company structure was now streamlined with just three product divisions: civil aircraft, military aircraft and guided weapons.

From the shareholders' viewpoint the decision not to launch the Three-Eleven was far from troublesome. Where profits

in 1970 had been weak, in the years between 1971 and 1976 they grew steadily from £4.1m to £40m. Commercial aircraft revenue was a declining feature while military aircraft, guided weapons and, to a lesser extent, space and satellites were the real money-makers. The reason for this large increase in profits was that a number of projects were emerging from the development stage into production and delivery.

Queen's Award

In 1974 as a mark of the Military Aircraft Division's export prowess it received the Queen's Award for success in exports.

The citation referred to BAC's success in exporting the Lightning, Strikemaster, Canberra and Jaguar. Between 1971 and 1974 exports of these had increased by £14.5m, accounting for 80 per cent of the Division's sales. Over that same period the value of aircraft and spares sold accounted to £80m. The Strikemaster, which was wholly funded by BAC, earned £45m in sales to nine countries in 1974, while Lightning sales to Saudi Arabia and Kuwait brought in £80m.

BAC, in its entirety, had been awarded the Queens Award on three previous occasions, but this was the first time that one Division had received such an accolade. In 1975 the Guided Weapons Division doubled the previous year's honour by receiving two Queens Awards, one for Exports and one for Technological Innovation.

Tornado and Concorde

In August 1974 the first MRCA (later Tornado) prototype flew and its multinational flight test programme began. The Tornado was to prove a money-spinner for BAC and its successors. On the civil front, on 24 May 1976 Concorde entered airline service with British Airways and Air France. This was the culmination of an immense task: the

One of the money-spinners of the Guided Weapons Division in the later years of BAC was the Rapier missile system. BAE Systems

All six types of the Military Aircraft Division on the apron at Warton in 1975. All of these aircraft contributed substantially to BAC's profitability. From top left: Strikemaster, Lightning F.3, Canberra B.2 WH952 (the Tornado chase aircraft), the first British Tornado prototype, XX946 (now in camouflage), Jet Provost T.3A XM352 and Jaguar GR.1. BAE Systems via Warton Heritage

BAC's achievement, five of the seven BAC aircraft at the final Farnborough Air Show before the company's nationalization in 1976: (from left) Concorde G-BBDG, Jaguar International XZ362, RSAF Strikemaster 1124 (temporarily G-BECI), One-Eleven N111NA and Tornado GR.1 XX950. BAE Systems

research, development, production and successful flight testing of the world's only supersonic airliner, the pinnacle of BAC's aviation engineering achievement.

Nationalization

In 1974 the Conservatives lost the General Election and a Labour Government was returned to power. The new Government was determined to nationalize certain major industrial sectors, including the aviation industry. For GEC and Vickers this meant they would each lose one of

the most important assets in their portfolio of interests. Vickers was to suffer a double blow as shipbuilding, the other major asset of their engineering portfolio, was also to be nationalized.

Just prior to nationalization in 1977 BAC had announced a record profit after taxation of £14.1 million. The Corporation's order book stood at a record £850 million. Trading profit on all 1975 group sales of £307.1 million amounted to £26.9 million. BAC exports in 1975 totalled a record £199.6 million. Notwithstanding the strength of military and guided weapons sales, there were

lean times for the Commercial Aircraft Division: owing to the decline in world airliner sales and lack of new projects 5,000 redundancies had been declared. But BAC was in a healthy condition and ready for nationalization, focusing on its core areas of missile and military aircraft sales.

The Government bill to nationalize both the aircraft and shipbuilding industries was eventually passed into law in March 1977. From 29 April 1977, BAC, Hawker Siddeley, their Guided Weapons Divisions and Scottish Aviation become British Aerospace.

CHAPTER THREE

BAC's Mature Civil and Military Aircraft Programmes

When BAC came into being in 1960 it inherited two airliner programmes that were well past their peak and one other that seemed certain to fail to penetrate its intended market. These were, respectively: the Bristol Britannia, where only three remained to be completed; the Vickers Viscount, where production had drastically slowed; and the Viscount's intended successor, the Vanguard, which had few orders and whose production life was to prove all too short.

There was also a military type, English Electric's exceedingly successful Canberra: although its production was virtually at an end, substantial refurbishment work was to continue right throughout the existence of BAC and then with British Aerospace until 1988.

Bristol Britannia

The final Filton-built Britannia was delivered to the RAF in March 1960, just a few months before the formation of BAC, and the last three Britannias were

delivered to the RAF in late 1960 from the second production line at Shorts in Belfast. Later, as part of BAC, Bristol continued to have an involvement with the type as it held design authority and RAF Britannias regularly returned to Filton for maintenance.

The Bristol Britannia seemed to have the makings of a success story when its flight trials began in 1952, but progress was hindered by the technical failings of its Bristol Proteus turboprops, which severely delayed its entry into service until 1957. By then major airlines were already introducing jet airliners such as the Boeing 707 and Douglas DC-8, so the market for large medium- to long-range turboprops had drastically diminished.

Bristol projected several Britannia developments, but the attraction of large jetliners spelled the end of production and only eighty-five were produced. In Belfast, Shorts' connection with the Britannia continued after the end of production as the wing and tail surfaces were incorporated into the Shorts Belfast

military freighter, and Filton manufactured the Belfast's wings. Bristol's reward for all its endeavours on the Britannia was a large loss, in the order of £7–8m.

Specification – Britannia 310	
Length:	124ft 3in (37.87m)
Wingspan:	142ft 3in (43.36m)
Height:	36ft 8in (11.18m)
MTOW:	180,000lb (82,000kg)
Cruising speed:	355mph (571km/h)
Range:	4,100 miles (6,600km)
Passengers:	114
Powerplant:	4 × 4,120ehp Bristol Proteus 755/761
Britannias built:	85 (55 at Filton, 30 at Shorts, Belfast)

Vickers Viscount

At the formation of BAC in June 1960, production of the once best-selling Viscount turboprop airliner had slowed to a trickle, though there were twenty-two more deliveries before production ceased in February 1964. These deliveries were to Lufthansa, Ghana Airways, Iran Air, All Nippon Airways, Austrian Airlines and finally CAAC of China. Twenty of these, including the last, were completed at Hurn while Weybridge built just two.

When the Viscount 700 entered service in the early 1950s it was ahead of

Britannia 312 XX367 landing at Filton on 29 April 1983, to celebrate the twenty-fifth anniversary of its maiden flight there. It started its flying career with BOAC as G-AOVM in June 1958, was sold to British Eagle barely six years later and was converted into a freighter. Purchased by the Ministry of Defence in November 1971, G-AOVM was re-registered as XX367 to the A&AEE at Boscombe Down, Wiltshire. The final owner was BCF Aviation in Zaire.
BAE Systems

its time: it was the first turboprop airliner – powered by the new Rolls-Royce Dart – and had no serious competitor. Airlines found that its impact on their routes was considerable: load factors increased substantially as people wanted to travel on the fastest and most comfortable airliner available. The order book benefited accordingly and the Viscount went on to become Britain's best-selling airliner. By the end of 1956 Vickers had received the order for the 200th Viscount. There were by then two production lines, one at Vickers' main factory at Weybridge and another at Hurn near Bournemouth, which together could produce ten aircraft per month.

The Viscount 700 was lengthened and developed into the Viscount 800 with greater capacity, of which a total of sixty-eight were sold to six airlines in Europe and New Zealand. The design was further refined into the Viscount 810, a logical development of the 800 which, although unaltered in size, was matched to the new Dart 525 engine that gave the airliner a maximum take-off weight of 72,500lb, 17 per cent greater than the 800's.

Specification – Viscount 810	
Length:	85ft 8in (26.11m)
Wingspan:	93ft 8½in (28.56m)
Height:	26ft 9in (8.15m)
MTOW:	72,500lb (33,900kg)
Cruising speed:	351mph (565km/h)
Range:	1,275 miles (2,050km)
Passengers:	56–64
Powerplant:	4 × 1,990ehp Rolls-Royce Dart R.Da. 7
Viscounts built:	444 (2 at Wisley, 163 at Weybridge, 279 at Hurn)

Continental Airlines was the first customer for the Viscount 810 and started services with it in May 1958. The 810 soon proved more economical than the airline's Convair 240/340s and DC-3/6/7s. Lufthansa, Austrian Airlines, Pakistan International, South African Airways and other airlines ordered a total of eighty-three. The final customer was CAAC of China, which ordered six 843s (Vickers allocated specific type numbers for each customer) and received the last Viscount from the Hurn production line in April 1964.

Vickers' speedy development of the Viscount made the most of its potential and resulted in sales to more than sixty operators in some forty countries, with over 150 operators later receiving second-hand examples. The aircraft was also in demand with Governments in

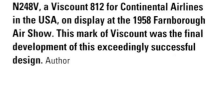

N248V, a Viscount 812 for Continental Airlines in the USA, on display at the 1958 Farnborough Air Show. This mark of Viscount was the final development of this exceedingly successful design. Author

The 438th and final Viscount at the Hurn factory. It first flew on 2 January 1964 and was delivered to CAAC of China the following April. BAC's Hurn plant built the majority of the Viscounts and One-Elevens. BAE Systems

Among the small number of Viscounts that returned to BAC for refurbishment was Arkia's 4X-AVB. It is seen here at the back end of the One-Eleven production line in the spring of 1973, with a One-Eleven 475 behind it. BAE Systems

an executive role and many served in the corporate market. However, unlike military programmes, civil aircraft generally provide much less upgrade and modification work for the manufacturer after production has ended. Whereas BAC (Preston Division) continued to profit from a large amount of Canberra refurbishment work for almost thirty years after production had ended, only a small amount of similar Viscount work returned to the Weybridge Division.

With 438 sales the Vickers Viscount remains Britain's best-selling airliner, yet for Vickers it was not the money spinner that might have been imagined, as the firm only made a profit of £17m.

Vickers Vanguard

The Vickers Vanguard grew out of a requirement first raised by British European Airways (BEA) in 1953, a few days before the initial Viscount 701 had entered service, which called for a faster airliner with 10 per cent greater economy than the developed Viscount 806 that was only due for delivery in 1957. Trans-Canada Airlines, another major Viscount customer, was also interested in this broad specification and Vickers' design teams began to examine options.

Many in the Vickers Project Office were convinced that the new airliner should be a jet, but BEA's view that it should be propeller-driven prevailed. The design evolved into the Vickers Type 950 powered by new the Rolls-Royce Tyne turboprops, capable of carrying 139 passengers in six-abreast seating together with a double-bubble fuselage that allowed for substantial underfloor cargo space. BEA decided on the name 'Vanguard', which the manufacturer accepted, and placed an order for twenty in July 1956 with delivery due in 1960. Trans-Canada Airlines (TCA) needed an aircraft with higher operating weights so Vickers strengthened the airframe and added higher-power Tynes to create the Vanguard 952 for the Canadian airline. BEA's aircraft were classed as the Type 951 and TCA's as the Type 952, but BEA decided to take advantage of the higher weights and greater payload of the Type 952, so fourteen of their order became Type 953s with the greater payload of the Type 952 but the lower-powered Tynes of the Type 951.

Construction took place at Vickers-Armstrongs' Weybridge works and the Vanguard prototype G-AOYW made a maiden flight in Vickers' livery to the company's test airfield at Wisley on 28 January 1959, piloted by Jock Bryce and Brian Trubshaw. The Vanguard's test programme proved troublesome as it had vibration and stalling problems, and more than 2,000 stalls were carried out before an acceptable performance was achieved.

The second Vanguard, G-APEA was the first aircraft for BEA and was demonstrated to the airliner's only other major customer, Trans-Canada Airlines, at Montreal at the end of June 1959. G-APEA initially flew without a dorsal fin and in the original BEA colours. For demonstration flights the livery was modified to 'Vickers Vanguard' titling. BAE Systems

Four Vanguards at the Wisley Test Centre in early 1960. These four aircraft (from the left) G-APEC, -EB, -EA and -ED were all later delivered to BEA as part of their twenty-three strong Vanguard fleet. Problems with the Rolls-Royce Tyne engines severely delayed their entry into service with BEA. BAE Systems

In November 1959 G-AOYW was fitted with a dorsal fin to prevent rudder 'hunting' and this became standard on all subsequent aircraft. In May 1960 however, the whole test programme, which was virtually complete, was suspended owing to compressor problems with the engine, and Rolls-Royce ordered all Tyne-powered aircraft to be grounded. This delayed scheduled deliveries to BEA and led to the airline having to charter a number of Viscounts to fill the gap. However, on 4 July 1960, just a few days after BAC's formation, G-AOYW recommenced test flying with modified engines and other Vanguards soon joined the prototype, enabling certification to be granted on 2 December 1960. Deliveries to BEA and TCA began almost immediately.

Even though the Vanguard was very economical and enabled TCA to introduce fare reductions, by 1960 both passengers and airlines wanted jets and many major European airlines had ordered the Sud Aviation Caravelle twin-jet for short/medium-range routes, even though its passenger and freight capacity was far less than the Vanguard.

Several large US carriers considered the Vanguard but decided to wait for the development of suitable jets such as the Boeing 727. Those American airlines that did choose a turboprop of the Vanguard's size ordered the Lockheed Electra, which entered service with American Airlines and Eastern Airlines in January 1959, well ahead of the Vanguard. The Electra was not a success though, due to accidents caused through wing failures early in its career; only 170 were produced, with sales mostly in the USA, Canada, Australia and New Zealand.

When G-AOYW took to the air for the first time in 1959, forty Vanguards were already on order from BEA and TCA, but only three more were ever ordered. As a result, only forty-four Vanguards were built and the last delivery was that of CF-TKW to Trans-Canada Airlines on 3 April 1964.

Specification – Vanguard 952	
Length:	122ft 10½in (37.45m)
Wingspan:	118ft (35.97m)
Height:	34ft 11in (10.64m)
MTOW:	141,000lb (64,000kg)
Cruising speed:	400mph (640km/h)
Range:	2,070 miles (3,330km)
Passengers:	139
Powerplant:	4 × 5,545ehp Rolls-Royce Tyne R.Ty: 512
Vanguards built:	44 (all at Weybridge)

In Service

By the summer of 1961, both BEA's and TCA's aircraft were established in service on both high-density domestic and international routes. But on the European routes the BEA's new Vanguards often had to compete with Caravelles, which were seen as more chic by the passengers even though the Vanguard was much more efficient and, owing to its double-bubble fuselage, could carry a large amount of freight.

While the Vanguard's two operators put these sturdy workhorses to good use as passenger airliners, as early as 1966 one of Air Canada's (formerly TCA) was converted to all-freight operation, known as the 'Cargoliner'. BEA improved on this idea in 1968 by having G-APEM modified by Aviation Traders: all the windows were removed, a strengthened floor was fitted and a large forward freight door was installed. Aviation Traders modified a

CF-TKU, one of Trans-Canada Airlines Vanguards, at Wisley. All the Vanguards were built at Weybridge and flown from the short runway there to Wisley for flight testing. The Vanguard was a commercial failure, securing orders for only forty-three aircraft from two customers. BAE Systems

Nine of BEA's Vanguards were converted into dedicated freighters with a freight door installed in the front fuselage and renamed 'Merchantmen'. They proved invaluable to operators in this configuration. One is now preserved at the Brooklands Museum at Weybridge. BAE Systems

Vickers lost £17m (at 1960 prices) on the Vanguard. According to Vickers' Technical Director, Charles Gardner, the Vickers Board was well aware of the Vanguard's lack of appeal early on in its production and contemplated cancelling it, but concluded that penalty payments and the closure of the Weybridge site would imperil the future of Vickers as an aircraft manufacturer, and was determined to face the losses. With hindsight, Sir George Edwards opined that instead of a totally new aircraft in the shape of the Vanguard there should have been a further development of the Viscount.

second aircraft and BEA itself then converted seven more of its Type 953s. These were given the name 'Merchantman', though BEA crews jokingly called them the 'Guardsvan'.

Air Canada withdrew their Vanguards from passenger service in October 1971 and their sole Cargoliner in mid-1972. The last BEA Merchantman flight was flown by G-APEJ on 2 December 1979. All these aircraft now joined the second-hand market, but as they were propeller-driven were not readily marketable. Operations by a number of second-tier carriers took the aircraft to unusual climes with airlines in Iceland, Indonesia,

France and Sweden, and also with British carriers such as Invicta and Air Bridge. The last Vanguard passenger flight was operated by Merparti Nusantara Airlines of Indonesia in 1987.

The trusty Merchantman remained in service for almost another decade and the final operator, Hunting Cargo Airlines, presented G-APEP to the Brooklands Museum at Weybridge, where it had made its maiden flight from the Vickers-Armstrongs factory on 29 November 1961. G-APEP made a dramatic landing on the remaining 2,500ft of runway at its birthplace on 16 October 1996, where it is now preserved.

English Electric Canberra

The Canberra's success is all the more remarkable when one considers that this was the first aircraft to be designed by English Electric since the small Ayr flying boat of 1924. English Electric's wartime production had consisted of manufacturing Handley Page Hampdens and Halifaxes, which led to the licence-building of Vampires for de Havilland post-war.

As the war drew to a close, English Electric set up its own design department led by Teddy Petter. Numerous designs were projected, and in late 1945 a design was submitted to the Ministry of Supply to meet specification B3/45, powered by two Rolls-Royce Avons. In January 1946, a contract was placed for four English Electric A1 prototypes, much to the surprise of the more established names in the industry who were piqued that the contract was not awarded to them, but to a firm with no track record in designing and producing ground-breaking aircraft. Three years and four months later VN799, the first English Electric A1, made its maiden flight, piloted by Roland Beamont, the company's Chief Test Pilot.

The first Canberra, VN799, on pre-first-flight engine runs at Warton. This first aircraft can be distinguished by its rounded fin and fin fillet.
BAE Systems via Warton Heritage

Four Canberras on the flight test apron at Warton. They are the prototype T.4 WN467, the prototype B.5, which later became the B(I).8 prototype, PR.3 WE135 and B.2 VX165.
BAE Systems via Warton Heritage

and the Canberra entered RAF service in the following May. The Canberra met and exceeded requirements, and there were few problems to delay their introduction into service.

Production of the Canberra B.2 was underway at the English Electric factories when, owing to an intensification in the Cold War and onset of the Korean War, three other aircraft firms – Avro, Handley Page and Short Brothers and Harland – were each contracted to start production. (This represented an interesting reversal for Handley Page who were now licence-building an English Electric aircraft.) Avro and Handley Page each built seventy-five B.2s while Shorts, after producing sixty B.2s, went on to build forty-nine B.6s and twenty-three PR.9 photo-reconnaissance variants. In addition, Shorts converted thirty B.2s into U.10 and U.14 unmanned target drones.

The Canberra B.2 was followed by the B.5 prototype, VX185, which was

Production Begins of Canberra Bombers

The first prototype Canberra B.2, VX165, first flew on 23 April 1950. This, the first production version of the Canberra, was a light bomber armed with six 1,000lb bombs in an internal bomb bay, and carrying a crew of a pilot under a distinctive broad and shallow canopy, and a navigator and a bomb aimer behind him. As production had been ordered straight off the drawing board the first production example, WD929, flew in October 1950

The Canberra B(I).8 was a substantially redesigned ground-attack variant of the original Canberra bomber able to carry varying loads of bombs, rockets and cannon. Its redesigned canopy – offset to port and higher up than before – provided a much better view for the pilot. BAE Systems via Warton Heritage

An example of one of the research uses for which Canberras were employed: WV787 with a spray rake at the tail fitted for airborne icing tests. The Canberra would fly ahead of an aircraft and spray water behind, which would then ice up the trailing aircraft so that its de-icing equipment could be tested. Crown Copyright

however soon superseded by the next mark, the B.6, which entered production immediately and entered service in June 1954. A modified version of the B.6 known as the B(I).6 was produced in small numbers and served with 213 Squadron. This version, intended for ground-attack and interdiction (hence the 'I' in its designation), carried a ventral pack in the rear half of the bomb bay, containing four 20mm cannon and a large quantity of ammunition, and was fitted with underwing pylons to carry two 1,000lb bombs or two packs of 2in rockets. With the ventral gun pack installed the aircraft was still able to carry three 1,000lb bombs.

Next in the ever-growing list of variants came another ground-attack interdictor, the Canberra B(I).8, which had a heavily revised nose to better suit it for the low-level flight that the role entailed. This Canberra carried a crew of two; the pilot was situated further back and higher up than on earlier versions, seated beneath a fighter-type cockpit canopy offset to the left. The navigator sat below and ahead of the pilot in a swivel chair, this arrangement giving the pilot greatly improved visibility and the navigator a ground view. Additional stores up to 2,000lb could be carried on underwing pylons and a camera pack or ventral gun pack could be installed in the bomb bay, making the aircraft extremely versatile in the range of roles that could be undertaken.

The prototype B(I).8, VX185, was converted from the B.5 prototype and first flew on 23 July 1954, followed in June 1955 by the first production aircraft, WT326. The Canberra B.15 and B.16, both refinements of the B.6, were next to follow and were converted from B.6s at Filton as part of BAC's need to provide work to the Bristol plant.

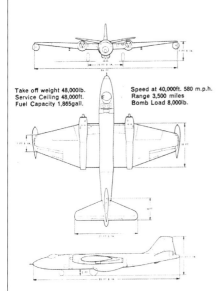

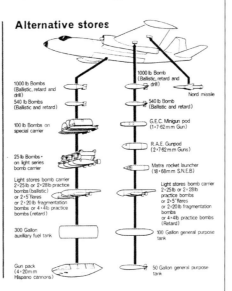

The Canberra today . . .

An economical interdictor reconnaissance bomber for use through the 1970's

Alternative stores

Take off weight 48,000lb.
Service Ceiling 48,000ft.
Fuel Capacity 1,865gall.

Speed at 40,000ft. 580 m.p.h.
Range 3,500 miles
Bomb Load 8,000lb.

1000 lb Bombs
(Ballistic, retard and drill)

540 lb Bombs
(Ballistic and retard)

100 lb Bombs on special carrier

25 lb Bombs • on light series bomb carrier

Light stores bomb carrier
2•25lb or 2•28lb practice bombs (ballistic)
or 2•5"flares
or 2•20 lb fragmentation bombs or 4•4lb practice bombs (retard)

300 Gallon auxiliary fuel tank

Gun pack
(4•20mm Hispano cannons)

1000 lb Bomb
(Ballistic, retard and drill)

Nord missile

540 lb Bomb
(Ballistic and retard)

G.E.C. Minigun pod
(1•7·62mm Gun)

R.A.E. Gunpod
(2•7·62mm Guns)

Matra rocket launcher
(18•68mm S.N.E.B)

Light stores bomb carrier
2•25lb or 2•28lb practice bombs
or 2•5"flares
or 2•20lb fragmentation bombs
or 4•4lb practice bombs (Retard)

100 Gallon general purpose tank

50 Gallon general purpose tank

The Canberra has proved an outstandingly successful military aircraft and is in use today on tactical bombing, day-and-night interdiction, counter-insurgency and various antipersonnel missions, as well as photo-reconnaissance, pilot training and target towing duties.

New marks, constructed during refurbishing of B.2s have recently entered RAF service for special duties in operational roles extending throughout the 1970s, and other refurbished marks have entered service with two new air forces, bringing to sixteen the number of countries now flying this highly versatile aeroplane.

Its continued use on operational duties for many years is thus assured.

Although no longer in continuous production, Canberras released from operational service in the RAF are being rebuilt in the original BAC production factories for export with a renewed operational life.

A BAC advertisement promoting the Canberra in 1970. BAE Systems

The United States Air Force's interest in the Canberra resulted in a licence agreement with Glenn Martin of Baltimore to produce the aircraft for the USAF. It would have been cheaper for the USAF to have purchased British-built aircraft for fitting out in the USA, but political considerations meant that it was decided to have a production line in the USA. The major production version for the USAF was the Martin B-57B, of which 202 were built. These differed considerably from the earlier B-57A/RB-57A, which resembled the Canberra B.2. Both the Australian Air Force and USAF used their Canberras/B-57s in anger, flying sorties in the Vietnam War.

The more the B-57s were developed the less they resembled the British design, and in their final manifestation as the RB-57F had lengthened wings with a span of 122ft, an extended nose and a considerably larger tailplane, plus two additional wing-mounted engines each developing 3,300lb. These versions were used for strategic reconnaissance, for which they had an endurance of ten hours and an operating ceiling of 100,000ft.

Specification – Canberra B(I).8

Length:	65ft 6in (19.96m)
Wingspan:	65ft 6in (19.96m)
Height:	15ft 7in (4.75m)
MTOW:	56,750lb (25,740kg)
Cruising speed:	450kt
Combat range:	850 miles (1,400km)
Powerplant:	2 × 7,500lb Rolls-Royce Avon RA.29
Canberras built:	1,376 (643 by English Electric/BAC at Preston, Accrington, Samlesbury and Warton 643, 75 by Avro, 75 by Handley Page, 132 by Shorts, 48 in Australia by the Government Aircraft Factory and 403 Martin B-57s in the USA)

The Canberra also played a key role in the RAF's photo-reconnaissance force, and indeed the last examples of the aircraft to remain in service were PR.9s, which were retired as late as 2006. The initial PR version, the PR.3, was created by slightly lengthening the fuselage of the B.2 to accommodate a forward camera bay, and fuel capacity was increased by using part of the bomb bay for additional tankage, the smaller bay being retained for photographic flares. The PR.3 prototype, VX181, first flew at Salmesbury in March 1950 (ahead of the prototype B.2) and the type entered service with 541 Squadron in early 1953.

The PR.3 was followed by the PR.7, and the final reconnaissance mark was the PR.9, which was developed by Shorts at Belfast. Externally it resembled the B(I).8 with a fighter-type cockpit, but incorporated a fully opening nose rather than a hatch to permit crew entry; unlike the B(I).8, it had an ejector seat for the navigator as well as the pilot. It had redesigned wings of increased span and greater chord on the sections inboard of the engines, which were now Avon 206s of 11,250lb thrust. With the modified wing and higher-powered engines, the PR.9 was able to reach a much higher altitude.

A grand total of 1,376 Canberras was built (including licence-built) of which 782 served with the RAF. Twenty-one different versions were built, operated by twenty-one countries. In addition to 143 newly built export aircraft 115 ex-RAF aircraft were rebuilt and exported.

Export and Licence-Built Marks

The type had good export potential, which is evidenced by the list of overseas customers: Venezuela, Peru, Ecuador, France, Sweden, West Germany, New Zealand, Rhodesia, South Africa, Argentina, Ethiopia and India, all of which ordered British-built Canberras, and Pakistan and Nationalist China, which bought aircraft of American manufacture. Whereas most of the Canberra's customers received aircraft built by the parent company, there were two notable exceptions, Australia which built forty-eight and the United States which also established a production line.

Canberra: Post-Production Earnings

When English Electric became part of BAC in 1960 the production of the Canberra was coming to an end, although a handful of PR.9s were still in production at Shorts in Belfast. Although production at Samlesbury had ceased, fifteen aircraft were constructed as the last on the line to hold against further orders: this proved a wise decision as orders were soon received for these, and the final delivery of a newly built Canberra was to the South African Air Force on 3 February 1964.

Completion of production did not signal the end of activity, however. Large numbers returned to the factories for maintenance, refurbishment and modification for new roles as new marks for the RAF and as test beds for UK research establishments. This was also the case with overseas operators of the Canberra,

A good example of the large amount of money English Electric made out of the Canberra, an 'old account' project until nationalization in 1977. Originally delivered to the RAF in 1953, this Canberra B.2 was sold back to BAC in July 1966 and reworked to become a B.56 for the Peruvian Air Force as 242. Test flown as G-27-99, it was delivered in April 1969 but written off in December 1972. BAE Systems

who also frequently returned theirs. In fact, owing to the continued demand for Canberras in the 1960s, BAC purchased large numbers of RAF aircraft that were surplus to requirements.

It was originally intended that the RAF's Canberra would be replaced by the TSR2 in the late 1960s. Following the cancellation of the TSR2 in 1965, the Canberra's replacement was planned to be a mix of the General Dynamics F-111 and the Anglo-French Variable-Geometry (AFVG) aircraft. However, the French withdrew from the AFVG project in mid-1967 and, owing to huge cost overruns, the Labour Government cancelled the F-111 in January 1968. Finally, in December 1968 go-ahead was given for the Anglo-German-Italian Multi-Role Combat Aircraft (MRCA), dubbed by some wags who were pessimistic about its ever entering service as the 'Must Refurbish Canberra Again'. In fact, the MRCA succeeded and went on to become the highly successful Tornado.

The refurbishment work provided BAC and then BAe with an excellent income stream throughout the 1960s, 1970s and 1980s. Prior to the cancellation of TSR2 English Electric had often sub-contracted out modification work on the Canberra, but with the huge loss of work caused by the end of that programme the work was brought 'in-house'.

The refurbishment programme was carried out at BAC's Samlesbury factory where the Canberras had originally been assembled and flown. Aircraft for refurbishment were either flown into the plant or, where necessary, dismantled and delivered by road. The actual refurbishment work consisted of a complete breakdown of the aircraft's structures into its three parts – wings, tail and fuselage. All paint was stripped, equipment removed, time-expired parts replaced and engines sent for overhaul by Rolls-Royce or the RAF. New electronics or other equipment could be fitted to suit customer requirements. BAC also agreed to provide spares support for a further ten years. Depending upon the customer's requirements, work would take between a year and eighteen months. Upon completion the aircraft would make a short flight from Samlesbury to Warton where test flying took place wearing 'B' registration marks (for example, G27-182). Following the satisfactory completion of pre-delivery trials, the Canberras were delivered from Warton to the customer's air force.

A good example of the ongoing value of this practice can be seen with the Venezuelan Canberras. The first export order for the Canberra was placed in 1952 when Venezuela purchased six B.2s following a demonstration earlier that year. In 1957 the Fuerza Aérea Venezolano (FAV) ordered eight B(I).58s (the export version of the B(I).8) and two T.4s; these

aircraft were delivered in 1957–58. In 1965 a further order was placed for twelve B.2s and two PR.3s, these coming from stock that BAC had bought back from the RAF. In 1975 BAC started work on a contract to refurbish twenty-four Venezuelan Canberras; having been delivered by sea, following rework they departed by air between 1977 and 1980, by which time BAC had become part of the nationalized British Aerospace. All the Venezuelan Canberras that were not written off in service returned to English Electric/BAC for overhaul at least once, and many returned more often for overhaul or modification to a superior specification.

Other foreign air forces that purchased refurbished Canberras from BAC were Ethiopia, Peru, Argentina, South Africa and West Germany. The Argentine Air Force deployed Canberras against the United Kingdom in the Falklands War, but lost two of them in the process.

Surplus RAF B.2s were heavily modified from 1963 with a new large and bulbous radar nose, and many other blisters and bulges. This highly specialized conversion was known as the Canberra T.17 and was used by an RAF/RN unit for special electronics countermeasures training. The TT.18 followed in 1965; this was also a B.2 conversion, for use as a target-tug aircraft and operated by the various RAF and RN units. Yet another mark was the T.19 target aircraft, a modification of the T.11 that had been developed to train Javelin crew in radar interception. The final Canberra mark, produced in 1971, was the T.22: PR.7s that were rebuilt for the Royal Navy's Fleet Requirements Unit. Work did not cease at this point however, for in 1976 BAC was awarded a contract to rework fifty aircraft of six different marks for the RAF.

This continuing demand provided plenty of work at Samlesbury until 1988, when the final Canberra rework was completed. As an 'old account' aircraft it will have earned considerable sums for English Electric (GEC from 1968).

With nationalization in 1977 and the formation of British Aerospace, the 'old account' arrangement ceased.

The RAF's trainer Canberra T.4s flew their last flights at RAF Marham in September 2005, ahead of the retirement of the photo-reconnaissance Canberras in 2006. A ceremony to mark the closure of No.39 (PRU) Squadron took place at RAF Marham on 28 July 2006 – in the last months of their service these Canberras had been operational over Afghanistan. The three surviving RAF Canberras made their final flights on 31 July when they were delivered to Delta Jets at Kemble. After the Canberra left RAF service, the other remaining full-time military operator, the Indian Air Force, announced the withdrawal of the Canberra from combat service from March 2007, after fifty years of service.

Roland Beamont demonstrated one of the Argentine B.62s, a modified B.2, at the Farnborough Show in 1970; it was given British registration G-AYHP for the occasion. Two of Argentina's Canberras were shot down in the 1982 Falklands Conflict but not this one, which is preserved at the Museo Nacional de Malvinas in Cordoba, Argentina. BAE Systems

CHAPTER FOUR

The Corporation's Research Aircraft

When BAC was formed the inherited projects included three research aircraft: the Bristol 188, Hunting H.126 and the BAC 221. The Bristol 188 originated in a requirement issued in 1953 for a supersonic research aircraft able to cruise at high Mach numbers. Had its development and construction been more straightforward than they were, it might have flown well before the formation of the Corporation. The Hunting H.126, which first flew in 1964, was intended to operate at the other end of the speed spectrum to investigate the effectiveness of jet-flap in lowering take-off and landing speeds. The final member of the trio, the BAC 221, a rebuild of the first Fairey Delta 2 that also first flew in 1964, was designed to research the properties of the slender delta wing at different angles of attack as part of the Concorde development programme.

Bristol 188

At the 1962 Empire Test Pilots' School dinner, BAC Filton's Chief Test Pilot, Godfrey Auty, received the dubious honour of being voted the 'man most likely to eject in the coming year'. The aircraft he was to fly on 14 April 1963 was the Bristol 188, a stainless-steel supersonic research aircraft built under contract to the Ministry of Aviation. It was intended to fly faster than any other British aircraft and to gather a huge amount of information for research purposes.

No other British aircraft had posed such challenging manufacturing problems, and the very fact that these were solved meant that the project had already accomplished its first objective. The aircraft was comparatively conventional in appearance, yet every portion of its structure, every bolt, every fluid seal and cable connector, and even the manner in which flight data was measured and recorded, had all been the subject of years of painstaking development. The 188 was intended as a focal point for a major advance in the technology of high-speed aircraft and, although the world of missiles and spacecraft into which it emerged was very different from that of 1954 when the project was initiated, it had not completely been overtaken by events.

The Experimental Requirement 134T called for an aircraft capable of flight at Mach 1.8 to Mach 2.5 (later envisaged as even Mach 2.7) with sufficient fuel to maintain this speed long enough for steady, as well as transient, conditions to be investigated. It was clearly desirable to be able to fly at full speed under

One of the Bristol 188s under construction at Filton. Most of the airframe was made of stainless steel, which proved hugely problematic to use. Sir George Edwards claimed that after BAC's experience with using it there was a clear determination not to use it on Concorde.
Bristol Aero Collection

This photo of the first Bristol 188, XF923, shows the thinness of the wing and the large diameter of the Gyron Junior engines. The large projections on the engine nacelles were for the fire extinguishers. The projection to the left of the rear fuselage is the tail parachute housing. Bristol Aero Collection

Despite all the expectations of its research potential, XF923 made only nineteen flights before being withdrawn from use; it never even flew supersonically. The Bristol 188 was let down by the Gyron Junior's engine tending to surge, and its higher than estimated fuel consumption. Bristol Aero Collection

conditions of severe kinetic heating for sustained periods; maximum endurance was also required in order to increase the data gathered per sortie. The Ministry demanded the ability to take off and land conventionally (unlike the American X-planes, which were air-launched from 'mother' aircraft). The basic configuration of the aircraft was determined by the need to accommodate the pilot, a large quantity of fuel, undercarriage, instrumentation and engines arranged that so new intakes, nozzles and engines could be installed with minimum difficulty. Bristol found that this tied in particularly well with their choice of an essentially unswept wing, with the engines outboard in self-contained nacelles.

Several manufacturers prepared designs to meet ER134T: Armstrong Whitworth,

Bristol, English Electric, Hawker and Saunders-Roe. The winner of the competition in 1953 was Armstrong Whitworth, but as this firm was heavily involved in the Gloster Javelin fighter programme for the RAF, the contract was passed to the runners-up, Bristol. The contract was for two aircraft plus a structural-test specimen, with the first flight scheduled for 1957. Three more aircraft were added to the programme in 1955 to support the Avro 730 supersonic bomber project, which was to be powered by Armstrong Siddeley P.176 engines; these were also selected for the Bristol 188.

Then, however, came the infamous 1957 Defence White Paper, which declared manned aircraft to be obsolete so axed almost all future warplanes apart from the English Electric Lightning

fighter and the Canberra replacement that later emerged as the TSR2. The Avro 730 was cancelled, and although the 188 survived the order was reduced back to two plus the test specimen. The cancellation of the Avro 730 and the planned supersonic development of the Javelin also led to the end of activity on the Armstrong Siddeley engine so, after several others including the Rolls-Royce Avon had been considered, it was decided to use the de Havilland Gyron Junior. The engines of the 188 were required not only to power the aircraft, but also to be capable of infinite variation to achieve peak efficiency over all Mach numbers from zero to more than Mach 2.5. The DGJ.10 version of this engine, rated at 10,000lb dry thrust or 14,000lb with reheat at sea-level, appeared to fit the 188 admirably.

The second Bristol 188, XF926, did achieve supersonic flight but was withdrawn from use after fifty-one flights without achieving the aim of Mach 2.5. It is now preserved at the RAF Museum, Cosford. Bristol Aero Collection

Technical Description

The wing shape evolved as a result of extensive flutter and wind-tunnel investigations, particularly into trim and stability. This testing also confirmed the use of a tailplane mounted at the top of the vertical tail. Exceptionally slender, the fuselage had a cross-section determined by the pilot and his ejection seat and the retracted mainwheels, and length adequate to accommodate the fuel, systems and payload.

Nearly all the airframe was made of stainless steel, as the 188 was expected to be the first British aircraft designed to fly so fast that kinetic heating prohibited the use of the more usual aluminium; Bristol joined forces with Firth-Vickers to produce the steel. The scale and complexity of the challenge to produce the material and then make aircraft from it delayed the project considerably. Bristol subcontracted the manufacturing of the complete tailplane, fin, rudder, outer wings, ailerons and cockpit canopy to Armstrong Whitworth Aircraft in Coventry, a member company of Hawker Siddeley and the original winners of the contract, who had conducted their own research into this field prior to the award of the contract.

As a research tool the 188 contained a large amount of flight recording equipment, and information was sent by live telemetry to a ground control room as well. The aircraft was under continuous radio control from the ground, tracked and positioned by a radar station that passed the aircraft's position to the ground control room at Filton. A pilot was based in the control room with a duplicate set of aircraft instruments at the control console to give advice to the test pilot flying the actual aircraft, and to act as a flight test observer.

The first airframe constructed was the static-test specimen, which was taken by road to RAE Farnborough in 1960. The first flying airframe, XF923, was rolled out on 26 April 1961 but did not make its maiden flight until almost a year later, flying from Filton to the A&AEE Boscombe Down on 14 April 1962. Despite several systems failures the flight had passed safely. XF923 made only nineteen flights, including four appearances at the 1962 Farnborough Air Show, before being placed into storage in early 1963 at Filton having never achieved supersonic flight.

Specification – Bristol 188	
Length:	71ft (22.6m)
Wingspan:	35ft 1in (10.69m)
Height:	13ft 4in (4.06m)
MTOW:	30,000lb (13,600kg) (projected)
Maximum speed:	Mach 1.88
Range:	n.k.
Crew:	1
Powerplant:	2 × DH Gyron Junior PS50 14,000lb thrust with reheat

The Gyron Junior engines were a major source of problems for the aircraft, a situation exacerbated by the fact that few other aircraft were fitted with the engine so few resources were available for its development. The second Bristol 188, XF926, first flew on 29 April 1963 and soon achieved supersonic speed, but continual problems with engine intake surging, and fuel consumption far higher than envisaged, crippled the reach of the programme. The second 188 hit a top speed of Mach 1.88 in its total of fifty-one flights, but the grand intention of the original requirement was never achieved.

Both 188s languished at Filton until November 1966 when they were sent to the ranges at Shoeburyness to be expended as gunnery targets. Fortunately XF926 was saved from destruction and sent to the Cosford Aerospace Museum. A disappointing end to an ambitious and expensive project, which had cost £20 million.

Hunting H.126

The second of BAC's research types, the Hunting H.126 jet-flap research aircraft, made its maiden flight from RAE Bedford on 26 March 1963. At the controls was S.B. Oliver, Chief Test Pilot of Hunting. BAC had issued a statement prior to the first flight:

A new research aircraft, the H.126, built by Hunting Aircraft, is undergoing ground checks in preparation for its first flight. The H.126 is designed to a Ministry of Aviation specification to investigate the principle of using jet engine exhaust gases as a 'jet flap' to increase lift and so improve landing and take-off performance. A single-seat aircraft powered by one Bristol Siddeley Orpheus turbojet, it will be piloted on its first flight by Hunting Aircraft's chief test pilot, Mr S.B. Oliver. The Orpheus provides power for both forward propulsion and lift. The greater part of the efflux from the engine is ducted into the wings and ejected as a thin sheet from the trailing edge and over the full-span flaps which act as a jet deflector. The stream follows the flap as it is lowered, thus considerably increasing lift. This part of the efflux produces thrust as well as lift, and further thrust is provided through nozzles low down on each side of the fuselage just aft of the wing.

The Hunting H.126, XN714, on its first flight from the RAE Bedford on 26 March 1963, piloted by Hunting's Chief Test Pilot, 'Ollie' Oliver. BAE Systems

The H.126 on the ground at RAE Bedford, liberally covered in wool-tufts used to indicate the airflow over the aircraft. XN714 is now preserved at the RAF Museum, Cosford. Crown copyright

The H.126 has conventional flying control surfaces, the ailerons being in effect the outboard section of each flap. They are supplemented by yaw and pitch nozzles at the tail for control at very low airspeeds. Independent roll nozzles are fitted at the wing tips, operated by an autostabilising system. Design of the H.126 posed a number of engineering problems associated with the large volumes of hot gas to be passed through the fuselage and mainplane to the trailing edge. Despite the high temperatures in the ducting, the primary structure of the wings and fuselage is of conventional light-alloy stressed-skin. This has been made possible by efficient insulation of the ducting and by the use of a heat-reflective shield around the inside of the wings and fuselage. The flaps presented a particular problem in that only the top surfaces are subjected to the hot exhaust gases while the bottom surfaces remain relatively cool. The method of construction employed allows

differential expansion to take place, while maintaining the correct profile.

The H.126 is fitted with extensive test instrumentation, most of the rear fuselage being occupied by automatic-observer equipment and associated apparatus. The jet-flap principle is of great potential importance as a means of reducing the take-off and landing speeds of the aircraft of the future, and the research programme which lies before the H.126 is, therefore, of major significance to the progress of aircraft design technology.

The H.126, registered XN714, was rolled out in August 1962 and Oliver conducted limited taxiing trials at Luton before the aircraft was taken by road to Bedford in December. Owing to very poor weather conditions that winter the H.126 did not get out onto the runway until 19 March, when it put in some fast taxiing – with

the wheels several feet off the ground on occasions – before proceedings were halted by an anti-spin chute that streamed but failed to jettison.

Specification – Hunting H.126	
Length:	50ft 2in (15.29m)
Wingspan:	45ft 4in (13.82m)
Height:	15ft 6in (4.72m)
MTOW:	10,740lb (4,870kg)
Minimum speed:	32mph (51km/h)
Range:	n.k.
Crew:	1
Powerplant:	1 × Bristol Siddeley Orpheus BOr.3 Mk.805 4,000lb thrust

On the afternoon of 26 March Oliver found everything, including the weather, to his liking. With flaps at 0 degrees, he took the H.126 off at about 80 knots after a run of some 600 yards. Afterwards he said 'Taking this plane off is an entirely new sensation; it just floats off the ground, and then you go up like a lift.' He cruised around in a slightly nose-down attitude for some eighteen minutes, and upon his return he climbed down from the lofty cockpit and announced that it had been 'a perfect, no-snags flight'.

Hunting carried out about six months of preliminary flying with the H.126, which then briefly visited Boscombe Down for trials in the blower tunnel to test emergency canopy jettison. The H.126's only public display was at the 1965 Paris Air Show. XN714 was then based at RAE Bedford from June 1966 for an extensive research programme, before going to Hawker Siddeley's Hawker Blackburn Division test airfield at Holme-on-Spalding Moor for servicing and preparation for transport to the USA for tests at the Ames Flight Center in California. However, the H.126 never flew again: although it was flown to the USA in a Shorts Belfast in April 1969, it was never reassembled in California and in May 1970 it returned to Holme-on-Spalding Moor for storage. On 30 April 1974 it was sent to the Cosford Aerospace Museum for preservation and display.

BAC 221

The Fairey Delta 2 was developed in the early 1950s to research supersonic flight. It showed great potential, and on 10 March 1956 Peter Twiss set a world absolute speed record of 1,132mph

(1,821km/h) in the first FD.2, WG774, surpassing the previous record by 310mph (499km/h). Fairey projected a much developed version of the aircraft as a fighter, but following the 1957 Defence White Paper there was no more development of this superb design. Britain lost the opportunity to develop a superb aircraft while its French rival, Dassault, built the similar Mirage, which became an exceedingly successful fighter/bomber.

By the mid-1950s the RAE was researching possible configurations of the slender delta wing that was considered to be suitable for a supersonic transport, and numerous models were made for wind-tunnel investigations. The data on lift, drag and stability obtained with these models provided the major part of the aerodynamic design of Concorde. To check the accuracy of this data, and establish the correlation between tunnel models and full-scale results, there was a need for a full-scale research aircraft. As a result the Ministry decided that one of the two Fairey Delta 2s could be rebuilt as this research machine.

Between 1958 and 1960 Fairey and the RAE discussed the possible extension of FD.2 research by fitting a new wing of the curved 'ogee' planform, which preliminary tunnel investigations had indicated as having a favourable combination of lift, drag and stability characteristics at Mach 2. But in 1960, with the reorganization of the UK aviation industry, Fairey Aviation was taken over by Westland Aircraft who were to concentrate henceforth on helicopters. The modification of the FD.2 was passed to Hunting Aircraft. Finally,

in July 1960 Bristol took over the programme to produce a modified FD.2 as part of BAC's redistribution of work to Filton, which was bereft of work.

In August 1960 BAC proposed two types of modification of the FD.2: a substantial conversion with an optimum ogival wing, a 6ft (1.8m) fuselage extension and a much taller undercarriage, or a minimum conversion without the fuselage extension and retaining the existing landing gear. The Ministry opted for the first to create an aircraft better suited for the research task and to provide a necessary increase in fuel capacity.

Having completed 503 flights as a FD.2, the former world-record holder, WG774, was delivered to Filton on 5 September 1960 for conversion into the BAC 221. Work on the conversion started in April 1961. The additional 6ft section was spliced into the original fuselage and accommodated a much lengthened nose undercarriage, additional fuel and instrumentation. The cockpit was essentially unchanged, and although the original metal canopy was used for initial flying it was later replaced with a Perspex moulding. The flying controls were modified to take into account the different handling characteristics of the longer and therefore more slender aircraft's handling, and an auto-throttle was added to reduce cockpit workload. The 221's lengthy nose undercarriage was designed and manufactured at Filton, the main legs was based on those of the Lightning.

Though the BAC 221 might initially appear to be an aerodynamic scale model of the Concorde, its wing had a different twist, camber and droop, and was mounted higher on the fuselage than Concorde's. The BAC 221 was intended to explore the behaviour of a slender delta wing at angles of attack high enough to generate a powerful vortex above the leading edge; such a vortex increases the lift available at high angles of attack from a sharp-edged wing with this type of planform.

The BAC 221's Rolls-Royce Avon RA.28R was basically a reheated version of the engine used in the Vickers Valiant bomber. The reheat system was rudimentary, with simple on–off control and a

The roll-out in October 1963 at Filton of the former Fairey Delta 2, WG774, rebuilt as the BAC 221. Bristol Aero Collection

The BAC 221 airborne on its first flight, on 1 May 1964 from Filton piloted by Godfrey Auty. Note that the landing gear is down and that the droop-nose is lowered in the landing configuration.
Bristol Aero Collection

The BAC 221 airborne from Filton, fully painted in blue and now with a clear-view canopy. WG774 is now preserved at Yeovilton. BAE Systems

two-element, two-position nozzle. The original FD.2 air intake arrangement, with leading-edge root intakes, was precluded by the need for a continuous, sharp leading edge extending forward along the fuselage. Therefore BAC relocated the intakes on each side of the fuselage, beneath the wing root and curving the ducts upwards in bulges above the wing to enter the body symmetrically above and below the centreline of the engine.

Specification – BAC 221	
Length:	57ft 7in (17.55m)
Wingspan:	25ft (7.62m)
Height:	11ft 4in (3.45m)
MTOW:	13,884lb (6,278kg)
Maximum speed:	Mach 1.6
Range:	830 miles (1,335km)
Crew:	1
Powerplant:	1 × Rolls-Royce Avon 28R 13,100lb thrust with reheat

The BAC 221's basic research instrumentation comprised an automatic observer, a crash recorder and a camera at the top of the fin to photograph the wing tufting that indicated airflow at low speeds. There was also a substantial amount of other, more sophisticated, instrumentation.

As the Ministry was determined to save money (and no contribution to the cost of the 221 was made by France) all systems development – hydraulic, electrical, fuel, and so on – had to be carried out on the actual aircraft rather than with specially built rigs that would have eased the task and saved time. As a result although the 221 was rolled out in October 1963 it did not fly until 1 May 1964 when Godfrey Auty, Chief Test Pilot of British Aircraft Corporation (Filton Division) took it aloft. Initially only the nose and tail were painted, but by the time it appeared at the Farnborough Air Show in September

that year it was painted a glossy blue all over to provide a good background to the tufted wings.

Flight clearance was carried out at Filton. Initially the aircraft was kept subsonic to explore handling at low speeds and prove the systems. Then the 221's flight envelope gradually was extended to its limits. On completion of the trials by BAC's Godfrey Auty, 'Willie' Williamson and an RAE pilot it was delivered to RAE Bedford on 20 May 1966 and then disappeared from public view, apart from a second appearance at that year's Farnborough Air Show. At Bedford it embarked on research into slender delta approach and landing and the use of auto-throttle. Having completed 288 flights, it was initially preserved at the Museum of Flight, East Fortune, but it was later moved to RNAS Yeovilton where it is displayed next to the British Concorde prototype G-BSST.

CHAPTER FIVE

The Vickers VC10 and Weybridge

The Vickers VC10 remains the largest all-British aircraft ever built, a record it is now unlikely to lose. At the time of writing it continues in service with the RAF and in 2012 will have been flying for fifty years, yet despite its long career only fifty-four were ever built, all at the Weybridge factory. Although it was a great engineering achievement it failed to penetrate markets and was a costly failure for Vickers-Armstrongs.

Vickers' partners in BAC, English Electric and Bristol, were unaffected by the VC10's poor sales as it was an 'old account' project, so the liability was not shared with them. English Electric and Bristol (which had lost so much on the Britannia) had certainly not wanted to be financially saddled with a project that, according to Vickers' Charles Gardner, they regarded as a potential loser. The two companies were proved right and Vickers was beset with heavy outgoings on the VC10 (and Vanguard) for a decade, which hampered its ability to invest in its other interests. Some relief came in 1960 when, to support the formation of BAC, the Government stepped in and offered financial support to Vickers for VC10 development, providing £6.4m for the VC10 and 50 per cent of the Super VC10's development costs.

Origins

In 1951 the Ministry of Supply approached Vickers to design a military transport aircraft based on the Valiant 'V' Bomber. BOAC also expressed interest as it was seeking a transatlantic jet airliner. At this point the transatlantic routes were being served by piston-powered aircraft such as the Lockheed Constellation and Douglas DC-7C, although the forthcoming Bristol Britannia turboprop appeared capable of offering shorter flight times.

The new specification called for an aircraft able to carry 120 passengers for 2,100 nautical miles and in September 1952 the Ministry ordered a prototype powered by Rolls-Royce Conways, to be registered XD662. The aircraft was to be called the V1000 in military guise while the civil version was to be the VC7. The V1000 design bore some similarity to the Valiant bomber but was substantially larger, with a fuselage 146ft (44.5m) long, a low-mounted 140ft (139.7m) span wing, four engines mounted in the wing roots and a conventional tailplane arrangement.

On 29 November 1955 the Conservative Government cancelled the V1000 stating bluntly 'The Minister of Supply has indicated that he could not devote money to the development of an aircraft without a home market, and that since BOAC does not require this aircraft, no home market exists.' (BOAC was happy with the Britannia.) Consequently the prototype, already 80 per cent complete, was scrapped. Thus at this crucial moment in the development of long-range airliners the British aircraft industry was prevented from competing with US manufacturers. As Vickers' Sir George Edwards remarked, it was 'a decision we shall regret for many years'. There was a huge amount of criticism in the House of Commons, the aviation press and by such bodies as the Air League, but to no avail.

The RAF had been forced to make budget cuts and so cancelled their order for six V1000s, replacing these with Britannias assembled at the Shorts factory in Belfast, an area of high unemployment. Shorts was 69½ per cent owned by the Government and the second Britannia production line situated there was in need of work owing to a lack of orders. BOAC now stated that it would be using Britannias and Comet 4s on their Atlantic routes in the years ahead. The airline showed little evidence of any coherent planning and failed to appreciate the activities of one of its major competitors, Pan Am, which had already ordered transatlantic jets in the shape of

A model of the Vickers V1000/VC7. This design had substantial potential and would have been able to carry 120 passengers across the Atlantic, entering service before the Boeing 707 or Douglas DC-8. However, in an exceedingly short-sighted move the project was cancelled in November 1955 when the prototype was 80 per cent complete. BAE Systems

The fuselage of the prototype VC10, G-ARTA, under construction in the huge north-side hanger at Weybridge. In the background there is a Vanguard fuselage, and the immediate foreground a Vanguard wing. BAE Systems

Conways with a large, unencumbered wing with leading edge slats and trailing edge flaps – the slats and flaps of the competing 707 and DC-8 were interrupted by their four podded engines. The advantages of the VC10 configuration were lower approach speeds, an impressive runway performance, reduced cabin noise, reduced fire hazard in the event of a crash (the fuel tanks being in the wings) and superior ditching characteristics.

Highly satisfied with the design, in January 1958 BOAC signed a contract for thirty-five 139-seat VC10s with options on a further twenty. In June 1960 BOAC converted these options to ten Super VC10s with transatlantic range and capacity for 212 passengers. This projected Super VC10 had much higher-rated Conways than the original, and a fuselage stretched by 28ft (8.53m) to raise the passenger seating to 212, larger even than the Boeing 707's capacity, thereby reducing operational costs.

During 1961 the order was altered to just fifteen standard VC10s (with four 21,000lb Conway 42s) and thirty Super VC10s (four 22,500lb Conway 43s) but, as BOAC had doubts about filling all 212 seats of the larger version, a smaller aircraft than originally proposed was devised with a fuselage stretch of 13ft (3.96m) and with capacity for only 174 passengers. The order was further reduced in January 1962 to just twelve standards (Type 1101 registered G-ARVA–C, and G-ARVE–M) and thirty Super VC10s, with eight of the Supers in a new combi-configuration with a large forward cargo door and stronger floor. The order for Supers was later reduced to seventeen Type 1151, registered G-ASGA–P and G-ASGR, and the combi version was abandoned.

Maiden Flight and Drag Problems

The prototype (Type 1100) VC10, G-ARTA, was rolled out at Weybridge on 15 April 1962, followed by a period of ground testing. On 29 June it made its

Boeing 707s and Douglas DC-8s. More grievously, it was rumoured that some BOAC executives had little confidence in the British aircraft industry and were in favour of ordering American airliners.

Within a few months BOAC was discussing the prospect of a Comet 5 with de Havilland but concluded that such a development could not compete with the Boeing 707's specification. Following Pan Am's lead, other world airlines were purchasing the new American jet airliner, and on 24 October 1956, less than a year after the scrapping of the VC7, the Government gave BOAC permission to order fifteen 707s as there was no equivalent British type available. The Government had taken the step of meeting Sir George Edwards to see if the VC7 could be resurrected, but the prototype had already been cut up for destructive testing, and the jigs and tools destroyed.

The VC10

Government approval for the BOAC order for 707s came with the caveat that no more dollars would be available for American aircraft and that any additional aircraft ordered would have to be British-built. BOAC then viewed the 707 as primarily for transatlantic services and

sought a smaller aircraft for the African and Far Eastern routes, so it issued a requirement for a jet airliner to service these 'Empire' routes.

The VC10 was designed to an exceptionally severe requirement written by and exclusively for BOAC. It detailed such critical examples as operating from Singapore to Karachi non-stop against a headwind, and in and out of 'hot and high' airports (that is, with very hot average temperatures and high above sea level, where the air is thinner) at Kano and Nairobi. Early versions of the Boeing 707 and Douglas DC-8 were underpowered and required very long runways in order to take off: for this reason the 707 could not serve on many of BOAC's 'Empire' routes, or take off with a full load from high-altitude airfields. To meet its specification the VC10 had excellent airfield performance but was heavier and higher-powered than its competitors. In the end, however, such was the demand for the American jet airliners that runways were lengthened to accommodate them, including those on the 'Empire' routes.

Vickers did not simply dust off the VC7 design; the VC10 was designed from a blank sheet of paper with many innovative features. It was a rear-engined T-tail design powered by four Rolls-Royce

G-ARTA and G-ARVA, the prototype VC10 and the first production VC10 for BOAC, seen at Wisley. They first flew on 29 July and 8 November 1962, respectively. Compare the rear of the engine nacelles of the two VC10s, G-ARTA with the original configuration and G-ARVA with the 'beaver tail' installation to reduce drag. The Gloster Javelin XA778 was normally based at Boscombe Down and was used for ASI pressure correction readings. Just visible in the background is the tail of the final Vanguard, CF-TKW, delivered to Air Canada in April 1964. BAE Systems

The final standard VC10 for BOAC taking off on its maiden flight from Weybridge on 8 July 1964; the huge VC10 final assembly hangars are in the background. Because of the limited length of the runway, aircraft had to be airborne by the hatched markings on the runway. BAE Systems

maiden flight very lightly loaded, piloted by Jock Bryce and Brian Trubshaw, using only 2,150ft of the 4,200ft runway. It landed at the Wisley Flight Test Centre, which was only three miles from Weybridge but had a much more generous 6,700ft runway. It then embarked on the test programme fitted with over ten tons of test equipment. Less than three months after its first flight, G-ARTA appeared at the 1962 Farnborough Show, making a favourable impression on the crowd. It was soon joined in the air by production VC10s destined for BOAC. Of these, G-ARVA–C and G-ARVE were all involved in flight testing while G-ARVF carried out 1,000 hours of route proving.

Vickers discovered that the aircraft's drag was greater than calculated, which would reduce its range, and so engaged on a programme to alleviate this. The modifications required were alterations to the rear of the engine nacelles and their pitch, to the leading edge slats and to the wing tips. G-ARVE, which made its maiden flight from Weybridge to Wisley in April 1963, was the first to incorporate these modifications.

G-ARTA and some of the other VC10s involved in the more critical test flying were fitted with escape chutes for the crew. This vertical chute was fitted above the forward freight door. It was a tunnel held in place by a smaller door fitted within the freight door; this was jettisoned by the firing of explosive bolts, whereupon the door would slide down below the slipstream, allowing the crew to slide down it and escape.

On 31 December 1963 G-ARTA took off to engage in stalling tests and was almost lost during this flight. While recovering from one of the stalls an elevator bracket broke, causing violent flutter. The aircraft was vibrating so badly that Brian Trubshaw, who was in command, thought it might break up. As the behaviour of the aircraft was so alarming the crew escape chute door was jettisoned at full cabin differential pressure. Consequently, the chute and the cabin floor had to withstand this differential pressure instantaneously because the freight bays were not vented. This resulted in the escape chute being crushed and much of it was torn out of the aircraft, making it unusable for the crew. Fortunately the aircraft was not lost and it made a slow return to Wisley where, following repair, it was back in

G-ARVJ flew BOAC's inaugural VC10 service from London Heathrow to Lagos on 29 April 1964. BAE Systems

the air on 7 February 1964. Despite this setback and the drag problem, the certification programme remained on schedule and the VC10 was certified on 23 April 1964.

BOAC's Attempt to Cancel its Super VC10 Order

In 1964 Sir Giles Guthrie became Chairman of BOAC and endeavoured to cancel the Super VC10s to replace them with more Boeing 707s, which the airline

stated were cheaper to operate. This information was soon in the public domain, adversely affecting possible VC10 sales. BOAC appeared before a Parliamentary Select Committee and implied that it had been forced to buy the VC10 that had not been designed for the Atlantic route. BAC's Managing Director, Sir George Edwards insisted on appearing in front of this Committee and established that the aircraft was designed for African and Far Eastern routes at BOAC's instigation, and that the airline had in no way been forced to 'buy British'.

Government intervention ensured that BOAC accepted the twelve standard VC10s and seventeen of the thirty Supers, while the RAF's order for eleven was increased to fourteen. BOAC demanded a Government subsidy to operate the VC10 while refusing to reveal its true operating costs. Its competitors were not slow to use this 'evidence' against the VC10, and it can be argued that BOAC's intransigence had an adverse effect on the VC10's sales.

In service BOAC found that the VC10 may have had slightly higher operating costs than the 707, but it also possessed greater passenger appeal, suffered from fewer fatigue cracks, less corrosion and had lower maintenance costs. On transatlantic routes the BOAC Super VC10s' passenger appeal was evident and they achieved 71.6 per cent load factors when the market average was 52.1 per cent: many passengers elected to fly on the VC10 in preference even to the later Boeing 747 'Jumbo

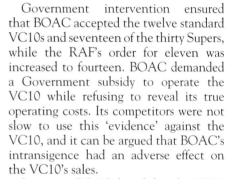

The first Super VC10, G-ASGA, taking off at the September 1964 Farnborough Air Show. After service with BOAC/British Airways it was stored at Abingdon for almost ten years before being flown to Filton and converted into a VC10 K.4 inflight-refuelling tanker, flying again in December 1994. It was scrapped in 2006. BAE Systems

Super VC10 G-ASGH in the final livery it wore. After being withdrawn from service it was bought by the RAF to be cannibalized for spares, stored at Abingdon for six years and scrapped in 1987.
BAE Systems

G-ARVC, one of five Standard VC10s that flew with Gulf Air from 1974 to 1978 until purchase by the RAF for conversion into flight-refuelling tankers.
BAE Systems

British United's first VC10, G-ASIW, undergoing ground testing at Weybridge prior to its first flight at the end of July 1964. The livery is not fully painted and when completed it did not wear the 'Jet' lettering. It was eventually sold to Air Malawi and scrapped in Blantyre, Malawi, in May 1981.
BAE Systems

Jet'. In 1975 BOAC's annual report stated that the VC10's revenue performance was the best in the fleet, superior to the 747 and the 707.

Specification – Type 1101 VC10	
Length:	158ft 8in (48.36m)
Wingspan:	146ft 2in (44.55m)
Height:	39ft 6in (12.04m)
MTOW:	312,000lb (141,500kg)
Cruising speed:	580mph (930km/h)
Range:	5,850 miles (9,400km)
Passengers:	135
Powerplant:	4 × 21,000lb Conway 42

Into Service

BOAC inaugurated services with G-ARVJ on 29 April 1964 with a flight from London to Lagos. By 30 July all of BOAC's standard VC10s had flown and seven had been delivered. The remainder followed soon after, with the final delivery (G-ARVB) on 6 February 1965.

The first Super VC10 (G-ASGA) made its maiden flight from Weybridge on 7 May 1964 in BOAC colours, piloted by Brian Trubshaw. As it had an important testing role to fulfil, half of the cabin was fitted out with flight-test instrumentation. By September 1964, when it appeared in 'Super VC10' livery at the 1964 Farnborough Air Show, G-ASGA had flown 140 hours on handling and stability trials. It carried out a full flight test programme including stalling trials fitted with a tail parachute and tests in

January 1965 carrying a spare engine in a nacelle under the right wing. G-ASGB was also employed on testing, with 'hot and high' trials at Torrejon, Khartoum and Johannesburg. The Super entered service with BOAC's transatlantic routes on 1 April 1965, when G-ASGD flew from Heathrow to New York.

G-ARVC was leased to Nigeria Airways, in their livery, for eighteen months in March 1966, but it was not until September 1969 that the airline had its own VC10 when G-ARVA was sold to it. Unfortunately it crashed at Kano only two months later. Only ten years after introduction into service, all bar one of BOAC's remaining standard VC10s were withdrawn from service. Of these, three were traded in for Boeing 747s and scrapped, while five were sold to Gulf Air with whom they served from 1974 to 1978, when they were bought by the RAF for conversion into flight refuelling tankers. G-ARVF became an executive jet for the United Arab Emirates and G-ARVM, which continued with BOAC until 1979, was donated to the RAF Museum at Cosford. G-ARVF is preserved at Hermeskeil in Germany, and the fuselage of G-ARVM resides at the Brooklands Museum.

Two of the Supers were lost through terrorist action, most notably G-ASGN blown up at Dawson Field in Jordan in September 1970; G-ASGO suffered the same fate in March 1974 at Amsterdam. Withdrawn from service in March 1981, fourteen of the surviving fleet of Supers were purchased by the RAF for spares

recovery and possible use as additional tankers, while G-ASGC is preserved at the Imperial War Museum, Duxford.

Specification – Type 1151 Super VC10	
Length:	171ft 8in (52.32m)
Wingspan:	146ft 2in (44.55m)
Height:	39ft 6in (12.04m)
MTOW:	335,000lb (153,000kg)
Cruising speed:	580mph (930km/h)
Range:	6,260 miles (10,070km)
Passengers:	163
Powerplant:	4 × 22,500lb Conway 43

Other Operators

Unlike the nationalized BOAC, British United Airways (BUA), an independent airline under the dynamic leadership of Sir Freddie Laker, showed great confidence in the VC10. BUA initially ordered four VC10s; though it later halved the order, it did in the end operate four VC10s, acquiring one from Ghana Airways and one from Laker Airways. The two BUA VC10s (G-ASIW and G-ASIX) were the first to incorporate a large forward freight door, which hinged upwards to give unobstructed loading to the forward cabin. In preparation for service with BUA on African and South American routes, G-ASIW left Gatwick on 13 September 1964 after appearing at the Farnborough Air Show. With its VC10s BUA turned BOAC's loss on the South American run into a profit and later introduced them on charter flights to the USA. BUA also received a third aircraft, G-ATDJ, originally destined for Ghana Airways, and later the refurbished prototype, G-ARTA.

Ghana Airways was the first export customer in February 1961, initially ordering three standard VC10s, subsequently reduced to two. The first Ghana VC10, 9G-ABO, flew on 27 January 1965 and was followed by 9G-ABP which was equipped, like BUA's machines, with the forward freight door. 9G-ABO flew the first service from London to Accra on 15 February 1965 and continued in use until 1980.

Middle East Airlines (MEA) would have ordered the VC10 but for difficulties

The first of five Super VC10s for East African Airways, registered 5X-UVA. This aircraft was delivered in September 1966 but crashed after an aborted take-off in April 1972. BAE Systems

in financing the purchase. Instead, MEA leased Ghana's second VC10 but this was blown up on the ground at Beirut Airport during an Israeli ground attack. Later, MEA leased the prototype VC10, G-ARTA, which, at the end of its development role in 1967, was flown back into Weybridge for a complete structural overhaul and conversion to airline standard. It was then leased to Laker Airways (which Sir Freddie had formed when he left BUA), which immediately subleased the aircraft to MEA as OD-AFA from January 1968 to March 1969; it was then returned to BAC, which sold it to British United two months later. With the merger of BUA and Caledonian in November 1970, it emerged in British Caledonian colours. While landing at Gatwick on 28 January 1972 G-ARTA landed heavily and bounced twice, badly creasing the fuselage fore and aft of the wings. The aircraft was beyond economic repair, and was broken up in 1975.

The three remaining British Caledonian (ex-BUA) aircraft were sold in 1973–74 to, respectively, the Sultan of Oman as a VIP transport, Air Malawi and RAE Bedford for research as XX914. The Omani aircraft flew back into Weybridge on 6 July 1986 and is preserved at the Brooklands Museum.

The day before the BOAC Super VC10 flew its inaugural transatlantic services on 1 April 1965, East African Airways ordered three Supers, later increasing the order to five. All the EAA aircraft had freight doors fitted and the fifth aircraft, 5H-MOG, was the final Super VC10

completed, making its maiden flight from Weybridge to Wisley on 16 February 1970 with Brian Trubshaw – taking a break from Concorde testing – at the controls. In service the EAA fleet had to contend with taking off from hot and high airports such as Nairobi – 5,327ft above sea level with temperatures typically reaching highs of 28°C – and were the only large airliners able to operate fully loaded from there at that time. One of the EAA Supers crashed at Addis Ababa in April 1972; in 1977 BAC repossessed the remaining four, and they were flown into Filton for storage.

The Double-Deck VC10 Proposal

On 2 July 1965 BAC announced the first details of a 265-seat development of the Super VC10. To accommodate this number of people BAC proposed a fuselage 33ft (10m) longer and a twin-deck layout with 80 per cent of passengers on the upper deck and the remainder on the lower. Two versions were projected: the first, with Conways as already employed in the VC10, could fly from London to New York fully loaded; the second, powered by larger Rolls-Royce RB178s, provided even greater range. This version of the VC10 could use the existing nose, wings, tail, and so on; all that was needed was a larger fuselage. However, post-TSR2, BAC could not even partly fund its development, so it could not proceed without Government assistance.

Development finally ceased when, in May 1966, the Labour Government refused to provide the £40m launch costs.

Chinese Interest

Following approaches from Beijing, in October 1972 a BAC sales team left for China to discuss a purchase of VC10s by the Chinese Government, which was dissatisfied with its Russian-built Ilyushin Il-62s. Following this visit BAC made a proposal for the re-opening of the production line to the Chinese: twenty aircraft to be supplied, with the first delivery three years and three months from the settlement of the contract. The rate of production would be six per annum, and at the end of deliveries components for at least ten more would be delivered to China, where licensed production would commence.

Such a deal was strewn with pitfalls and – unfortunately, since work was needed at Weybridge – did not proceed. BAC would have had to renegotiate contracts with subcontractors and equipment suppliers, and would also have needed the Chinese to accept a greater than three-year timeframe before receiving its first VC10. The unit price would have been greater than a Boeing 707 owing to the high price of re-establishing the production line.

RAF VC10s

The Royal Air Force required the VC10 to perform three principal roles: passenger transport, freight and casualty evacuation. The RAF originally ordered five VC10s in September 1961, increasing the order a year later to eleven; following the problems with BOAC, the order was further increased to fourteen in July 1964. Some of these aircraft remain in service at the time of writing, and the planned out-of-service date for them is currently 2013.

In September 1969 XR809 was loaned to Rolls-Royce for conversion to become a test bed for the Rolls-Royce RB211.

The first RAF VC10, XR806, at Wisley in late January 1966. It had first flown in November 1965 and was only delivered in April 1967; it flew with the RAF for thirty years. On the taxiway is One-Eleven D-ABHH, which was assembled at Weybridge and was an executive aircraft for the Helmut Horten department store group on Germany. BAE Systems

The first conversion of a VC10 to a flight-refuelling tanker was to the former G-ARVG of British Airways and later Gulf Air. Registered ZA141, it first flew from Filton in June 1982. It was withdrawn from use in February 2000. Author

ZA141 and ZA143 during flight-refuelling trials. The colour scheme shown on ZA141 was only used initially on that aircraft. Subsequent aircraft such as ZA143 appeared in hemp, and in later years in grey. BAE Systems

The twin Conways on the left side were removed and replaced with the large nacelle for the single RB211.

The RAF's VC10 C.1s were built as the Type 1106 and, though they have the standard aircraft fuselage, they have the fin fuel tank and the same model Conways as the Super. They also received a forward freight door, an Artouste APU and provision for flight refuelling. The first aircraft, XR806, made its maiden flight from Weybridge to Wisley on 26 November 1965 piloted by Brian Trubshaw. Both it and the succeeding aircraft, XR807, were used by BAC and RAF for extensive trials. XR808 was the first to be delivered to 10 Squadron at Lyneham, where it arrived in August 1966.

Employed in supporting the forces around the world, VC10 operations were greatly increased in April 1982 when the United Kingdom went to war to regain the Falkland Islands, which had been invaded by Argentina at the beginning of that month. The Falklands were liberated the following June, after which the VC10's flight-refuelling facility – never previously used – was reactivated to allow direct flights between RAF Brize Norton and the new airbase – RAF Mount Pleasant – that was hurriedly constructed on the Falklands. In a similar fashion the VC10s have played an important transport role in the two wars with Iraq and the war in Afghanistan.

Specification – Type 1106 VC10 C.1	
Length:	158ft 8in (48.36m)
Wingspan:	146ft 2in (44.55m)
Height:	39ft 6in (12.04m)
MTOW:	322,000lb (146,000kg)
Cruising speed:	580mph (930km/h)
Range:	6,260 miles (10,070km)
Passengers:	150 troops or 78 stretcher cases
Powerplant:	4 × 22,500lb Conway 43

RAF Tankers

By the late 1970s the RAF was considering how it might replace its ageing Handley Page Victor tankers. Five former Gulf Air VC10s and the four surviving

An RAF VC10 photographed in the current livery in The Netherlands in June 2010. All of the initial VC10s delivered to the RAF in the late 1960s now have a flight-refuelling capability. They are due to remain in service until the end of 2013. Mike Phipp

East African Supers were purchased by the RAF in 1977–78 for conversion into three-point flight-refuelling tankers, with additional fuel tanks installed in the fuselage. Although Weybridge carried out the design work, the modifications took place at the former BAC Filton plant. A new ventral hose drogue unit was installed in the rear underfloor freight bay and two flight refuelling pods under the wings. The standard VC10s became K.2s and the Super VC10s were designated K.3s. The standards had large apertures cut into their upper fuselages to allow for the installation of the new fuselage tanks, while the ex-East African Supers had their tanks installed through the fuselage freight door. The first K.2 conversion, ZA141 – formerly BOAC's G-ARVG – first flew on 22 June 1982 piloted by Roy Radford. (The aircraft had been stored for several years before conversion work started.) On its sixteenth flight ZA141 inadvertently entered a situation that required some dynamic piloting to recover. In so doing, an undiscovered crack in the structure resulted in the failure of part of the fin; as a result the fin and rudder were replaced using parts from XX914. The remainder of the VC10 K.2s and K3s soon followed from the Filton factory, and joined 101 Squadron at Brize Norton.

In 1991 an additional contract led to the RAF finally making use of five of the fifteen former BOAC Super VC10s that had been purchased from BOAC ten years earlier and stored at Abingdon. These were converted into three-point flight-refuelling tankers and designated K.4s; the remaining stored Super VC10s were broken up for spares. A substantial amount of work had to be carried out just to make these aircraft airworthy for a single flight – with gear down and slats and flaps locked – the short distance from Abingdon to Filton. Some of the aircraft had suffered so much corrosion that a large number of parts had to be replaced by newly made parts. Owing to the age of the aircraft (which lacked the large freight door of the ex-East African Supers) it was considered too risky to make a large aperture in the fuselage to fit additional fuselage fuel tanks, so the K.4s had to rely on their existing fuel tanks. As part of the same contract, between 1991 and 1997 the RAF's remaining thirteen original VC10s were modified by Flight Refuelling at Hurn into two-point tankers with underwing refuelling pods to become C.1Ks.

A number of VC10s have been withdrawn from service over the years, and at the end of 2010 the RAF's surviving fleet was thirteen strong: with eight C.1Ks, four K.3s and one K.4, they will be able to celebrate the golden jubilee of the type's maiden flight in 2012.

VC10: Conclusion

Even Vickers had not been very optimistic about the sales prospects of the VC10 and its partners in BAC, English Electric and Bristol, wisely decided that they did not want to share the liability, so it became an 'old account' project. Vickers had taken a risk in going ahead with the VC10 tied to a BOAC specification, but had considered that after fulfilling the airline's order it would need only twenty-seven more orders, sixty-two in total, to break even. Another influencing factor was the expression of a very different sentiment to that prevalent in the early twenty-first century. VC10 work was needed for the Weybridge factory following the end of the Valiant production in 1957 and the run down of Viscount production. Without it the factory might face closure, so work was needed and the VC10 would fill that gap.

From early 1964 the VC10 suffered adverse publicity from BOAC, the airline that had specifically commissioned it, and the lack of confidence from its main customer must have had a negative impact on sales. Its chances of making inroads into the market after the Boeing 707 and Douglas DC-8 were established in service were weak, especially as these two types continued to be developed and improved. With perhaps fifteen more orders the production line would have remained open until 1972, and would have been able to fulfil the order from the Chinese without the prohibitive costs of restarting the production line. Sales could then have reached the eighties and Vickers would have recovered their investment over the life of the programme.

Weybridge After the VC10

With the end of VC10 production and the decision not to go ahead with the Three-Eleven at the end of 1970, the prospects for Weybridge did not look very bright. The site, one of the most famous in British aviation history, had no large project of its own. But it did still have other substantial projects in hand, such as the forward and rear fuselages for the Concorde production aircraft, keeping 1,200 Weybridge workers busy. The engineering effort involved in manufacturing the forward fuselages, complete with all flying controls and wiring, ready for onward delivery to either the Filton or Toulouse final assembly lines was equivalent to the manufacture of a complete BAC One-Eleven.

Concorde forward fuselage production at Weybridge. The four nearest fuselages are in the following order: G-BOAC, F-BTSC, F-BVFA and G-BOAA. A fifth fuselage can be seen behind, and two tail sections on the right. BAE Systems

One of the two large final assembly hangars at Weybridge in January 1970. At the back of the hangar is the final VC10, 5H-MOG, a Super VC10 for East African Airways. There were also three Hurn-built aircraft in for refurbishment: Uruguayan flag carrier PLUNA's Viscount 745 CX-BHA, former Autair One-Eleven G-AWXJ and Cambrian One-Eleven G-AVOE. BAE Systems

When BAC took over Hunting in 1960 it had also received design authority for earlier Hunting aircraft such as the Pembrokes that were operated as communications aircraft by the RAF. During 1970–71 fourteen Pembrokes flew in to Weybridge to receive new wing spars in the east-side erecting shops. Here XL954 is seen taxiing down the Weybridge runway after the completion of the work; in the background is the Brooklands control tower, which is still extant. BAE Systems

BAC's substantial Weybridge facilities were also employed in the testing of a structural test specimen of the Shorts SD-330 in 1975. BAC Weybridge produced the SD-330 flaps. BAE Systems

To help the Hurn operation and assist its own workload, thirteen One-Elevens were assembled at Weybridge in two batches in 1966 and 1969–70. As the wings, centre section, undercarriage and other parts were made at the Surrey site it was not especially complicated to send the Hurn-built fuselage sections and Filton-built tails there. A batch of six aircraft was produced in 1966, and throughout the late 1960s One-Elevens made frequent flights into Weybridge, notably development models for refurbishment to delivery standard. In 1969–70 a second batch of seven One-Elevens was completed there, ending with D-ANNO for Bavaria Fluggesellschaft. On 19 December 1970 it made its first flight, which was the final first flight of an aircraft completed at the famous Weybridge/Brooklands site. These One-Elevens typically carried out their production flight testing from Wisley, unlike Hurn-built One-Elevens that made their production test flying from their home ground.

One of the smaller tasks taken on at Weybridge in 1970 was the re-sparring of the wings of fourteen Hunting Pembrokes for the RAF. Following the discovery of fatigue cracks, the RAF had a choice of extending the lives of the Luton-built Pembrokes – for which BAC had design authority as owners of Hunting – or purchasing Beech Queen Airs. The RAF chose the former and the Pembrokes were flown in and worked on in the main erecting shop. The first to arrive was WV735 and the final example left in 1971. Other work for sister factories included the Jaguar reconnaissance pod for the Military Aircraft Division.

For Hawker Siddeley the factory continued to build 748 engine nacelles, which were similar to those originally manufactured for the Viscount, fuselage fuel tanks for the Victor tanker conversions at Woodford and tails for Lockheed Tristars. BAC's facilities were also employed on a Shorts SD-330 structural test specimen, which was tested at Weybridge. The initial design of the wing and detailed design of the centre section and fuselage top was carried out by BAC Weybridge design office.

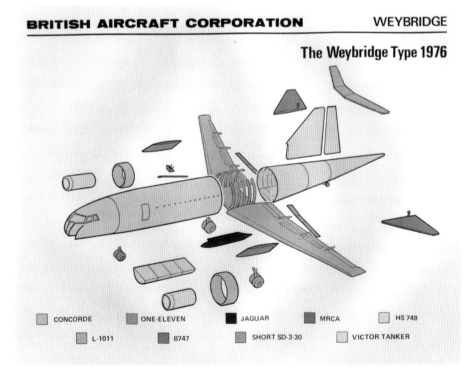

'Weybridge 1976' illustrates all the work taking place manufacturing sub-assembles on the site in 1976: Concorde forward fuselages and tails; One-Eleven wings, centre-sections and undercarriages; Jaguar reconnaissance pods; MRCA (Tornado) tails; Hawker Siddeley 748 engine casings; Lockheed L1011 Tristar engine casings and tails; Boeing 747 engine pylons; Shorts SD-330 flaps; and Handley Page Victor K.2 bomb bay fuel tanks. BAE Systems

CHAPTER SIX

One-Eleven to Three-Eleven

The BAC One-Eleven is the project that is perhaps most clearly identified with BAC, as its development and the bulk of its production was essentially limited by the short life of the Corporation. The decision was made to go ahead with the project in 1961, it made its first flight two years later, and it entered service in 1965; from 1977, despite some vain attempts, there was no further development although a low rate of production continued until 1984.

Throughout its life the One-Eleven received £19m of Government aid, with BAC matching this investment from its own resources. In 1977, at the time of nationalization, the Government had received approximately £4m in levies while the One-Eleven had made well over £250m in export sales and prevented imports by providing large numbers of aircraft to British operators. It was not only BAC that profited in the UK from these sales but also all the ancillary suppliers, as did all those employed, and those employed paid taxes back to the Exchequer.

In 1955, Hunting undertook a design study known as the H.107, for a four-abreast thirty-seater with two Bristol Orpheus engines, a moderately swept fin and a cruciform tailplane. At the time of BAC's acquisition of Hunting in 1960 the project had grown into a 80ft long, five-abreast with two Bristol Siddeley BS75 Orpheus engines of around 7,000lb thrust, a 500mph cruise speed, a range of 600 miles and a 'T' tail. This was evaluated by the project team and believed to be a sound design, and it was given the designation BAC 107. BAC carried out extensive market surveys during late 1960: eighty-nine airlines were visited in all parts of the world and some sixty indicated interest in the project, but they sought a larger, heavier machine with greater range and more power. To

provide this the Rolls-Royce Spey was chosen instead of the Orpheus, though this choice of engine was to prove a seriously limiting factor in the aircraft's later development.

It was on this basis that the project, as the BAC One-Eleven, was launched. The Corporation set down an initial production batch of twenty aircraft and abandoned the larger, more complex Vickers VC11 project described in the next section. Design was centred at Weybridge, with Luton designing and manufacturing the wing, and the tail design and manufacture being handled at Filton. The assembly line was planned for Hurn, where the bulk of the Viscounts were built.

The VC11

The decision to go ahead with the One-Eleven followed the cancellation of the Vickers VC11 in the spring of 1961. The VC11 had been designed in October 1959 to meet the BEA requirement for which the airline eventually chose the de Havilland 121, which later became the Trident. The VC11 was a scaled-down version of the VC10 with capacity for 138 passengers for short- to medium-range routes. In December 1959, in an unprecedented move, the Government agreed to contribute 50 per cent toward the development costs, which were expected to be £19.5m. After the formation of BAC development continued and the VC11 received a prospective launch order for fourteen aircraft from Trans-Canada Airlines. However, management soon judged that the VC11 was entering a crowded marketplace, which already had a number of competitors: the Boeing 727, the Caravelle and the Trident. As the firm could not go ahead with both the VC11 and the One-Eleven,

the VC11 was cancelled. Fortunately, BAC was able to transfer the £9.75m Government launch cost grant to the One-Eleven.

The Launch and the First Orders

On 9 May 1961 BAC held a press conference to launch the new jet and announced its first order for ten series 200s (there never was a series 100) from British United Airways – an impressive start for a major British airliner, launched with the announcement of an order from Britain's major independent airline, not BEA or BOAC. The One-Eleven was not designed for a single customer, unlike the Trident and VC10, which were tailored to BEA and BOAC needs, respectively. As a result this new jet had a far wider appeal from the outset.

The schedule was ambitious, with the first flight planned for the second quarter of 1963, certification by mid-1964 and deliveries to BUA that autumn. Sir George Edwards stated that BAC saw a total market of 1,000 aircraft and that they would be happy with 40 per cent, leaving a sizeable market to any other entrants.

Orders began to roll in and by the time of the first flight on 20 August 1963 the One-Eleven had amassed sixty orders from airlines, especially in the USA where Braniff, Mohawk and American Airlines had all chosen it in preference to home-grown offerings. American had ordered a heavier Series 400 One-Eleven, and toyed with having Pratt & Whitney JT8D-5 engines instead of Speys, as initially fitted to the competing Douglas DC 9-10. BAC produced two comparable specifications and contracts, one for each power unit, but American eventually decided to stay with the Rolls-Royce

The prototype One-Eleven, G-ASHG, made its maiden flight on 20 August 1963 and embarked on the flight-test programme. Tragically, while carrying out stalling tests on 22 October it entered a deep stall from which it could not be recovered and it crashed, killing all seven crew on board. BAE Systems

engines. This had serious ramifications for the future of the aircraft, unfortunately, for the Spey could not be developed much further: the lack of additional power stymied the One-Eleven's development, while the competing DC-9 and Boeing 737 grew and grew in size and received more and more orders.

Specification – One-Eleven 200	
Length:	93ft 6in (28.5m)
Wingspan:	88ft 6in (26.97m)
Height:	24ft 6in (7.47m)
MTOW:	79,000lb (36,000kg)
Cruising speed:	548mph (882km/h)
Range:	2,130 miles (3,430km)
Passengers:	89
Powerplant:	2 × 10,410lb Rolls-Royce Spey 506

The Flight Test Programme

Shortly after it first flight, on 20 August 1963, G-ASHG positioned at the BAC Flight Test Centre at Wisley, Surrey. The test programme set off at a cracking pace, with G-ASHG making fifty-three flights of eighty-one hours in sixty days. The first phase of the flight programme was devoted to a preliminary assessment of the aircraft. On 22 October, G-ASHG took off from Wisley for stalling trials piloted by Mike Lithgow. It successfully executed four stalls as part of its test profile before entering a fifth at 15,000–16,000ft, which resulted in it entering a stable (or 'deep') stall, from which recovery was impossible despite the best efforts of the crew, all seven of whom died in the crash.

In their statement about the crash in November 1963, BAC stated that there would be alterations to the wing leading edge to improve the nose-down pitching characteristics, and a fully powered elevator to provide a direct mechanical linkage between the pilot's control and the elevator. It was later decided that a stick-pusher would be installed so that on the approach to the stall the control column would be automatically pushed forward to introduce a downward elevator force and stop the aircraft from entering a stall.

Restarting the Test Programme and Into Service

With the loss of G-ASHG and the shock to all those involved, the test programme came to a temporary halt since there were no One-Elevens in the air at the time. There was a two-month gap before the first production aircraft, G-ASJA, took to the air from Hurn on 19 December 1963. The following February the second production aircraft, G-ASJB, made its first flight, joining G-ASJA at Wisley.

The problems besetting the testing were exacerbated when G-ASJB was written off following a landing accident at Wisley in mid-March. Matters were hardly improved when, on the anniversary of the One-Eleven's first flight, G-ASJD, the aircraft specially modified to carry out the stalling trials, was crash-landed on Salisbury Plain owing to pilot error. The aircraft was dismantled on site and roaded back to Hurn for rebuild while another One-Eleven had to be prepared to take over its task. These various accidents undoubtedly lost the aircraft sales from 'blue chip' carriers such as Alitalia and Iberia. Eventually, however, the One-Eleven was certified on 5 April

G-ASJJ, one of British United's One-Eleven 200s, 'beating up' BAC's Flight Test Centre at Wisley, Surrey. G-ASJJ first flew in February 1965 and was delivered two months later. It crashed at Milan-Linate in January 1969. BAE Systems

N1543 of Braniff seen at Hurn before delivery; this became the first One-Eleven delivered to an American customer on 16 March 1965. From the second from the left BAC test pilots Johnnie Walker and Peter Marsh, and Captain George Cheetham of Braniff; others unknown. BAE Systems

Serious Competition

Meanwhile, in the USA the Douglas DC-9-10 made its maiden flight in February 1965 and gained certification in November 1965. Douglas had orders from a wide spectrum of airlines including Air Canada, Bonanza, Delta, Eastern Hawaiian, KLM, Swissair and TWA, many of which had been courted by BAC and some of which had come near to ordering the One-Eleven. The order from Eastern was very significant because it was then the largest airline in the world. BAC had virtually bagged the order, but Douglas had offered the short-term lease of DC-9-10s and developed the stretched DC-9-30 for later delivery to Eastern. This early stretch of their basic design was to give them the edge in winning orders over the One-Eleven, since BAC was unable to offer a stretched aircraft at that time.

The One-Eleven 300/400 Series

In preparation for the American Airlines order, in May 1963 BAC had announced two developments, the 300 and 400 series, which could carry heavier payloads over longer range. The difference between these two versions was that Federal Aviation Administration (FAA) set a two-crew weight limit of 80,000lb, above which an third crew member was required. Fortunately the ruling was abolished in 1966, and from that time the 300 series classification was dropped and only the 400 series classification used.

The first 400 series development aircraft, G-ASYD, took to the air on 13 July 1965 from Hurn and immediately engaged on its test programme. On 16

1965, entering service with BUA four days later.

Although the One-Eleven was now in service BAC had a lot of work to do to bring the aircraft up to delivery standard, and the final BUA delivery was only in November 1965. The Duke of Edinburgh visited Braniff's Dallas base on 25 April 1965 to inaugurate the One-Eleven at a special dedication ceremony, and the aircraft entered service later that day.

The user-friendly aspects of the One-Eleven were soon apparent to the airlines that had chosen it. The combination of airstairs, auxiliary power unit, waist-high baggage holds and single-point pressure refuelling meant the operators were able to set new standards of short-haul productivity in terms of quick turnarounds and very high utilization rates. In the first year of operations the seven delivered averaged 3,960 landings each, and Braniff's aircraft were averaging a daily flying utilization of 9 hours 26 minutes over fourteen route segments. The true working day was nineteen hours, and the One-Eleven's reliability the best ever for a new type. Other airlines including Aer Lingus, Zambia Airways, British Eagle and the American carriers Mohawk and Aloha of Hawaii also received One-Eleven 200s.

The One-Eleven series 400 prototype G-ASYD in 'BAC One-Eleven 400S' markings at Wisley in the summer of 1965. This was its second livery and one of the many it carried during its life as a test aircraft and demonstrator. BAE Systems

The largest customer for the One-Eleven was American Airlines, whose order for the series 400 version eventually grew to thirty aircraft. This photo of passengers boarding an American aircraft was actually posed at Hurn for publicity purposes.
BAE Systems

In Service with American Airlines

American Airlines became the third American operator to introduce the One-Eleven, but was the first to inaugurate the series 400 into service. The American aircraft had the distinctive bare-metal finish of the airline's fleet, and their first was delivered just before Christmas 1965. The remaining twenty-nine aircraft followed at close intervals, with the final delivery in December 1966 – an average of one every twelve days, all built at BAC's Hurn plant. But as so often with the One-Eleven story, while American praised the aircraft in operation, before long passenger demand was such that the airline needed a larger type: American replaced their One-Elevens with Boeing 727s after only six years.

September G-ASYD's sister, G-ASYE, made her maiden flight from Hurn; after shakedown trials it was delivered to Marshall's of Cambridge in November for the fitting of an executive interior in the front cabin and airline seating in the back, ready for three extensive world sales tours. In a hectic six-month period from November 1965 to May 1966 G-ASYE travelled 160,000 miles with 334 separate flights.

Specification – One-Eleven 400	
Length:	93ft 6in (28.5m)
Wingspan:	88ft 6in (26.97m)
Height:	24ft 6in (7.47m)
MTOW:	88,500lb (40,000kg)
Cruising speed:	548mph (882km/h)
Range:	2,250 miles (3,620km)
Passengers:	89
Powerplant:	2 × 11,400lb Rolls-Royce Spey 511

The 300/400 in Service with UK Airlines

British Eagle had taken over Kuwait Airways' order for three 300s, but were followed at the end of 1965 by Laker Airways, which ordered three One-Eleven 300s for delivery in the following year and soon increased its order to four aircraft. Channel Airways, a British inclusive tour and charter operator based at Southend, received two 400s specially built with an additional window exit over the wing, like in the 500 series, which meant that Channel were now allowed to pack up to 99 passengers into the aircraft. Yet another British airline, Autair of Luton, ordered three 400s in late 1967, receiving them in time for the busy 1968 summer period; Autair was later to become Court Line and a short-lived 500 series user.

G-AVBY, one of Laker Airways' four series 300s, was leased to Air Congo in May 1967 prior to entering service with Laker in February 1968.
BAE Systems

In addition to airline customers, many One-Elevens were ordered from the production line as executive aircraft. **N270E was delivered to Engelhard Industries in September 1967.** BAE Systems

Originally built for Philippine Air Lines, this One-Eleven was leased to Spanish operator TAE as EC-BQF from March 1969 until February 1970. Seen here at Wisley, this aircraft was one of the thirteen One-Elevens assembled at Weybridge. BAE Systems

Around the World

The One-Eleven failed to penetrate into the 'blue chip' airline market in Europe, where the DC-9 had rather more success. However, in March 1967 Bavaria Fluggesellschaft became the first German One-Eleven operator, by leasing a 400 originally built for Philippines Airlines (PAL); it later ordered two 400s. Additional 400s joined the fleet in subsequent years as traffic grew, and were then superseded by the lengthened series 500s. PAL had placed an order for two 400s in November 1964 and later ordered the 500. Gulf Air of Bahrain became the first operator in the Middle East and, in a precedent for an Eastern Bloc country, Tarom, the state airline of Romania, ordered six 400s in 1968; this eventually led to more orders and licence production.

The One-Eleven 400 proved a hit in Latin America and initially had an near-monopoly of the market. It sold widely, if in very small individual orders, being operated by Austral of Argentina, TACA of El Salvador, LACSA of Costa Rica, LANICA of Nicaragua, and the Brazilian line, VASP. Austral and LACSA later graduated to the 500 series, as did many others.

The Stretched One-Eleven – the 500 Series

The One-Eleven's entry into service was a great success, with many airlines reporting large increases in passenger load factors and high utilization. Additionally, the world tour had allowed many potential customers to see the aircraft at first hand and be convinced of its versatility and sturdiness as a short-haul workhorse. However, these would-be customers were also being courted by Douglas with the DC-9 and Boeing with the 737, and since the American aircraft could carry more passengers and as air traffic trends indicated substantial increases, BAC came under pressure to produce a larger version. Many potential orders – notably Swissair – were undoubtedly lost because no clear stretch capability was on offer.

In June 1966 British European Airways (BEA) demonstrated its patriotic fervour by expressing an interest in ordering Boeing 727-200s and 737-200s. (It is ironic to reflect how keen BEA now was to replace the Trident, which had been designed exactly to their specification and had entered service only two years earlier; admittedly, the 727-200 was a larger and superior aircraft.) Fortunately the Labour Government told BEA to think again and order British aircraft. As a result, the lengthened BAC One-Eleven 500 was developed for BEA as an equal to the 737 and was further developed and sold well elsewhere.

Boeing had launched its 737-100 in February 1965 and three days later Lufthansa ordered twenty-one machines. The 737 had the same fuselage width as Boeing's larger 707 and 727, with scaled-down 727 wings. The engines, like the DC-9's, were Pratt & Whitney JT8Ds giving 14,000lb thrust, 2,000lb more than the Spey 512 on the One-Eleven 500. Before the first flight in April 1967 Boeing, like Douglas, introduced an extended capacity version, the 737-200 (with a maximum capacity of 124 seats) and quickly won an order for forty from United Airlines. Shortly after, the inaptly named Britannia Airways ordered three 737-200s, going on to order twenty-four more Boeings 737-200s in the years that followed and later to operate 737-800s.

Having told BEA to 'Buy British', the Government prevaricated for a year in its financial support for the One-Eleven 500, which was tied up with compensation payments to BAC for the cancelled TSR2 and the Government's desire to nationalize BAC and Hawker Siddeley. As a result of this delay Aer Lingus, which would have waited for the stretched One-Eleven, went ahead and ordered Boeing 737s. Eventually the Government had to provide developments costs of £9m – to be repaid by a levy on sales – to enable BAC to finance a stretched version. A total of eighty-six Hurn-built and nine Romanian-assembled One-Eleven 500s were built, amply repaying the Government's investment through export earnings and frustrated imports.

The Two-Eleven Proposal

Proposals from BAC for a variant of the VC10 eventually evolved into the Two-Eleven as competition to the Boeing 727-200 that BEA wanted to order. The Two-Eleven was a very much scaled-up expansion of the One-Eleven design: 156ft long, seating 203 passengers and powered by two of the new 40,000lb thrust Rolls-Royce RB211s. It was intended that the Two-Eleven would be assembled at Hurn, even though much of the fabrication would take place at Weybridge. BEA indicated to both BAC and the Labour Government that the Two-Eleven exactly met its needs, but a go-ahead decision was thwarted by the Government's commitment to continue with the Anglo-French-German Airbus project. Therefore, in December 1967 the Two-Eleven project was axed and BEA had to make do with the Hawker Siddeley Trident 3B. With hindsight it is easy to question the wisdom of BAC's decision to expend so much time, energy and money in pursuing the Two-Eleven project, especially when likely customers such as Air France and Lufthansa had already chosen the Boeing 727-200, which flew in July 1967 and entered service at the end of that year.

The Origins of Airbus and BAC's Role

In the late 1960s it was clear that VC10 work was running out and the military focus had passed to the Preston Division following the TSR2 cancellation. Sir George Edwards could foresee that BAC might become only a manufacturer of military aircraft and guided weapons, and how difficult it would be to maintain the viability of the Weybridge and Hurn plants without a major civil project. BAC was not part of the tripartite Airbus project: the Government had decided that Hawker Siddeley should be the British Airbus partner, as BAC was partner to Sud Aviation on Concorde. At that time the British aircraft industry was quite capable of producing a relatively straightforward civil airliner by itself, without collaboration with other European aircraft industries. Accordingly, BAC embarked on building a new civil airliner of its own (the Three-Eleven).

This went against the recommendations of the Plowden Committee established in December 1964 by the Labour Government to examine the future place and organization of the aircraft industry. One of its main decisions was that henceforward the industry should only proceed with projects in collaboration with other European countries. (Though

An artist's impression of the proposed BAC Three-Eleven. This would have had a capacity for approximately 245 passengers on short and medium-range routes. If it had gone ahead, manufacture would have taken place at Weybridge, final assembly at Hurn and flight testing at Fairford. BAE Systems

Rolls-Royce was exempt from this decision.) Sir George Edwards' response was that he had not seen the French industry directed that it could not go it alone with projects. On joint projects, French officials always insisted on project leadership, which they achieved on Concorde, Airbus and Jaguar. Where the French failed to secure project leadership, as on the AFVG and the European Fighter Aircraft, they withdrew.

BAC Three-Eleven

Deprived of the opportunity to develop the Two-Eleven, BAC embarked on the Three-Eleven, which evolved into an advanced-technology, wide-bodied airliner carrying 245 passengers in eight-abreast seating with a range of 1,450 miles. Outline design work was completed by mid-1968 and the Three-Eleven emerged with a fuselage 19ft 9in wide, twin rear-mounted Rolls-Royce RB211s and a T tail. It was 183ft 7in long with a wingspan of 147ft. The fuselage width was equivalent to the American Douglas DC-10 and Lockheed Tristar three-engined widebodies. An advantageous feature of the design was the two-crew flightdeck, contrasting with the American tri-jets and the Airbus A300, which all settled for two pilots and a flight engineer.

BAC then undertook a thorough market survey to assess the size of the market, the interest of airlines in the aircraft type and possible refinements that potential customers would require. As a

result of this research BAC concluded that the total market was in the order of 800 by 1985, though this figure was later revised upwards to 1,150. The firm estimated that it should be able to make sales of 240–280 against competing types. BAC was planning that if it could give an internal go-ahead to the project in April 1969 there could be a first flight in September 1972 and certification the following year.

Design work would take place at Weybridge and, though major sub-assemblies of the Three-Eleven were

A mock-up of the BAC Three-Eleven fuselage cross-section exhibited at the 1969 Paris Air Show. BAE Systems

to be built at Weybridge and Filton, final assembly would have been at Hurn in newly constructed final-assembly hangars, with flight-test at Fairford, where Concorde flight-testing was based. Weybridge was ruled out for final assembly owing to the wholly inadequate runway, which was only 3,600ft long and where, because of the close proximity of a railway embankment, landings could only be made from the south and take-offs from the north.

In order to spread the risk and conform to the Government's agenda for collaborative aircraft programmes, BAC sought risk-sharing partners for large parts of the aircraft from Britain and internationally. This had the dual purpose of reducing the liability to BAC, and could be used as an influence for orders from airlines in countries where parts were manufactured. Discussions led to preliminary agreements with a large number of British and international firms including Scottish Aviation, Shorts, Fairey (Belgium), Dowty Rotol, Romania, Canadair, Kawasaki Heavy Industries and Soko Mostar of Yugoslavia.

The Corporation calculated that the development costs would be approximately £150m and that up to £30m would be needed to establish the production line; Rolls-Royce would also require aid for the RB211 engine. BAC requested that the Government provide funding for half of the development costs, £75m.

BAC agreed not to proceed with the Three-Eleven unless it could gather fifty options to purchase. By September 1970 it had accumulated forty-three orders, including twenty from BEA. There was intense lobbying of the Labour Government, especially of Tony Benn, the Minister of Technology, and many believe that if Labour had won the June 1970 General Election the project would have received the launch aid needed. The new Conservative Government was broadly in favour of going ahead with the project in its initial months in power, but on 3 December 1970 announced that

An exhibition display illustrating the attributes and various seating options of the Three-Eleven. The decision not to proceed with it left BAC with no new airliner programme, and spelled the end for any future large British airliner programme.
BAE Systems

it would not provide support it. The Government had had to consider not only the needs of BAC, but also those of Hawker Siddeley, who were major sub-contractors to the Airbus, and Rolls-Royce – the financial collapse of the latter happened only a few months later, and required huge Government subvention. BAC had lost out again, having spent £4m on the stillborn project, with the immediate result of 900 redundancies at Weybridge and Hurn, mainly among the design staff.

The One-Eleven 500 Series

Meanwhile, despite attempts to develop the Two-Eleven (and later the Three-Eleven) the One-Eleven 500 was designed and built to fulfil the BEA requirement. BEA sought a relatively short-range aircraft and so only a modest rise in maximum take-off weight to 91,000lb from the 87,000lb of the series 400 was required. Almost two years behind stretched versions of the competition, the series 500 was launched on 27 January 1967 with an

order for eighteen series 510s from BEA, to be used mainly on services within West Germany. BEA insisted on compensation from the Government for having to order aircraft that were not its first choice and the Government meekly agreed – a great weapon for Boeing and Douglas salesmen!

The new version had the fuselage extended by 13ft 6in in two sections, one forward of the wing of 8ft 4in, and one aft of the wing of 5ft 2in. This allowed for four extra seat rows, increasing normal capacity from seventy-nine to ninety-nine, though 500s sometimes carried as many as 119 passengers. The wings had small extensions of 2ft 6in each. Overwing exits were doubled to two either side, underfloor hold volume was increased and the structure was strengthened. The APU was increased in power and Spey 512 engines with 12,000lb thrust were installed.

The 500 Series Test Programme

On 4 February 1967, G-ASYD flew from Wisley to Hurn to be converted into the aerodynamic prototype of the 500 series. It was cut into three, a 100in extension was fitted forward of the wing and a 62in extension aft, together with the extended wing tips. Structurally complete on 28 April, it first flew six weeks ahead of schedule, on 30 June 1967. It then embarked on the test programme based at Wisley and carried out the bulk of the certification work.

G-ASYD was joined by the first production series 510 for BEA, G-AVMH, which flew on 7 February, 1968. This aircraft was used to confirm the performance and fly at maximum weights, which

The One-Eleven series 400 prototype was rebuilt as the series 500 prototype at the Hurn factory by the addition of fuselage plugs either side of the wing and extensions to the wing tips. The conversion work took less than six months and G-ASYD made its maiden flight as the series 500 prototype on 30 June 1967. BAE Systems

The first production series 500 was a 510 built for BEA's eighteen-strong order. G-AVMH flew at Hurn in February 1968, immediately joining the test programme at Wisley. BAE Systems

G-ASYD could not as it was a conversion and not built to full series 500 structural strengths. From August to November 1968, G-AVMH tested all the specific BEA changes to the 510 series aircraft, which included a specially altered flight deck layout. Brian Trubshaw claimed that BEA's changes were equivalent to the cost of another aircraft! The 510s either met or handsomely exceeded the entire range of its contractual performance, but across the Atlantic the equivalent Douglas DC-9-30 had entered service eighteen months earlier, in February 1967.

BEA's aircraft first entered full scheduled services on 17 November 1968. They were delivered in a 97-seat, single-class configuration and gradually took on all the German services. In 1971 One-Eleven services were expanded and a division was set up in Manchester to fly all BEA flights from there to European destinations. On merging with BOAC to form British Airways on 1 April 1974, BEA brought twenty-five One-Elevens to the combined operation – its original order plus four Cambrian 400s and three 400s that BEA had purchased for services out of Birmingham just prior to the merger.

In 1978 BA indicated its intention of purchasing 737s and, although British Aerospace contested this strongly, offering a One-Eleven 600 and/or 700 series, the order was eventually placed for nineteen Boeing 737s. The 600 series was a 500 with refinement to its wings to improve lift; the 700 was a lengthened and re-engined version of the 600. One commentator has written that BA never seriously considered BAC's One-Eleven 600 and 700 proposals. Presumably to placate British Aerospace in 1978, when

placing the Boeing order BA ordered three One-Eleven 500s.

BEA's initial reluctance to adopt the One-Eleven proved to be misplaced, for the airline used a total of forty-four 400s and 500s between September 1968 and August 1998, when the last survivors left the BA fleet.

Further Development of the 500 Series

The One-Eleven 510 led to the much more significant 500D series, which was aimed specifically at the burgeoning European Inclusive Tour (IT) industry – package holidays, as they are generally known. This market was one that independent carriers could easily enter in those heavily regulated times and some airlines, for example BUA, had introduced One-Eleven 200s on these services as early as 1965, followed by others such as British Eagle in 1966.

However, with the delivery of Britannia Airways' Boeing 737s, it was clear that BAC needed to work fast to preserve a healthy share of the UK market before other domestic airlines followed Britannia's lead. BAC had enough knowledge of the One-Eleven's structural performance limits to allow significant increases in the design weights for the 500D, increasing the MTOW to 104,500lb and introducing Spey 512-14DWs with 12,550lb thrust. These improvements allowed operations with up to 119 passengers at ranges that satisfied 95 per cent of the Inclusive Tour demand at the end of the 1960s. When BAC offered the 500D in 1968 they

finally had a product that could properly compete with Douglas and Boeing.

The thoroughness of this development paid off well, since the 500D with its additional performance, range and lower seat/mile costs was bought by BUA, Caledonian, Court Line and British Midland Airways (BMA) in the UK, in addition to several German charter companies; the aircraft also gained sales in Central and South America, the Bahamas and the Philippines. To quantify the performance improvements, the early 510s built for BEA could only carry a full payload of 23,000lb over 800 miles, while the 500D was able to carry a slightly greater payload over 1,500 miles.

Specification – One-Eleven 500	
Length:	107ft 0in (32.61m)
Wingspan:	93ft 6in (28.5m)
Height:	24ft 6in (7.47m)
MTOW:	104,500lb (47,000kg)
Cruising speed:	541mph (870km/h)
Range:	2,165 miles (3,483km)
Passengers:	119
Powerplant:	2 × 12,550lb Rolls-Royce Spey 512

British Independent Operators

In early 1968 British United Airways (BUA) announced an order for four 500s which were delivered in the following year; three more joined their fleet in 1970. Only a few days after the BUA order, Caledonian joined them by ordering three 509s. At the end of 1970 British United and Caledonian merged to form British Caledonian Airways, creating a large fleet of short- and long-fuselage One-Elevens: at the time of the merger the combined fleet was eight 200s and twelve 500s of differing types. Eighteen years later British Caledonian Airways was itself taken over by British Airways, which then inherited thirteen 500s.

Though Court Line's period of operating the One-Eleven was comparatively short, it made an indelible mark because the airline decided to rename itself and totally overhauled its brand. The

Eight British-made airliners on the tarmac at Gatwick: a series 200 and two 500s of British Caledonian in the foreground, and in the distance a Dan-Air One-Eleven, a VC10 and three Comets. BAE Systems

Each of Court Line's eight One-Elevens was finished in a pastel colour – pink, orange or turquoise – with a silver logo and white wings. Quite a change from the generally staid British liveries of the time! Each aircraft was also given a Halcyon fleet name: Halcyon Sun, Halcyon Breeze, Halcyon Sky and so on. BAE Systems

German charter airline Bavaria Germanair's One-Eleven 500 D-AMAS at the airline's maintenance base at Munich. Also in the photo is BAC's Hawker Siddeley 125 executive jet G-AVPE. BAE Systems

airline, formerly named Autair, ended its scheduled services and branded itself as Britain's premier holiday airline. So with new aircraft, a new name, a striking new livery and uniforms to match it was poised to seize a large slice of the newly affluent short-haul holiday market. But by 1974 the world economic downturn, fuelled by huge rises in the price of oil, put paid to Court, which ceased operations in August 1974. The One-Elevens were repossessed and were swiftly passed on to other airlines.

European Operators

The One-Eleven 500s made an impression on the German charter market with orders from Paninternational, Germanair and Bavaria Fluggesellschaft, which was already using 400s. The latter two merged in 1977 to form Bavaria Germanair with a fleet of seven 500s and two 400s of various marks, and further merged to become Hapag-Lloyd two years later, which operated the aircraft until 1979. In May 1974 Cyprus Airways started One-Eleven operations with a leased 500 from BAC and in 1977–78 the airline took delivery of three new 500s, operating them until 1995 when they emigrated south to start operations with Nationwide Air Charter of South Africa.

Caribbean and Latin American 500s

The shorter-bodied 400 series had made its mark in the Caribbean and in Latin America, and the 500 soon followed in its wake. After leasing two 400s from BAC, Bahamas Airways bought two 500s and a 300 in 1969–70. Aviateca of Guatemala ordered a 500 in November 1970 and started operations only one week later with a leased 500 – their own aircraft was delivered in March 1971 and served until the end of the decade. Starting One-Eleven operations with a 400 in 1967, LACSA of Costa Rica received another two years later. Delighted with their One-Eleven experience, they soon decided on the larger 500 series and ordered three 500s, which were delivered at yearly intervals from 1971. In 1973 these were joined by a fourth, and the fleet continued in use on scheduled routes throughout the Caribbean until 1982. Transbrasil, previously Sadia, of Brazil operated a large fleet of 500s on domestic Brazilian services from late 1970 until early 1978.

Austral of Argentina began One-Eleven operations in 1967 with the delivery of the first of four 400s; these were followed by three 500s two years later. Needing more aircraft for their extensive domestic network serving twenty cities, Austral bought seven second-hand 500s and leased more One-Elevens. But by the early 1990s Austral sought a replacement for the type and replaced them with McDonnell Douglas MD-80s, a super-stretched DC-9 development. All the 500s were broken up in Argentina except for two 500s that European Aviation bought, which escaped back to Hurn. European's plan was to hush-kit the pair to comply with the stringent Stage 3 noise regulations that came into force in April 2002, but that programme was not viable so they never flew again and were scrapped there in early 2000.

PAL's One-Eleven Years

Philippines Air Lines was, like Austral, an early and loyal customer of the One-Eleven. It started with 400s in 1966, gradually replacing them with 104-seater

One of Transbrasil's One-Eleven 500s outside a production hangar at BAC's Hurn plant. BAE Systems

Philippines Airlines was a loyal operator of the One-Eleven 400 and 500, operating them from 1966 until 1992. Its One-Elevens proved their structural strength as one of them was twice subjected to terrorist bombs in the same rear toilet and, despite substantial damage and depressurization, made safe landings. This aircraft was on each occasion given temporary repairs, flown back to Hurn for rebuilding, and returned to service. BAE Systems

500s in the 1970s. With the takeover of two local operators PAL became the sole national airline, so more capacity was needed and eight second-hand 500s were gradually added to the fleet, the last arriving in 1980. The fleet was used mainly for domestic services, which were expanded considerably in the 1970s when new local airports were built. The last One-Eleven was retired in 1992 and replaced by 737s. Two flew half way round the world back to their birthplace at Hurn, but never flew again.

One-Eleven Sales Valued at £300m in 1970

On 6 August 1970 BAC announced that orders had now reached 200 with the placing of orders for four 500s from Philippines Airlines, two more for

Court and an additional machine for Paninternational. One year later, on 3 November 1971, the 200th One-Eleven was delivered to PAL. The value of sales and spares had now reached over £300m, two-thirds of which had been for export.

By late 1970, with the demise of the Three-Eleven project and the end of VC10 production, the Concorde – a collaborative project with Aérospatiale – and One-Eleven were BAC's only remaining civil programmes. There was no prospect of any others.

The Final Development – the One-Eleven 475

With re-engining of the One-Eleven vetoed by the BAC board, the company reviewed the characteristics of the One-Eleven and decided that with a minimal

investment a new version could be devised for a niche market. This One-Eleven would have new aerodynamic and structural improvements and very high performance that would be of major interest in Third World countries. From this came the series 475, announced in January 1970, using the body of the 200/400 but retaining the extended wing, leading edge and powerplant of the 500, with undercarriage refinements for rough-field operation. This provided an aircraft of eighty-seat capacity, able to operate from 4,000ft strips and ideal for 'hot and high' operations.

The Conversion of G-ASYD to the 475 Series Prototype

On 8 May 1970 G-ASYD flew into Hurn for conversion. The fuselage plugs that had been inserted when it was extended to the series 500 length were removed, and the main wheel bay was reconfigured to accommodate bigger wheels and tyres, giving a noticeable bulge. All tribute was due to the BAC engineers who completed the task one month ahead of schedule, and on 27 August 1970 Roy Radford took G-ASYD into the air from Hurn's runway 26 for a 'third' first flight, now as the series 475 prototype.

BAC flew various demonstration tours of the 475, often flying into strips that had never previously been visited by jets. Strenuous efforts were made to break into

For its tests to prove the performance of the One-Eleven 475 in rough-field operation, BAC constructed a 1,500ft test strip on a disused runway at Waterbeach in Cambridgeshire. In May–June 1971, G-ASYD made twenty-five take-offs and landings in conditions of pouring rain, hot sunshine, high crosswinds and tailwinds of up to 20 knots, simulating 'hot and high' airfields. Certification for this kind of operation was achieved in September 1971. BAE Systems

ZE433, a One-Eleven 475 originally delivered to Air Pacific in 1972, returned to the UK in 1984 and was employed until 2008 as a radar trials aircraft. It is currently stored at Boscombe Down. Author

G-BLHD (LHD = last Hurn delivery) flew in May 1984 and was the final One-Eleven to fly from the former BAC (by this time British Aerospace) plant. BAE Systems

the Japanese market, to such an extent that a special version of the 475 designated as the series 670 was devised to meet the stringent local requirement to operate fully loaded out of 4,000ft runways. G-ASYD was refitted for this task and demonstrated in Japan, but to no avail. The 475 series had all the hallmarks of a 'Regional Jet' – a twin-jet airliner able to carry 70–100 passengers out of airports with short runways at the cost of an equivalent propeller-driven aircraft – for which there is now a substantial market but which had not been developed forty years ago.

The 475 in Service

The first and second production series 475, for Faucett of Peru, first flew in March and July 1971, and were both based at Wisley for the final parts of the 475's certification. The first was demonstrated at the 1971 Paris Air Show before delivery in July. The second was demonstrated at Farnborough 1972, painted in BAC house colours, and was only finally delivered to Faucett in July 1974.

Based at Lima, the first aircraft began revenue services in September 1971, on key Peruvian domestic routes radiating from the capital to serve seven major cities. Peru boasted a number of unpaved runways, notable among which was Iquitos, deep in the Amazon jungle, and Cuzco, at 10,500ft above sea level in the Andes; both required the special abilities of the 475. Further orders were received for a single aircraft from Air Malawi, which served for twenty-one years and was joined in 1980 by a former Hapag-Lloyd 500, which was sold to Okada Air twelve years later. The two Air Pacific One-Eleven 475s served for more than eleven years in the Pacific before returning to the UK in March 1984, joining the RAE at Bedford and the ETPS at Boscombe Down.

Sadly, the 1973 oil crisis had an adverse effect on air-traffic prospects in the Third World more than anywhere else, and curtailed interest in an aircraft of this size and capability for many years.

Production of the One-Eleven actually stopped at the end of 1972, leaving a stockpile of six unsold aircraft. The Omani Air Force ordered three in July, which were fitted with a large, VC10-sized freight door, 120 × 73in (3 × 1.8m), in the forward fuselage to give them a dual passenger/freight role. The last of these aircraft was only withdrawn from use in 2010.

Besides the freight-door equipped Omani machines, one windowless dedicated freighter 475 was built on the Hurn production line for Tarom. This proved very useful in transporting equipment from Hurn and other BAC sites during the later setting up of a licence production line in Romania. Only three other 475s were built. One was delivered in May 1978 to Saudi-Arabia as an executive aircraft. The last two machines lingered complete but unflown at Hurn, while there was consideration of them being used by the RAF's Queen's Flight, but unfortunately this did not come to fruition.

With the announcement in July 1983 of British Aerospace's decision to close the Hurn factory, it was decided to fly the two as yet unflown 475s. The first flew on 2 February 1984 as G-BLDH (LDH = last delivery Hurn) in a special colour scheme, with a blue cheatline and 'BAC One-Eleven 475' titling, and the final British-built One-Eleven made its maiden flight on 9 May as G-BLHD (LHD = last Hurn delivery). They were fitted out with executive interiors and long-range tanks by McAlpine Aviation, and then sold to Indonesian and Saudi owners, respectively.

G-ASYD continued in use with British Aerospace until 1994, carrying out experimental and communications flying. Then it was very appropriately donated to the Brooklands Museum where there was still half of the original 3,600ft runway remaining. On 14 July 1994 it made a well-rehearsed short landing there, and it is now on show to the public.

Specification – One-Eleven 475	
Length:	93ft 6in (28.5m)
Wingspan:	93ft 6in (28.5m)
Height:	24ft 6in (7.47m)
MTOW:	98,500lb (45,000kg)
Cruising speed:	541mph (870km/h)
Range:	2,300 miles (3,700km)
Passengers:	89
Powerplant:	2 × 12,550lb Rolls-Royce Spey 512

The Lack of One-Eleven Development Beyond the 500

Between 1967 and 1978 BAC and its successor, British Aerospace (BAe), examined a number of proposals to develop the One-Eleven. Although most of the developments were based on extending the fuselage to improve payload/range for commercial carriers, some were for military applications and there were civil and military collaborative proposals with Japan. None of these came to fruition but some of them had real potential and would have given the type the power and improved performance needed to compete with the Americans. But the promise of the One-Eleven was wasted. BAC should have developed the One-Eleven further and, if Rolls-Royce was unable to provide the necessary power, chosen another company to do so.

The decision to develop the aircraft would have required the BAC Board to make a substantial investment in the project. But throughout its sixteen-year existence the Corporation had to fight for survival against many vicissitudes. The One-Eleven itself had a troublesome development that delayed it severely, the VC10 failed to penetrate the civil market and in 1965 a major blow was struck by the Labour Government's cancellation of TSR2, BAC's main military aircraft programme. The loss of TSR2 put the organization into a parlous state: there were many redundancies and the Luton factory, which made the One-

Eleven's wings, was closed and the work transferred to Weybridge. The problems were exacerbated by the Government's lengthy negotiations over TSR2 cancellation compensation, which interfered with and delayed their financial support for the One-Eleven 500. Throughout this period the Labour Government continued to propose purchasing all of BAC as a step to merging it with Hawker Siddeley, which had a deleterious effect on project development and investment.

Other problems confronting the Corporation were the result of a change in its make-up. In 1960 BAC was formed by the merger of three companies, Vickers-Armstrongs, English Electric and Bristol. But in 1966 Rolls-Royce purchased Bristol, enabling them to take over Bristol Siddeley Engines and become the sole British aero-engine manufacturer. This purchase gave them a 20 per cent holding in BAC, which was unwelcome to the Corporation. Eventually this holding was bought from the receiver by Vickers and English Electric (now owned by GEC) after Rolls-Royce's bankruptcy in 1971, giving them equal shares in the Corporation. So now there was GEC's Sir Arnold Weinstock, a vigorous industrialist of the times with a say-so over half of the BAC board but no background or interest in the aircraft industry. It is recorded that at a meeting of the Board in April 1971 Weinstock saw no reason for One-Eleven production to continue and opined that BAC was finished in the civil market. It is in the light of this tough, if not downright hostile atmosphere, that BAC had to make its investment decisions. As a result no major developments of the One-Eleven took place. This attitude also put paid to the production of aircraft at BAC's expense that had not been ordered, which tied up capital but gave BAC the advantage of being able to offer early delivery dates and clinch a deal.

In 1977 with the formation of the state-owned BAe from BAC, Hawker Siddeley Aviation and Scottish Aviation, the new Board examined their projects and in July 1978 decided to develop the mothballed Hawker Siddeley 146 project as the BAe 146; this spelled the end for any investment in the One-Eleven. But all was not over for this sturdy jet, since BAe then followed another road and began licensed production with Romania.

Post-BAC Developments – Romania and the Tay Re-Engining

The Romanian connection with BAC/BAe began with an order in February 1968 for six One-Eleven 400 series for Tarom, the Romanian national carrier. Tarom later ordered five 500s, which were delivered in 1977 and were the first One-Elevens to fly with Spey hush-kits designed to reduce the noise levels.

In 1978 BAe and Romania agreed to enter into a licence production contract. The partnership was indicated by the aircraft being branded as ROMBAC One-Elevens, 'ROM' for Romania and 'BAC' for the original BAC. The agreement included the sale of three complete aircraft, to be built at Hurn. But the main part of the deal was twenty-two aircraft sets of structural components, equipment, details and raw materials, to be supplied for the Romanian production line. After the twenty-second aircraft, indigenous One-Eleven production was to be established and Romaero, the Romanian aircraft manufacturer, encouraged to produce as many One-Elevens as it could sell.

The three Hurn-built aircraft comprised a single 500 for delivery in January 1981 followed by a 475 Freighter in June and another 500, the last One-Eleven completed at Hurn – although there were still the two unflown 475s in the factory, which had been completed prior to the Romanian 500 and were only flown just prior to Hurn's closure in 1984.

The first ROMBAC One-Eleven – the series 561 – flew in September 1982 from Baneasa and the next eight followed at approximately yearly intervals, with the final machine flying in April 1989. With this slow rate of production ROMBAC was never really a reliable supplier of aircraft and the nine built 561s were all initially delivered to Tarom. Had production really developed as planned, sales could have taken place to other operators.

The Romanian intention was to build new One-Elevens fitted with Rolls-Royce Tays, and they sought to work with the Dee Howard re-engining programme in the USA. The Dee Howard Company flew the first of two One-Elevens with Tays three years behind schedule in 1990 and demonstrated it at that year's Farnborough Air Show. However, the attempt to produce a One-Eleven powered by Tays came to an end in late 1992. The reasons for this failure were the long duration of the programme, lack of substantial orders for conversions, some technical constraints and the lack of full support from BAe and Rolls-Royce. British Aerospace also lost confidence with Romaero, and ended their joint agreement in July 1993.

The Final One-Eleven Years

In the first years of the new millennium One-Elevens still served with Nationwide in South Africa, and in Nigeria. More importantly with the UK's European

Aviation the One-Eleven found a dynamic champion, which demonstrated the strength of a great airframe and how much potential still remained in a far from new design. European's involvement with the One-Eleven began when it bought sixteen of BA's One-Eleven 510s in 1993. Some were used as spares, some sold and some used on services. In 1994 European began purchasing more One-Elevens, and eventually it operated fourteen of them. European even sought to extend the life of that aircraft beyond the imposition of the Stage 3 noise regulations, but was unable to make this viable. At the end of 2011 there were only six One-Elevens flying in the world, including one operated by the RAE's successor, Qinetiq, at Boscombe Down.

Conclusion

The BAC One-Eleven was the only civil project conceived and produced solely by the British Aircraft Corporation, and which stayed in production throughout BAC's existence. The earnings from it were a major factor in keeping the Corporation afloat during its troubled history: from a Government investment of £16m, export sales of the One-Eleven up to nationalization in 1977 earned £160m and home sales or prevented imports were to the value of £100m.

It is self-evident that the One-Eleven should have been further developed – it obviously possessed the potential. Douglas outsold the One-Eleven with the DC-9, but it was bankrupted as a result. Let it not be forgotten that BAC did not over-extend itself, but went on to produce Concorde. The One-Eleven achieved substantial sales with 244 delivered (222 built at Hurn, thirteen at Weybridge and nine in Romania), bested in Britain only by the Hawker Siddeley 748, Viscount and BAE 146/RJ.

CHAPTER SEVEN

Concorde!

The Formation of BAC and the Development of Concorde

At the formation of BAC in 1960, the notion of a supersonic transport (SST) was no more than a feasibility study. It was developed by BAC and Sud Aviation (which later became Aérospatiale) to become a remarkable British and French icon, recognized throughout the world.

Within the short life of BAC from 1960–77, Concorde was designed, built, flight tested, certified and put into service. Many other firms were involved on both sides of the Channel, alongside BAC and the two other major players, Sud Aviation/Aérospatiale and Rolls-Royce, and the management and staff of BAC can feel proud of their major contribution to what was a huge technical achievement. British and French engineers succeeded where the engineers of the USA and the Soviet Union failed to produce viable supersonic transports. Had any member of the public been asked the question in 1960, 'Do you expect airliners to be travelling at the same speed or faster in 2011', the overwhelming response would have been the latter – 'faster'. Sadly, owing to a fall in demand and other factors Concorde was prematurely retired in 2003 and now the top speed for civil airliners has retreated to where it was in the 1960s. People from that time would never have credited that fifty years later the maximum speeds for airliners would be the same as they were then.

Although there were military aircraft that could fly at the speeds required for Concorde in the 1960s, Britain and France each had only one type of aircraft that could achieve this; these were, respectively, the Lightning and the Mirage, both of which could reach Mach

2 for short periods. In contrast, the enormity of the task facing Concorde's designers has to be acknowledged: they were to design an aircraft capable of cruising at Mach 2 for extended periods, carrying 100 passengers in comfort and capable of executing this several times a day.

The Supersonic Transport Aircraft Committee

When the de Havilland Comet entered service in 1952, British aircraft were riding the crest of a wave and only two years later the industry began to consider the feasibility of a supersonic airliner. As early as 1955 aeronautical designers determined that the most effective shape would be a slender delta, which would offer high-speed capability and good low-speed handling, albeit with the drawback of a very high angle of attack on landing.

In November 1956 the Supersonic Transport Aircraft Committee was formed with representation from both the aircraft and aero-engine industries and the British Government to promote research into supersonic airliners. This committee examined all aspects of supersonic airliner operation and tabled a report recommending the building of not one but two supersonic designs, one with a capacity for 150 passengers and transatlantic range at Mach 1.8 and the other to carry 100 passengers over medium-ranges at a speed of Mach 1.2. Many British firms made proposals that were considered by the Committee, but in March 1959 when the Committee submitted its report, design-study contracts were issued to just two, Hawker Siddeley and Bristol Aircraft.

Work started in late 1959 on competitive proposals, each looking into light alloy and steel (Mach 2.2 and Mach 2.7, respectively) designs. Hawker Siddeley

was asked to concentrate on a slender delta with integrated fuselage and wing shape, while Bristol was to design an aircraft with a distinct fuselage and a thin wing. In 1961 Bristol, by now part of BAC, was selected for a further development contract, and in August of that year the Mach 2.2, 130-seat transatlantic Bristol 198 powered by six Olympus turbojets was proposed and selected by the Government.

The project was examined by Sir George Edwards who, against much Bristol resistance, insisted that six engines were too many and the design evolved into the Type 223, a 100-seater slender delta concept with only four Olympus engines, recognizably similar to Concorde. This design and the similar work being done by Sud Aviation at Toulouse later resulted in the specification forming the basis of the agreement between Britain and France. In awarding the contract, the Conservative Government made it clear that owing to the magnitude of the task this was to be a collaborative project, preferably with the USA or France. However, the Americans were unimpressed at the concept of an SST flying 'only' at Mach 2 and were seeking Mach 3 as the speed for their own aircraft, which was being designed by Boeing.

Collaboration

Without a US partner the project might have been laid to rest, but Sud Aviation was seeking a replacement for their successful medium-range Caravelle jet airliner, and had devised a delta-winged, medium-range 100-seat Mach 2.2 airliner provisionally called the Super Caravelle. In March 1960 the Super Caravelle had been announced as an all-French project, with Sud and Dassault working in collaboration, but as the project would gain

Ceremonial rollout of the first French Concorde, F-WTSS, at Toulouse on 11 December 1967. It did not fly for another fifteen months. BAE Systems

Threats of Cancellation

The British Conservative Minister of Aviation, Sir Julian Amery feared that France might withdraw from the project unilaterally, so he insisted that the treaty signed by the two Governments to launch the project contained an extraordinary caveat: if either side withdrew from the agreement, then all the development costs would have to be borne by that country. Ironically, the threat of such a heavy financial penalty thwarted the incoming Labour Government's strenuous efforts to withdraw from the project, rather than deterring France from withdrawing.

According to Roy Jenkins, the incoming Minister of Aviation, within days of entering office the new Labour Government made plain its determination to scrap the project. Jenkins was aware of the binding nature of the contract with the French, but was told to inform the manufacturers and the French of British intentions. The Government deemed Concorde a 'prestige project of low priority' and on 27 October the British Ambassador to France called on M. Pompidou, the French Prime Minister, to convey Britain's wish to re-examine the Concorde project. The French politely but firmly pointed out the consequences of Concorde's cancellation to French industry, and the harm that would be done to Anglo-French relations.

Meanwhile, Jenkins had met Sir George Edwards and Sir Reginald Verdon-Smith to inform them of the Government's wishes. Their immediate response was that ending the project would bring about 2,300 redundancies, the majority from Filton, increasing to a total of 6,000 by the end of 1965. BAC Filton depended on Concorde, so cancellation might result in the site's closure. Sir George was also quick to point out that any future collaboration with the French would be endangered by cancellation.

Roy Jenkins met his French counterpart on 29 October to discuss the project's future, but the French position was that they had no intention of withdrawing; they also hinted at suing Britain at the International Court at the Hague, where Britain might incur huge

from international collaboration and be better able to compete with the USA, exploratory discussions between BAC and Sud on partnership were held in Paris in June 1961. At the 1961 Paris Air Show, Sud Aviation had displayed a model of their Super Caravelle Mach 2.2 supersonic airliner project. The wing was of the ogive configuration that BAC engineers also regarded as the optimum wing planform for this Mach number, and both Sud and BAC had chosen the Bristol Siddeley Olympus as the power-plant.

Co-operation had always taken place between the British and French aircraft industries, albeit that the British saw themselves as superior. (Fifty years later the picture is very different.) The French Air Force had operated licence-built de Havilland Vampires and Air France had bought Viscounts and Comets. Sud Aviation had expected an order from British European Airways for the Caravelle in 1957, but this was never received, for it was generally felt at that time that a British carrier should only operate British aircraft. However, in 1961, in an effort to promote links with Sud, BAC sub-contracted some VC10 tail assembly work to the French firm. When the first parts were delivered in 1963 this led to questions in Parliament as to why the work was not placed with a

British company. Notwithstanding, this small gesture helped cement relations between BAC and Sud Aviation.

Negotiations culminated on 29 November 1962 in the signing of agreements between the two governments and between BAC and Sud Aviation to build two Concorde prototypes followed by two pre-production aircraft and two airframes for static and fatigue testing. Initially there were plans to build two versions of Concorde, with Sud Aviation constructing a medium-range variant and BAC a long-range one, but wiser counsels soon prevailed and the medium-range aircraft was stillborn. The first flight was scheduled for the second half of 1966 and development costs were estimated at between £150–170m. However, the task facing the two countries, the airframe and engine manufacturers and ancillary suppliers, was immense and the first flight did not occur until 1969, by which time expenditure had escalated hugely and the total cost borne by British and French taxpayers eventually totalled £2bn. Aside from the technical challenges there were vocal critics in all aspects of the media throughout the whole length of the project, especially the British media who took every opportunity to criticize the project for its cost and apparent environmental dangers, even when these were not borne out in reality.

Concorde

MANUFACTURE BREAKDOWN   DETAIL FABRICATION

	COMPONENT	PIECE	PRODUCTION REALISATION	DESIGN ETUDE
10	FUSELAGE NOSE	POINTE AVANT	BAC WEYBRIDGE	BAC FILTON
11	FORWARD FUSELAGE	FUSELAGE AVANT	BAC FILTON	" "
12	INTERMEDIATE FUSELAGE	FUSELAGE INTERMEDre	SUD MARIGNANE	" "
13	FORWARD WING	ONGLETS DE VOILURE	SUD BOUGUENAIS	DTA UC
	CENTRE WING/FUSELAGE	PARTIE CENTRALE	SUD MARIGNANE	" "
14	{ Fr 46 to Fr 54 fus. / Fr 46 tu Fr 50 wing	" "	" "	" "
15	Fr 50 to Fr 54 wing	" "	SUD TOULOUSE	" "
16	Fr 54 to Fr 60 wing/fus.	" "	" "	DTA UT
17	Fr 60 to Fr 63 wing	" "	" "	SILAT
18	{ Fr 60 to Fr 69 fus. / Fr 63 to Fr 66 wing	" "	" "	" "
19	Fr 66 to Fr 69 wing	" "	" "	FIAT
20	Fr 69 to Fr 72 wing/fus.	" "	SUD St NAZAIRE	"
21	OUTER WINGS	VOILURE EXTREME	GAM DASSAULT	GAMD
23	ELEVONS	ELEVONS	ROHR	DTA UC
24	REAR FUSELAGE	FUSELAGE ARRIERE	BAC PRESTON	BAC PRESTON
25	NACELLES	NACELLES	BAC FILTON & ROHR	BAC FILTON
	NOZZLE	TUYERES	SNECMA	SNECMA
26	FIN	DERIVE	BAC WEYBRIDGE	BAC PRESTON
27	RUDDER	GOUVERNAIL	BAC FILTON	" "
51	LANDING GEAR MAIN	TRAIN PRINCIPAL	HISPANO SUIZA	HISPANO SUIZA
	NOSE	TRAIN AVANT	MESSIER	MESSIER

BAC FILTON Division	
ELECTRICS	ELECTRICITE
OXYGEN	OXYGENE
FUEL	CARBURANT
ENGINE INSTRUMENTATION	INSTRUMENT REACTEURS
ENGINE CONTROLS	COMMANDES
FIRE	FEU
AIR CONDITIONING DISTRn	DISTRIBUTION AIR CONDITIONNE
DE-ICING	DEGIVRAGE
SUD TOULOUSE	
HYDRAULICS	HYDRAULIQUE
FLYING CONTROLS	COMMANDES DE VOL
NAVIGATION	NAVIGATION
RADIO	RADIO
AIR CONDITIONING SUPPLY	ALIMENTATION CONDITnt D'AIR

The initial breakdown of design, production and systems on Concorde between BAC and Sud Aviation (later Aérospatiale) factories. BAE Systems

penalties. The French maintained this stance into the new year when the Labour Government was contemplating cancelling the BAC TSR2 and various Hawker Siddeley projects. So Concorde survived. According to Jenkins in his autobiography, he later discovered that had Britain persisted the French might have accepted cancelling Concorde.

BAC's Contribution

Manufacture of Concorde was shared between BAC and Sud Aviation (later Aérospatiale). France was granted a larger amount of airframe work as Britain had a greater share of the work on the Olympus engines built by Bristol Siddeley (later Rolls-Royce) and SNECMA. BAC built the three forward sections of the fuselage, the rear fuselage and vertical tail surfaces, the engine nacelles and ducting, the electrical system, sound and thermal insulation, oxygen system, fuel system, engine installation, and fire warning and extinguishing systems. Sud Aviation had responsibility for development and production of the rear cabin section, wings and wing control surfaces, hydraulic systems, flying controls, navigation systems, radio and air conditioning.

Flight-Test Programme

The flight-test programme required the testing of all systems and functionality in all aspects of the aircraft's flight envelope: throughout its entire speed, attitude and altitude range. Regular and sometimes lengthy groundings occurred from first flight onwards, for instance for the installation of updated engines, intakes and control systems.

The test programme demanded the testing of the air conditioning and pressurization, automatic flight-control system, avionics, droop nose and visor, electrics, engines and air intakes, flying controls, fuel, icing, internal and external noise, handling, hydraulics, performance, structure, undercarriage and brakes. Under all these headings there were many additional items, and assessments of simulated failures and the support provided by standby systems.

The first four Concordes were solely intended for flight testing and carried approximately 12 tons of electronic test instrumentation; this instrumentation could record 3,000 different parameters on magnetic tape in the aircraft for later analysis on the ground. In addition, basic flight information was continuously telemetered to a ground monitoring centre. This test equipment had itself to be tested, regularly modified and calibrated.

Specification – Prototype Concorde	
Length:	184ft 6in (56.24m)
Wingspan:	83ft 10in (25.55m)
Height:	37ft 5in (11.4m)
MTOW:	326,000lb (148,000kg)
Max cruise speed:	Mach 2.02
Range:	n/a
Passengers:	n/a
Powerplant:	4 × 28,000lb st Rolls-Royce/ SNECMA Olympus 593-1

Maiden Flights of the Prototypes

BAC had to establish a totally new flight-test centre for Concorde's hugely demanding test programme. The Weybridge Division test centre at Wisley was hopelessly inadequate to the task, with a runway too short for Concorde and a critical overrun in the westerly direction onto the busy A3 London to Portsmouth road. Although BAC Filton had a longer runway, Brian Trubshaw, as Director of Flight Test, insisted that the Filton runway was neither sufficiently long nor level enough. Therefore, at additional expense a test centre was established at nearby Fairford that remained in operation until the end of the main part of the test programme in November 1976, when it was closed and the remaining flight-test operations transferred to Filton, which was now deemed to be suitable for Concorde after all.

As design was developed, the aircraft had to be virtually redesigned twice to make it viable for transatlantic routes. As a result, the first two Concorde prototypes were very different from the final aircraft: they were shorter and lighter, and were each fitted with a metal visor with extremely limited vision that was raised over the front cockpit windows for supersonic flying. This was superseded by a much improved fully glazed visor design with the subsequent aircraft.

The first prototype registered F-WTSS (TSS = *Transport Supersonique*) was rolled out on 11 December 1967 at Toulouse in front of 1,100 VIPs and guests. They had to endure the cold while speeches were given by politicians including the British Labour Minister of Technology, Tony Benn, who conceded the French spelling of 'Concorde' rather than the English 'Concord'. It did not fly until Saturday 2 March 1969 when it made a 42-minute maiden flight from Toulouse with an all-French crew led by Trubshaw's opposite number, André Turcat. The first British prototype, G-BSST, first flew on 9 April 1969 and was watched by huge crowds as it took off for its 22-minute flight from Filton to Fairford, piloted by Brian Trubshaw. At the Paris Air Show two months later both Concordes appeared together in the air, and stole the show.

The French-built F-WTSS expanded Concorde's flight envelope, reaching Mach 1.05 on 1 October 1969 and Mach 2 on 4 November. The first British Concorde, G-BSST, had been scheduled to achieve Mach 2 ahead of the French prototype, but technical problems meant that F-WTSS achieved that too. Almost every flight at this time for the two prototypes established new achievements for Concorde.

Succeeding these two initial prototypes were two pre-production prototypes, G-AXDN and F-WTSA, which more closely resembled the final production standard aircraft. However, as they varied considerably from the prototypes and even from each other, much of the flight-testing had to be repeated. The third Concorde, G-AXDN, flew from Filton on 17 December 1971 and was noticeably larger than its two prototype predecessors, with an 8ft 6in longer forward fuselage and the much improved fully glazed visor to give the crew forward vision at supersonic speed. Less than two months later it reached supersonic speed, on 12 February 1972. The final pre-production aircraft, F-WTSA, was even longer than G-AXDN as it had an extended tail designed to reduce drag and was powered by production-standard Olympus engines. It first flew, from Toulouse, on 10 January 1973.

Following these four initial aircraft were two further aircraft built to approximately final production standard. It was these two production prototype Concordes that bore the brunt of the certification process. The first production prototype Concorde 201 (as the French-built Concordes were designated), F-WTSB, first flew at

A view of the first British Concorde, G-BSST, being assembled in the huge hangars at Filton. Despite initial predictions of large sales – airlines took out options on seventy-four aircraft – total production of the Concorde was a mere twenty aircraft, production shared evenly between Filton and Toulouse. BAE Systems

A Concorde forward fuselage being loaded into the bottom part of a transport container at Weybridge. The top part of the container is visible ahead of it. There is also a One-Eleven at the end of the hangar. BAE Systems

Brian Trubshaw and John Cochrane, Chief and Deputy Chief Test Pilots of BAC Commercial Aircraft Division, on the flight deck of the first British Concorde, G-BSST. BAE Systems

The first British Concorde prototype, G-BSST, at the 1970 Farnborough Air Show. Author

Concorde gathering at the BAC Fairford Flight Test Centre on 6 January 1972. The two Concorde prototypes, G-BSST and F-WTSS, with the pre-production G-AXDN in between. BAE Systems

The first Concorde to fly that resembled the production aircraft was French-assembled F-WTSA. It is seen here in landing configuration with its nose fully drooped and the undercarriage down. BAE Systems

Toulouse in December 1973, reaching Mach 1.57 on its maiden flight and Mach 2.05 on its second flight. Two months later, Concorde 202 (i.e. British-built) G-BBDG made its maiden flight of 105 minutes' duration from Filton to Fairford, piloted by Brian Trubshaw and reaching a top speed of Mach 1.4.

Certification

F-WTSC (later F-BTSC) and G-BOAC first flew, respectively, in January and February 1975 and were employed on endurance flights. G-BOAC flew four North Atlantic crossings during the same day on 1 September 1975. As the culmination of all the hard work by British and French aeronautical engineers, Concorde received its full airworthiness certificates from Britain and France in October and December 1975, respectively.

Concorde deliveries were equally shared by Air France and British Airways. The second pair of production Concordes flew in late 1975, the next four in 1976 and two more in 1977, giving both airlines the full complement of their original orders. The remaining four aircraft in production had no customers; three made their maiden flights in 1978 and the final Concorde flew from Filton in May 1979.

Specification – Production Concorde	
Length:	203ft 9in (62.1m)
Wingspan:	83ft 10in (25.55m)
Height:	37ft 5in (11.4m)
MTOW:	408,000lb (185,000kg)
Max cruise speed:	Mach 2.04
Range:	3,870 miles (6,230km)
Passengers:	100 (first class)
Powerplant:	4 × 38,050lb st Rolls-Royce/ SNECMA Olympus 602

Concorde's Sales

The original motivation for going ahead with Concorde was not to produce an expensive prestige product, but to leap ahead of the Americans and sell them all around to the world. Speed has always sold. Initial sales projection foresaw a market for over 200 SSTs, but this was based on the assumption that permission for overland supersonic flights would readily be granted. The reality was rather different, and country after country forbade supersonic overflights. Likewise, the burgeoning environmental lobby protested against Concorde on the grounds of cost and pollution.

Until such time as Concorde's performance could be guaranteed the manufacturers only took options, not orders, from airlines for the aircraft. The first of these was received from Pan Am, in those days a trend setter and the USA's

G-BBDG taking off. This Concorde, the final test aircraft, went supersonic on its first flight. Following the end of the test programme it was retained at Filton and used for spares by British Airways. It is now preserved at the Brooklands Museum, on the former BAC Weybridge site. BAE Systems

Sir George Edwards, Chairman of BAC, being congratulated by Sir Freddie Page, BAC Managing Director (Aircraft), on 13 October 1975 following the award of the British Certificate of Airworthiness to Concorde, which permitted its entry into passenger service. These two great men oversaw BAC's huge programme of civil and military aircraft. BAE Systems

British Airways Concorde G-BOAA. This is now preserved at the National Museum of Scotland at East Fortune. BAE Systems

The final Concorde built, which later became British Airway's G-BOAF. At the time of its first flight on 20 April 1979, when it was not allocated to a customer, it was painted all white and was registered G-BFKX. BAE Systems

premier airline. However, Britain's and France's two state airlines, BOAC and Air France, soon followed suit and by 1967, two years before the first flight, prospects for Concorde were buoyant as it had received seventy-four options from sixteen of the world's major airlines with the potential for substantial further sales. These options were, however, refundable and could only become firm contracts when guaranteed performance figures had been established by the flight-test programme. British Airways and Air France placed firm orders for five and four aircraft, respectively, in July 1972, by which time Iranair and CAAC of China had also taken out options.

Paradoxically, the cancellation of the Boeing SST project in May 1971 was very unhelpful to Concorde. Had the US SST flown, there would have been substantial pressure on countries to allow supersonic overflights of the USA, which would have helped Concorde. The Soviet Union produced their supersonic Tupolev Tu-144, which entered service ahead of Concorde, but this was a troubled aircraft,

and despite a subsequent huge redesign did not prove successful and had a short, intermittent service life.

Not long after the cancellation of the Boeing SST the world oil crisis was to play havoc with the market for Concorde. In January 1973 Pan Am and TWA cancelled their options and, following the lead of these then powerful, influential carriers, the other airlines' options were also soon withdrawn. There were understandable fears within BAC and Sud Aviation that the loss of the options would lead to calls for cancellation, but in July 1974 the French and British Governments agreed to the manufacture of sixteen production-standard Concordes (including the two production prototypes, F-WTSB and G-BBDG).

The loss of the options was bad publicity for BAC since it gave the erroneous impression that the company would stand or fall on the success or otherwise of Concorde. In actuality Concorde was only a minor contributor to BAC's profits, though it did take up a vast amount of factory space at both Filton

and Weybridge. On the plus side, BAC also gained prestige for its involvement in the project and was far more often in the public eye than its British counterpart, Hawker Siddeley.

BAC was paid by the Government for its major part in Concorde's success, though of course it was British and French taxpayers who actually paid for it. The total cost born by the taxpayers was £1.784bn, of which £278m was recouped from sales to British Airways and Air France.

BA and Air France received five and four aircraft, respectively, but with no further orders two British and three French-built machines remained unsold. Following the winding down of the sales campaign in September 1979 these five unsold aircraft were delivered to BA and Air France for a token payment.

Including prototype and pre-production machines, a total of twenty Concordes was built, ten each by BAC at Filton and Sud Aviation/Aérospatiale at Toulouse. As production did not progress beyond the sixteen production aircraft, further development could not take place. From the seventeenth aircraft onwards Concorde would have received full-span droop wing leading edges, extended wing tips, increased fuel tankage and engine improvements. These improvements would have offered quieter takeoffs, greater range and improved fuel consumption. If the original expectations of orders had been borne out by reality, then following the typical model of aircraft development there would have been further improvements offering even better performance.

In Service

Concorde's first services began on 21 January 1976, still within the existence of BAC, appropriately considering all of BAC's hard work to create what is still the world's only successful supersonic airliner. Owing to problems in the USA described later in this chapter, the initial routes were to perhaps unexpected destinations.

A BA Concorde at Bahrain in 1976. As Concorde was at that time banned from the USA, BA's inaugural route was to Bahrain. This was regarded as the precursor to a route to Australia, but this failed to materialize. BAE Systems

An Air France Concorde at Washington-Dulles Airport. Though initially unable to operate into New York, permission was granted to operate into the US federal capital. BAE Systems

There were synchronized departures from London and Paris at 11:40 GMT with British Airways' G-BOAA flying non-stop to Bahrain and Air France's F-BVFA to Rio de Janeiro via Dakar. Air France later introduced another South American route, serving Caracas via the Azores.

British Airways' route to Bahrain was regarded as preliminary to flying to Australia via Singapore. However, the extension to Singapore in December 1977 was short-lived owing to Malaysian opposition, and a joint operation to Singapore in co-operation with Singapore Airlines using Concorde G-BOAD with Singapore

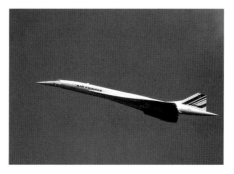

Air France initially operated a service to South America, but that too was short-lived. Here is F-BVFA taking off from Roissy/Charles de Gaulle in August 1998. Jean-Pierre Touzeau

Airlines' livery on the left side and BA's on the right proved uneconomical owing to poor load factors.

Into the United States

The US Congress initially banned Concorde landings in the United States on environmental grounds, but the US Transportation Secretary allowed trial services into Washington from February 1976 for a period of sixteen months. Regular services from both London and Paris to Washington Dulles airport began on 24 May 1976. The inaugural arrival of the French and British Concordes was quite a media event: they landed simultaneously on parallel runways and then stopped, posed either side of the Washington-Dulles Airport's huge control tower.

Continued opposition to Concorde operations into New York was finally countered in October 1977. British Aerospace and Aérospatiale (as the makers had now become) responded speedily and proving flights began on 19 October 1977 to be welcomed by huge crowds and equally large groups of protesters. When actual noise measurements at New York's John F. Kennedy airport proved Concorde to be within the legal limits, opposition collapsed. Services to JFK finally began on 22 November 1977 and it was this route that became the aircraft's staple. By 1982 Air France's only scheduled service was its regular Paris–New York return flights. With the reduction in its Concorde route network Air France had insufficient work for seven aircraft, so in May 1982 F-BVFD was withdrawn from service and broken up for spares.

BA and Air France Take Over Ownership of Concorde

In 1981, following lengthy negotiations between the Governments and manufacturers, BA and Air France took over full financial responsibility for the aircraft and spares. Consequently BA paid £16.5m to the Government and acquired spares worth £120m, all of its seven Concordes plus the partly cannibalized G-BBDG, which was grounded at Filton as an additional spares source. Having G-BBDG as a spares source paid dividends to BA in allowing the speedy replacement of the damaged rudder of G-BOAF when it lost part of it on a Round the World flight between Christchurch, New Zealand and Sydney in April 1989.

Concorde was run at a loss by BA in its early years and was the recipient of weighty media criticism as a result. Yet on one point everybody agreed: the iconic charisma of the aircraft was unique and captivating. In the mid-1980s the airline refined its Concorde marketing to promote the superiority and convenience of Concorde's speed in addition to the excellence of its food and wine. Crossing

the Atlantic in approximately 3½ hours, half the time it took a conventional airliner, the airline marketed a one-day Concorde London–New York round trip to top business travellers from Britain. Passengers could leave London Heathrow on the 10:30am (GMT) Concorde, arrive at New York Kennedy at 9:30am for business then return to London on the 13:45 pm (EST) flight. This marketing strategy paid dividends, for the 100-seat Concordes flew at well over the break-even point of 60 per cent on Atlantic routes.

Both operators dropped their Washington services in the 1990s and scheduled services were reduced to both airlines just operating into New York, which BA bolstered with a Barbados run during the winter months. BA in particular did not only fly its Concordes on its scheduled operations, but much more widely on its charters where it proved extremely popular and a regular crowd-puller at airports. These charters varied from trips to Nice for the Formula 1, Round the World flights or supersonic Round the Bay tours of the Bay of Biscay.

The Air France Concorde Accident

At the beginning of the twenty-first century Concorde had been in service for twenty-four years without serious incident. However, on Tuesday 25 July 2000 Air France Concorde F-BTSC was taking off with a group of German holiday-makers on a charter flight from Paris-Charles de Gaulle Airport to New York, from where they were to join a cruise, when it caught fire and crashed. Concorde services were suspended within a few weeks, and did not resume for over a year.

As F-BTSC was accelerating on its takeoff run it ran over a strip of metal deposited on the runway by a Continental Airlines McDonnell Douglas DC-10. This piece of metal penetrated one of the left front mainwheel tyres, which immediately burst and large chunks of rubber were blown into the underside of the wing. The force of these large chunks of rubber caused a shockwave in a fuel tank, which then ruptured from the inside.

A massive fuel leak, estimated as up to 100ltr per second, poured from the ruptured tank and ignited. This immediately upset the performance of the two engines

on the left side, causing them to surge. Even though the control tower informed the crew that the aircraft was on fire, the captain elected to continue with takeoff, as the aircraft had passed the point where there was sufficient runway remaining in which to safely stop.

As the Concorde lifted off, the underside of its left wing ablaze, undercarriage retraction was selected but it failed to operate. The Concorde was now in a critical condition, barely able to make 200kt at 200ft; with its landing gear down causing immense drag and with power from only two of the engines, it was unable to gain sufficient airspeed to fly. It reared up and stalled, crashing onto a hotel west of the airfield less than three minutes after takeoff, killing all 109 people on board and four on the ground.

Air France immediately cancelled all its Concorde flights. BA flights continued for three weeks until 16 August, when the French and British authorities officially withdrew Concorde's Certificate of Airworthiness. Tyre failure resulting in damage to the wings or landing gear was far from unknown with Concorde – there had been twelve incidents of it in Concorde's history. But on those occasions there had been no fire.

Return to Service

For Concorde to return to service the main requirements of the airworthiness authorities were that Kevlar linings be fitted to each vulnerable fuel tank to drastically reduce the rate of fuel leakage in the event of wing damage, and that new, more resilient Michelin tyres be used. BA's G-BOAF was the first Concorde to incorporate these modifications. After extensive ground trials it flew out of Heathrow on 17 July 2001. It was routed over the Atlantic, accelerating to Mach 2, and landed at RAF Brize Norton. Three days later a flight of similar duration was made out Brize Norton, returning to Heathrow. These flights proved that the Kevlar linings did not affect the fuel system's operation, and Concorde could now re-enter service. Meanwhile the first Air France Concorde to be brought up to modification standard flew on 27 August. On 5 September 2001 Concorde was re-certified by the British and French authorities and definite plans could be made to restart services.

A view of Air France Concorde F-BVFB landing. In this view it is possible to appreciate how chunks of punctured tyre could hit the fuel-filled wing and cause an over-pressure which punctured the wing. The fuel flowing from this hole ignited and as the aircraft was past the point at which it might safely stop on the runway, the Captain went ahead with the takeoff. Author

In an attempt to engender confidence, a repeat performance of Concorde's original triumphal arrival at New York in 1977 was arranged when BA and Air France resumed passenger flights on Concorde on 7 November carrying a full load of celebrities, corporate customers and the media. After being grounded for more than a year, BA's G-BOAE and Air France's F-BVFB arrived at JFK just fifty minutes apart and parked nose to nose as a symbolic gesture of their joint return to commercial service. New York's mayor, Rudi Giuliani, went so far as to jump aboard G-BOAE to welcome it back following the disastrous events of 9/11 only two months previously.

After 9/11 there was a serious downturn in transatlantic flying and when services resumed in November 2001 the numbers wanting to fly at Concorde prices had drastically reduced: BA could attract sufficient business for only one transatlantic flight each day. Ironically, in the late 1990s BA had spent approximately £20 million on upgrades for five of its seven Concordes to enable them to fly until 2009, by which time they would have reached 8,500 supersonic cycles. Additional similar schemes could have prolonged their flying life until 2013.

However, Air France had already announced that it planned to retire its Concorde fleet in 2007. Then, in February 2003, Air France's resolve to continue operations was seriously weakened when one of their New York flights was endangered by crew error following a fuel leak and another aircraft lost part of its rudder. BA had suffered the rudder problem on five occasions, and had even replaced all the rudders in its Concorde fleet, yet this had still not put an end to the problem.

Concorde Services End

British Airways and Air France made simultaneous announcements on 10 April 2003 that they would retire

24 October 2003: three Concordes landed in succession at Heathrow on the final day of BA's services. Here the trio can be seen taxiing after the event. Rob Ware

The final Concorde built, G-BOAF, which made the final flight of the type back into Filton and preservation on 26 November 2003. Author

The final Concorde flight occurred on 26 November 2003, with the final Concorde built, G-BOAF, returning for preservation at its birthplace at Filton. It made a last, brief, supersonic flight, carrying 100 BA flight crew, over the Bay of Biscay, then a 'lap of honour' above Bristol before touchdown and was welcomed by huge crowds including employees from Rolls-Royce's Patchway factory and the Airbus (former BAC) factory at Filton.

Concorde later that year. The reasons given were low passenger numbers following the Paris crash, the slump in air travel following 9/11, and rising maintenance costs.

Both airlines – especially British Airways – made the most of the last flights, continuing their New York schedules and making a large number of enthusiasts' special charters. Air France's last flight was in June but British Airways continued with operations and provided a remarkable spectacle with three aircraft landing in quick succession at Heathrow in front of huge crowds in the late afternoon of 24 October 2003.

The Final Flights

The two airlines' Concordes had not yet made their final flights for they were destined for museums around the world. Gradually they left Heathrow and Paris, Charles de Gaulle respectively, though some could not fly out as they had never received the modifications following the Paris crash.

Conclusion

When the two airlines had announced their intention to end services, Noël Forgeard, President and Chief Executive Officer of Airbus, paid tribute to the original manufacturers and said 'The Airbus's predecessors, Aérospatiale and British Aircraft Corporation created the Concorde some forty years ago and we are proud of this remarkable achievement.'

Concorde provided supersonic passenger travel for twenty-seven years. Alongside Sud Aviation/Aérospatiale, the British Aircraft Corporation must always be remembered for its achievement in creating this unique aircraft.

CHAPTER EIGHT

BAC's Very Profitable Guided Weapons

On its formation BAC inherited two major surface-to-air missile systems, the English Electric Thunderbird and Bristol Bloodhound, and a wire-guided anti-tank missile, the Vickers Vigilant. English Electric had two other significant projects under development, the *Blue Water* nuclear surface-to-surface system and the anti-aircraft PT428. Hunting Aircraft, which was bought by BAC in 1960, had no guided weapons, but in 1962 BAC made a deal with Fairey Aviation – which had left the aviation business – and took over its Swingfire anti-tank missile and Jindivik target drone.

Guided weapons appeared to be the poor relation in the early years of the Corporation since its commanding figures, the Chairman, Lord Portal, and Managing Director, Sir George Edwards, were aircraft men not schooled in the world of missiles. However, the Guided Weapons Division was to earn the respect it deserved in later years when its profitability grew, providing a greater than proportional contribution to BAC's success, employing one-quarter of the firm's resources yet delivering one-third of the profits.

Old Account Versus New Account with Guided Weapons

As part of the horse trading during the negotiations at the formation of BAC, decisions were made as to which projects should remain the financial responsibility of the parent companies and which should pass on to the new conglomerate. The Bloodhound Mk 1 and Thunderbird Mk 1 were regarded as old account while the far superior Mk 2 models of each became new account – BAC's. The Vigilant also became new account. The Vickers Vigilant remained as an 'old account' product. The Vigilant was a private venture project (i.e. entirely funded by Vickers, without any Government support) and it remained on the Vickers balance sheet.

Settling In

With the formation of BAC there had to be rationalization in all aspects of the operation, including guided weapons. English Electric seemed to have the better hand by far as one of the two larger investors in BAC with its 40 per cent holding, double that of Bristol. Lord Caldecote of English Electric was appointed Chief Executive of Guided Weapons and many at Bristol were suspicious of an English Electric takeover. Both firms had two factories each, Bristol at Filton and Cardiff, English Electric at Luton and Stevenage. Bristol continued working on its Bloodhound, while English Electric at Luton and Stevenage progressed with Thunderbird, PT428, *Blue Water* and later on Vigilant and Swingfire. For a time the Bristol team felt very vulnerable to closure in favour of English Electric with their modern, purpose-built factory at Stevenage, but in the event the Bristol team continued in being.

A display of the BAC Guided Weapons Division's missiles in 1964. From the left: ET316 (which became Rapier in 1966), Swingfire, Bloodhound, Vigilant and Thunderbird. BAE Systems

A *Blue Water* battlefield nuclear missile mounted on a Bedford 3-ton truck. This missile was showing great potential when it was cancelled in August 1962. BAE Systems

Vickers Vigilant

Vickers had been heavily and famously involved in weapons design throughout its history and in the Second World War its *Upkeep* 'bouncing bomb' was used in the famous attack on the German dams by 617 Squadron (which became known to the public as the 'Dambuster' Squadron). Later in the war 617 Squadron employed Vickers' *Grand Slam* bombs against the German battleship and U-boats pens on the French coast. Post-war, Vickers established a Guided Weapons department which then developed in succession three Government-funded projects: *Red Rapier* (a long-range surface-to-air missile), *Blue Boar* (a TV-guided bomb) and *Red Dean* (a radar-guided air-to-air missile); however, each of these was cancelled and by June 1956 the department was without work.

To provide work for the small team remaining, the Vickers Board financed a private-venture, portable wire-guided missile with a range of approximately 1,500yd. The V.891 Vigilant could provide infantry or vehicles with a powerful weapon against tanks and other armoured vehicles. Wire-guidance enforced limited range but removed virtually all risk of jamming. A single round could be contained in a man-portable box, where the front end opened to expose the missile and provide a stand, while the operator with the sight could be some distance away. The range of designs included several different magazine formats or a fixed mounting on an armoured vehicle.

The British Army and Ministry of Defence could foresee no requirement for Vigilant despite competition from French, German and Swiss manufacturers. In a demonstration on the Larkhill ranges in September 1958, eleven missiles were fired at tanks of which seven hit the target, three were near misses and one failed – an impressive achievement by a missile still under development. Despite the success of these trials, resistance to its adoption continued in higher circles, though eventually 100 were ordered for evaluation and a production run of 300 was initiated at Weybridge, with the final fifty built at Stevenage.

Cancellation of PT428 and *Blue Water*

Even before the BAC aircraft divisions were hit by the cancellation of TSR2 there were cancellations of missile projects. The first to feel the axe was the PT428, a lightweight anti-aircraft, eighteen-round missile battery, designed to be air portable and easy to establish on the ground. Remarkably it was to have 'Blindfire' capability: able to operate at night and in poor weather. However, the MoD regarded it as too sophisticated and likely to prove very costly, so cancelled it in February 1962 in favour of the less sophisticated, American-made General Dynamics Mauler; however, the Mauler was itself axed a year later. All was not wasted by the cancellation of PT428, as the research and development for it paved the way for the highly successful Rapier.

Whereas there had been some expectation that PT428, which was only in the early stages of development, might not be proceeded with, the cancellation of *Blue Water* only six months later had far greater ramifications. It was the biggest single project at English Electric's Guided Weapons Division. It was performing well and appeared to have great potential. *Blue Water* was a surface-to-surface battlefield nuclear missile with a range of 70 miles. It was intended to be a mobile missile, air-portable and able to be mounted on a 3-ton Bedford truck. In August 1962, after the expenditure of £32.1m (1962 prices), and just as it was showing promise it was cancelled by the Conservative Government on the grounds of cost, range limitations and lack of export orders. The British Army purchased the larger and less capable Honest John missile from the USA. This cancellation threatened the viability of the Stevenage plant and closure was considered, with the centre of activities moving to Bristol. However, as it transpired the Luton plant was closed, along with the painful loss of 1,000 jobs.

A Vigilant wire-guided missile just launched from a twin magazine. The Vigilant began as a Vickers private venture, and when Vickers joined BAC it remained an 'old account' product so the parent firm was to benefit directly from its success. MBDA

A closely guarded Vigilant display at the 1963 Paris Air Show, with a single Vigilant launcher and an operator destroying a tank. BAE Systems

At a further demonstration in front of NATO officers in Italy in May 1959, the weapon scored eleven hits and two near-misses out of thirteen shots, all against difficult targets at 400–1,400yd. While one of the operators was experienced, the other was a novice. The demonstration started with the arrival of a small helicopter carrying an operator and two complete Vigilant rounds in their carrying cases (total weight per package, 48lb). The operator then made a 50yd sprint to the firing point, and had the rounds rigged and ready for action in about a minute.

In late November 1961 Vickers finally received an order from the British Army for 6,000 Vigilant missiles (later increased to 12,000). This order was cold comfort to the small Weybridge missile team, who in the preceding month had been told of their disbandment and the transfer of production to the much larger factory at Stevenage. This move took place early the following year.

Over 17,000 Vigilants were manufactured at Stevenage, continuing until the late 1970s. It was also licence-built as the Clevite for the US Marine Corps. Vigilant was exported to Switzerland, Finland, Libya, Saudi Arabia and Abu Dhabi. As an 'old account' product, over the course of its lifetime it handsomely repaid Vickers' initial £1m investment.

Swingfire

Swingfire was a wire-guided anti-tank missile with range of between 150–4,000yd. It was designed to be mounted on a veicle, and was steered by its jet nozzle. It was initially developed by the Royal Armament & Research Development Establishment (RARDE) and passed to Fairey for development. As part of the Government's reorganization of the industry, a joint BAC-Fairey company, British Aircraft Corporation (AT) Ltd (AT: anti-tank), was established in 1961 to develop it, with BAC having the controlling interest.

Production was originally intended to take place at Fairey's Heston plant, but following the cancellation of *Blue Water* it was diverted to Stevenage, while Bristol built the ground control system. Trials was started by Fairey in December 1960 and were completed by BAC in September 1963. Full production began in 1966, and continued until 1993. Two variants of Swingfire – the infantry-operated Beeswing and the air-launched Hawkswing – were cancelled during 1975 for budgetry reasons.

Initially equipping British Army Ferret scout cars, armoured personnel carriers and Striker tracked reconnaissance combat vehicles, Swingfire entered service in 1970. It was exported to Belgium, Egypt, Iraq, Kenya, Nigeria, Portugal, Qatar, Saudi-Arabia and Sudan. Continuing development extended its life such that it was only withdrawn from service in 2005.

Bloodhound and Thunderbird

From the formation of BAC in mid-1960 until March 1963 and the establishment of BAC's Guided Weapons (GW) Division, the two dominant partners in BAC's GW portfolio, Bristol and English Electric, warily circled each other. Formerly deadly rivals in the surface-to-air missile market, they lived in mutual dread of the Ministry cancelling Bloodhound (Bristol) in favour of Thunderbird (English Electric), or vice versa.

Bloodhound and Thunderbird both originated from a post-war requirement for air defence missiles. This rivalry had been exacerbated just prior to the inception of BAC when the Government set up the Penley Committee to examine which missile to axe; the Committee came down in favour of Bloodhound. However, just as the RAF preferred the Bloodhound, so the Thunderbird had strong support from the Army: in the end, neither was cancelled and so the rivalry persisted. However, it was Bloodhound that was first into service and sold overseas while Thunderbird failed to penetrate export markets except for an interim supply of ex-British Army examples to Saudi-Arabia while it waited for the delivery of American Hawk missiles.

Bloodhound

Shortly the end of the Second World War in 1945, the Bristol Aeroplane Company started looking into the guided-weapon field. This private work soon changed to officially sponsored development for the Ministry of Supply, which recommended an alliance with the electronics engineering firm Ferranti, and for many years the two companies were equal partners in the development of *Red Duster*, later renamed Bloodhound, surface-to-air missile. As the manufacturers did not possess a supersonic wind tunnel, over 500 missile test vehicles were flown between 1951 and 1959.

Bloodhound was manufactured at Bristol's Cardiff factory. It was really a small, extremely high-performance aeroplane, fitted with a proximity-fuzed warhead that would detonate when close to the target – a direct hit was not necessary. Bloodhound was fitted with a Ferranti guidance system activated by the directional radar beam

A Swingfire being fired; the wire cable guiding the missile is visible. Development of the Swingfire was started by Fairey, but following the aircraft industry's reorganization in 1960 BAC and Fairey formed a joint firm to develop it, in which BAC had a controlling interest. MBDA

A RAF Bloodhound battery. The Bloodhound Mk 1 entered service with the RAF in 1958. It was later superseded by the air-transportable and more effective Bloodhound Mk 2, which remained in service until 1991. MBDA

Whereas the RAF had Bloodhound for air-defence, the British Army had Thunderbird for the same task. It looks extremely formidable in this photo. MBDA

from the ground, after which the individual missile-borne equipment automatically locked onto its target. During its attacking flight the missile's radar computed the movements of the target into an ever-correcting collision course employing the Bloodhound's flight controls. Bloodhound was fired from a zero-length launcher (i.e. no longer than the missile itself) by four Gosling solid-fuel boost motors with cruise propulsion provided by a pair of 16in Thor ramjets manufactured by Bristol Siddeley. The Goslings were jettisoned after launch, and the Bloodhound attained Mach 2+ in just two seconds.

Much work was put into simplifying the design to reduce manufacturing costs, with the launcher using an anti-aircraft gun base and its operating equipment. Bloodhound production was established at a factory in Cardiff in 1956, but as part of BAC's rationalization this highly regarded plant was sold to Bristol Siddeley Engines only ten years later when, thankfully, the majority of employees remained employed.

Initially designed for the Army, which was then responsible for air defence, the Bloodhound was transferred, along with the air defence role, to the RAF. The Bloodhound Mk 1 entered service with the RAF in 1958, eventually equipping eleven squadrons, and was exported to Sweden and Australia. Whereas the Mk 1 was essentially a static missile to be installed at permanent sites, the later, improved, Bloodhound Mk 2 was designed to be air-portable. While the Mk 1 only had a range of 20 miles, the Bloodhound 2 had more than double the range, greater operational altitude, a 35 per cent increase in speed to Mach 2.7 and improved guidance, and was able to intercept fast targets at heights well below 1,000ft. Development of Bloodhound Mk 2 began in 1960 and continued until 1965, with export orders from Sweden (again) and Switzerland. The Bloodhound was only withdrawn from RAF service in 1991, after thirty-three years of service.

Thunderbird

In 1949 a development contract was placed with English Electric for a complete land-based, mobile anti-aircraft weapon system. Thunderbird emerged as a semi-active radar-homing missile, with a receiver aerial located at the front of

a guidance package that was mounted within the large dielectric nose-cone.

Each Thunderbird battery had its own surveillance and height-finding radars, and a battery command post that could control up to six firing troops. Each such troop had a launch-control post, a target-illuminating radar and three missile launchers. A complete Thunderbird defence could be deployed in under three hours in all weathers, by day or night. Regiments had an average success rate of 90 per cent during exercises, with firings taking place against high-speed aircraft targets that were manoeuvring and changing course when the missiles engaged them.

The Thunderbird Mk 1 went into service with the British Army in 1960 and continued in service until 1966, when it was replaced by Thunderbird Mk 2. The Mk 2 offered increased range, improved low altitude cover and greater resistance to countermeasures. It was highly mobile and air transportable, and entered service with the British Army in Germany in 1966, continuing in use until 1976. Thirty-seven Thunderbirds were supplied to Saudi-Arabia as a stop-gap missile until the delivery of the American Hawk system; although Libya ordered Thunderbird, in the event the contract was never finalized.

BAC Guided Weapons Division

In order to build on the strengths and end the warring between the Bristol and English Electric Guided Weapons Divisions, the first of BAC's divisions, the BAC Guided Weapons Division, was established in March 1963. It was branded by its products, which originated from each of BAC's partners unlike the other divisions of the firm formed nine months later. These divisions were simply the renaming of the original firm: English Electric Aviation becoming BAC (Preston Division), Vickers-Armstrongs (Aircraft) becoming BAC (Weybridge Division), and so on. It was not until 1971 that divisions defined by product were formed amongst the aircraft part of BAC, when the Civil Aircraft and Military Aircraft Divisions were formed.

The Chairman of the Guided Weapons Division was Lord Caldecote; George Jefferson became the Chief Executive and later succeeded to Caldecote's role.

George Jefferson was the driving force leading the Guided Weapons Division. Initially Managing Director, he later became Chief Executive.
BAE Systems

The establishment of the new Guided Weapons Division required goodwill on all sides, which was not always forthcoming. Over time the barriers were eroded through a combination of shrewd management and interchange of staff.

Rapier

After the Ministry had cancelled PT428, BAC continued working on a cheaper, privately funded, optically tracked version (internally called Sightline) retaining the capability for Blindfire. It was designed to combat fast aircraft at altitudes as low as 100ft and up to 10,000ft. This version, designated ET316 by the Ministry, was to be complementary to the American Mauler system; however, Mauler proved to have many problems and in 1965 it too was cancelled.

In 1966 the name Rapier was given to ET316, after the Guided Weapons Division had come up with the unfortunate soubriquet 'Mongoose'. According to Pat Adams, Guided Weapons Division Company Secretary 1964–75, no one was certain as to what the plural of Mongoose was and the less contentious and more elegant name of 'Rapier' was preferred. Rapier was to prove markedly different

A Rapier and a USAF Sikorsky Super Stallion HH-53C 31648 at the 1974 Farnborough Air Display. This shows to advantage the small size of the Rapier and how it could be loaded onto this helicopter. BAE Systems

A Rapier battery well dug in and ready for deployment. The Rapier was almost called Mongoose but fortunately wiser counsels prevailed. Rapier proved to be an excellent investment and by the time BAC was nationalized had earned £600m. MBDA

from previous products in the firm in that it was a truly divisional project, shared between both Stevenage and Bristol.

Rapier's Performance

Rapier was designed to be very accurate, rather than using the large and heavy proximity fuzed warheads used by its competitors, which resulted in a larger, heavier and slower missile. Instead, Rapier relied on the direct impact of a lighter charge on its target.

However, the armed forces complained about the limited usefulness of a clear-weather system with optical tracking in the poor weather conditions in Northern Europe and soon demanded an all-weather version with radar-tracking. As a result the requirement was changed in 1966 to include Blindfire capability, thus reverting in many ways to the original PT428 specification. Fortunately BAC had designed ET316 so that it could incorporate a Blindfire capability, and by 1974 Blindfire radar tracking of targets in darkness or poor visibility was available to allow operation when optical tracking would be impossible.

be loaded on the ships in the UK, the Rapiers were inaccessible throughout the voyage south. However, they were quickly put into action in the midst of Argentine air raids, two Sea Kings taking just three hours to lift the Rapier units to high ground around the San Carlos Water beachhead, and by the end of that first day, all were operating. Rapier successes were initially exaggerated but in reality there was one definite hit, two probables and two possibles. The systems were sited too high for the attacking aircraft and could not be depressed far enough down to engage them; in addition, there was no spares support and as a result two units were cannibalized.

By the time of BAC's nationalization in 1977 Rapier had earned the company £600m in export sales. The basic towed version of this missile was ordered by the armies of Britain, Australia and Zambia, the Iranian Air Force, Brunei, the RAF Regiment and the defence forces of Abu Dhabi and Oman. By mid-1979 some 10,000 Rapier missile rounds had been built and around 3,000 fired. Developed versions of Rapier remain in production in 2011 with MBDA, which has taken over BAC/BAe's guided weapon interests.

Sea Wolf

The BAC Guided Weapons Division received the design contract for the PX430 shipboard short-range surface-to-air missile in June 1967, following a Bristol proposal. A year later PX430 – intended to replace the Royal Navy's Shorts Sea Cat missiles – was named Sea Wolf, and a development contract followed in 1969. This was shared with Marconi, who were responsible for the associated radars and control system, and Vickers Shipbuilders for the missile launcher. BAC became prime contractor in 1970 as initial trials began at the Aberporth missile range in Wales.

Sea Wolf was intended to be the final line of defence against both sea-skimming and high-angle anti-ship missiles, and against aircraft. Once a target has been identified as hostile, all phases of launch and guidance are automatic. Both the missile and the target are tracked by radar, and the system guides the two

Rapier was highly mobile, requiring in its basic form the use of only two Land Rovers. One Land Rover towed the launcher trailer and carried the tracker, radio equipment, four missiles in sealed containers and three members of the firing crew. The other towed a trailer carrying nine more missiles and transported additional equipment and two crew. Rapier had a towed weight of less than one ton, contrasting favourably with lightweight anti-aircraft guns that might weigh seven times more and could not be transported by helicopter. It had a range of 4 miles, up to a height of 2 miles and was capable of hitting a Mach 1+ target.

The performance and reaction time of Rapier ensured a high kill probability

against subsonic or supersonic targets from ground level up to 10–11,000ft, yet the missile could be operated by one man, with a second man standing by as relief operator and to assist in reloading. The system could also be deployed more quickly by mounting the tracker semi-permanently on the Land Rover that transports it.

The Rapier missile system entered service with the British Army and the Royal Air Force and was rushed into its first action in the Falklands conflict with Argentina in 1982. Twelve early-model optical Rapier fire units were operated by an Army Air Defence Regiment as, in order ease logistics, all Blindfire radar trackers were left behind. First to

A Sea Wolf being launched from a Royal Navy Type 22 frigate. These frigates have twin Sea Wolf launchers. As a short-range supersonic missile, it enables ships to defend themselves against aircraft and anti-ship missiles. The complete weapon system, including tracking radars and fire control computers, operates automatically. MBDA

A Sea Wolf launch from a Type 23 frigate. These frigates carry thirty-two Vertical Launch Sea Wolfs in a silo on the foredeck. In vertical launch form, the missile has an additional boost rocket motor that is jettisoned once the missile is out of the silo. MBDA

together for the interception. Sea Wolf is even able to intercept shells fired from 4.5in guns, which are even smaller than itself.

Sea Wolf entered service in 1979 and was on active service on Royal Navy ships during the Falklands conflict and in the Gulf War. Used in anger for the first time on 12 May 1982 off the Falkland Islands, the system downed two Argentine A-4 Skyhawks while another Skyhawk flew into the sea as it attempted to evade the missiles.

Initially developed for use in a manually loaded six-round launcher on the Type 22 'Broadsword' class frigate, Sea Wolf later appeared in a silo-based vertical-launch guise, which was fired for the first time in 1990. Vertical launching provides all-round coverage and greater fire-power against multiple targets; vertical-launch Sea Wolf equips the Navy's Type 23 'Duke' class frigates and some supply vessels. In vertical-launch Sea Wolf the propulsion system combines a booster and a rocket motor, whereas the original Sea Wolf only has the rocket motor.

Sea Wolf also operates with the Malaysian, Chilean and Brazilian navies.

It is planned to remain in use on British warships until 2018, by which time it will have served for almost forty years.

Sea Skua

In October 1975, not long before BAC was nationalized, the go-ahead was given to develop Sea Skua: an all-weather, lightweight, sea-skimming anti-ship missile with a 15km range. This missile was designed to be carried on the Westland Lynx helicopters entering service on the Royal Navy's destroyers and frigates. The

A Westland Lynx with BAC Sea Skua missiles. On the eve of the Farnborough 1976 Air Show, Westland received permission to hang four real Sea Skua development rounds on its armament-development Lynx, XZ166. BAE Systems

Launch of a Sea Skua from a twin launcher from a fast patrol boat – a very potent weapon for such a small vessel. The pieces trailing the missile are the remnants of the launcher's frangible front-end cover. MBDA

naval version of the Lynx would carry a semi-active radar seeker operating with a Ferranti Sea Spray radar. The Lynx/ Sea Skua combination was developed to replace the smaller Wasp helicopters armed with Aérospatiale AS.12 missiles that were then in service, to provide long-range defence against missile-carrying fast patrol boats, hydrofoils or hovercraft.

Following target location by the Sea Spray radar, the missile is released, dropping clear of the launch aircraft before the solid-fuel boost and sustainer motors ignite. The Sea Skua descends in stages to the sea-skimming height before homing onto the target with a semi-active homing head. It possesses a warhead effective against vessels of up to 1,000 tons' displacement; a concerted attack by more than one helicopter could cripple a larger vessel. The warhead has a slightly delayed action, allowing penetration of the target before detonation.

In April 1982, the Royal Navy rushed some early missiles into use in the Falklands conflict, before formal evaluation and acceptance procedures had been completed. Eight Sea Skuas were launched and all scored direct hits. The Sea Skua formally entered service with the RN in 1983 and was used in both the First and the Second Gulf Wars. The Sea Skuas fired in the First Gulf War were specially modified to enable them

to attack small patrol boats with a low freeboard; twenty were fired from RN Lynxes, sinking or damaging eleven Iraqi ships.

Later development of Sea Skua fell to BAC Guided Weapons Division's successors, namely British Aerospace Guided Weapons Division, later Matra BAe Dynamics and now MBDA. A ship-launched variant was developed as a private venture, with the first trial firing carried out at the end of 1988 at Aberporth; this version was later ordered by Kuwait. The helicopter-launched version was the first British missile to see service with German armed forces and it has also been exported to Brazil, Malaysia, South Korea and Turkey.

Into Space

The Guided Weapons Division's work was not only concerned with missiles, but also with a wide number of applications of which perhaps the most notable was the work with satellites. Initially the work was spread around several sites, but from 1967 it was centralized at Bristol.

BAC's first major involvement in satellites came in 1962 with the UK1–4 series, built to research the ionosphere. BAC had first entered this market with some contributory work on the UK1 and UK2 satellites (on entering orbit

they became Ariel 1 and 2, respectively), though they were actually built in the USA. On UK3, the first space research satellite to be completely developed and built in Britain, BAC was main contractor, with responsibility for the spacecraft structure, overall integration and ground-check equipment, while GEC supplied the electronics. UK3 was launched in May 1967 in California and on entering orbit was renamed Ariel 3, performing well within specification during its short, two and a half year life. It was succeeded by UK4 (later Ariel 4), for which BAC was again prime contractor.

In the meantime BAC's rapidly growing space expertise was used by ESRO (European Space Research Organization) as a sub-contractor to MBB to develop systems for the HEOS (Highly Eccentric Orbiting Satellite) A1 launched in December 1968. This led to work on HEOS A2 and ESRO's Cos-B satellite, whose scientific mission was to study in detail the sources of extra-terrestrial gamma radiation.

Other satellites were to follow with varying involvement from BAC, which shared the work with the American Hughes Aircraft Corporation and European aerospace firms, while on the later Intelsat 4 and 4A Hughes and BAC were the sole partners. The Intelsat series launched during 1971 and 1972 was a great success and took over transmission of worldwide television and telephone communications. BAC's relationship with Hughes burgeoned to such an extent that it constructed sixteen sets of satellite hardware for Hughes. As a result of these successes and the growing significance of this area of activity, a Spacecraft assembly facility and a large Space building were constructed at Filton in 1969.

As a major contributor to Prospero, Britain's first technology satellite, BAC was awarded responsibility for design and manufacture of structures, handling and test equipment and power supplies. This was launched at Woomera in October 1971.

In January 1971 BAC led the formation of STAR (Satellites for Technology Applications and Research)

A Paris Air Show display of some BAC space vehicles, including the nose of a Skylark rocket and a GEOS Intelsat 4 satellite. Note the BAC Union Flag logo. BAE Systems

consortium and the Corporation joined with companies from seven of the nine other ESRO member nations, namely Contraves (Switzerland), CGF-Fiat and Montedel (Italy), Sabca (Belgium), Ericcson (Sweden), Fokker VFW (Netherlands), Dornier Systems (Germany) and Thomson CSF of France. As a result the firm was awarded the contract for the GEOS satellite, which orbited above the equator probing the earth's magnetosphere. The STAR consortium later won contracts for other satellites, which received varying amounts of BAC input.

BAC airframe and the Guided Weapons Divisions provided substantial support to Rockwell for the US Space Shuttle, with staff based in California for more than two years. There were high expectations of a permanent contribution to this technologically advanced programme, but in the event the British Government withdrew support and the Germans stepped into BAC's place.

MUSTARD Project

In 1966 BAC had proposed its own space transporter, the Multi-Unit Space Transport and Recovery Device (MUSTARD) for European development in competition with the NASA Space Shuttle. Although seemingly a GW project, the research originated from BAC's Preston Division based on a Government-funded research contract.

MUSTARD consisted of three near-identical units stacked together, with two units acting as first-stage boosters and the third vehicle as the actual spacecraft. The booster units would have separated from the orbital unit and been flown back to Earth, landing conventionally. It would have delivered a 6,600lb payload to a 300nm polar orbit for a take-off weight of 936,000lb. The motors of all three stages would burn for take-off, with the tanks of the orbital stage topped up from the two non-orbiting boosters. MUSTARD appeared to be more efficient than the Space Shuttle design, in which no provision was made for the salvage of the boosters. However, the project did not proceed as the British Government did not offer it any further support following the initial research contract.

Skylark

The Skylark upper-atmosphere research and earth-resources survey rocket was designed by the RAE Farnborough and the Rocket Propulsion Establishment for Geophysical Year in 1957–58. The launch of the initial Skylark, which could only transport 100lb to a height of 95 miles, took place at the Woomera range in Australia in 1957, at a time when Britain still had expectations of taking part in a space programme with intentions to launch its own satellites. By 1964 the UK rocket programme had so expanded that it was passed to BAC Filton, which took over design authority.

As an example of the rocket's work, in June 1968 a Skylark rocket was successfully launched 115 miles into space from Woomera with a large X-ray telescope on board. During the flight the telescope made several sweeps of the sky, searching for a new type of X-ray star. By that time, 183 Skylarks had been used for various research purposes.

Skylark continued to be employed, built by Astrium, despite losing all Government support in 1977. It remained a significant, inexpensive research tool

A Skylark ready for launch at the Spanish National Rocket Range at Arenosillo, near Huelva.
Bristol Aero Collection

The launch of the 441st and final Skylark in Esrange, Sweden on 2 May 2005. The final Skylark mission, MASER 10, carried a suite of experiments to study the effects of microgravity, including a biological investigation of the protein actin, and a study of interfacial turbulence in evaporating liquids. This final flight drew to an end the British space programme. MBDA

that was used for a wide range of research topics, from X-ray astronomy to the fertilization of frogs' eggs. The 441st and last Skylark was launched from Sweden in May 2005. In this final developed form, it was able to carry a 440lb payload to an altitude of 360 miles, and on one launch from Brazil even reached a height of 625 miles.

Other Activities

The GW Division had a large number of other significant and income-producing activities. These included the complex automatic air-intake control systems for Concorde, the MRCA/Tornado trials programme test equipment, and the Jaguar's nav/attack system. Another activity was the construction of nose cones for missiles, TSR2, Concorde and Tornado.

The GW Division also took over the work of importing, fitting out and modifying the Jindivik pilotless target drone. This had previously been handled by Fairey Engineering Ltd but now became the responsibility of BAC (AT) Ltd, jointly owned by BAC and Fairey Engineering.

Designed and produced at the Government Aircraft Factories, Melbourne, Australia, the Jindivik first flew in 1952 and incorporated a wealth of British equipment: a Bristol Siddeley Viper 8 engine, Elliott autopilot, radio control system and various trials equipments. Therefore, it made sense for the UK to import the bare airframes and have them completed locally by a subcontractor. Production and testing continued at the Fairey Engineering factory at Ringway, Manchester, and approximately 150 were assembled there between 1960 and 1977, when work was transferred to RAE Llanbedr, Anglesey.

Conclusion

At the time of nationalization the GW Division had become a leading missile and space enterprise, making a far larger than proportional contribution to the overall profitability of the group. Many of its products were exported and in 1975 the Division won a double accolade by receiving two Queens Awards, one

A Jindivik pilotless target drone in the Fairey Engineering hangar at Manchester Ringway in June 1961. The assembly and modification of the Australian-designed and built Jindivik became the responsibility of BAC (AT) Ltd, a joint BAC-Fairey company, after 1960. R.A. Scholefield

for Exports and one for Technological Innovation.

As nationalization hung over the aircraft industry in the mid-1970s, BAC was unsure whether guided weapons would be included and seriously investigated forming a separate company for this enterprise to continue owning it. However, when it became clear that guided weapons would be included, any such thoughts ceased. In April 1977 the GW Division, along with the airframe divisions, became part of the newly minted British Aerospace as British Aerospace Dynamics. Part-privatized in 1981, by 1989 it was fully privatized. Its subsidiary, British Aerospace Space Systems, was sold to Matra Marconi Space in 1994 and is now Astrium, a British-French-German combine. In 1996 BAe Dynamics Guided Weapons Division was merged with a division of Matra Defence to form Matra BAe Dynamics. Finally, in 2001 Matra BAe Dynamics merged with Aérospatiale-Matra Missiles (of EADS) and Finmeccanica of Italy to create MBDA.

CHAPTER NINE

Jet Provost to Strikemaster

In the complex merger of the three firms that formed BAC, the founding companies agreed which programmes should remain the responsibility of the original firms: the profit and loss from these 'old account' products would remain with each founding company. Those programmes where the profit and loss was to be BAC's became 'new account' products. However, no such distinction prevailed with Hunting, as it was not a founding company but had been acquired by BAC in 1960: all profits or liabilities from its programmes became the Corporation's.

BAC inherited Hunting's Jet Provost trainer together with an ambitious project for a Viscount replacement, the twin-jet H.107. Production and development of the Jet Provost remained unchanged at the Luton factory, but the Viscount replacement was soon taken over by the Corporation to become the BAC 107. In May 1961, after much internal debate, the Corporation decided to proceed with the 107 as the larger BAC One-Eleven, with project design centred at Weybridge and final assembly at Hurn. Hunting at Luton

was to play a substantial part in the One-Eleven, designing and manufacturing the wings, ailerons and flaps.

The Jet Provost

The Jet Provost was developed from the Percival Provost, which had entered service as the standard basic trainer for the RAF in 1953. Piston-powered, it provided side-by-side seating for the instructor and student pilot. (Percival, a division of the Hunting Group, became 'Hunting Percival' in 1954 and dropped the 'Percival' name altogether in 1957.) In 1951, even before it entered service, Hunting decided to capitalize on its experience by proposing a jet-powered version, the Jet Provost, using 70 per cent of the piston Provost's components.

The Jet Provost was intended to train pilots from the very outset of their flying careers, to carry them through the elementary and basic stages and to include a proportion of the syllabus handled by advanced jet trainers. In March 1953,

ten Jet Provost T.1s, powered by the 1,750lb thrust Armstrong Siddeley Viper, were ordered to allow an RAF evaluation of its suitability. An eleventh was also constructed as a company demonstrator.

Hunting's objective in designing the Jet Provost was to produce handling characteristics paralleling those of operational jet aircraft, but retaining modest circuit, approach and stalling speeds, and simple handling. It incorporated a retractable tricycle landing gear, air-brakes and instrumentation, all in line with modern jet aircraft, but these did not detract from its overall simplicity. The maiden flight of the prototype XD674 took place uneventfully at Luton on 16 June 1954. Following an initial test and development programme with the company, the prototype was submitted to Boscombe Down for official trials in November 1954.

The clear potential of the Jet Provost justified the construction of four improved development aircraft, designated as T.2s, which took advantage of an extra 110lb thrust from the Viper 8 engine, had a cleaned-up rear fuselage contour and a slightly enlarged jet pipe. The long-legged undercarriage of the T.1, the main units of which were directly adapted from the piston Provost, were replaced by shortened gear.

The final T.1, XD694, became the prototype T.2; two of the T.2s were civil-registered and one of these, G-AOHD, completed an extensive sales tour of South America and was later dispatched to Australia, where it remains to this day. Another T.2 toured India and Pakistan.

A Percival Provost T.1 and a BAC Jet Provost T.5. The Percival Provost was the RAF's standard basic trainer from 1953; it was superseded by the Jet Provost, of which the T.5 was the final trainer development. These two aircraft XF877 and XW422 are now in private ownership. Adrian Pingstone

Hunting Jet Provost T.1 'XD693' – actually G-AOBU – and BAC Jet Provost T.5 G-VIVM. This shows the development of the design from the T.1 to the T.5. XD693 made its first flight in June 1955; it was retained by the manufacturers and used as a test aircraft and demonstrator. G-VIVM, formerly XS230, was built as the penultimate Jet Provost T.4 for the RAF, but it was retained by BAC and converted on the production line to become the T.5 prototype. Author

During the tours the Jet Provost was often flown from stony, rough fields, drenched runways, from airfields up to 10,000ft above sea level and in very hot weather. No difficulties were experienced and performance was equal to estimates. Comprehensive service trials took place between 1955 and 1956, and a contract for a production batch of 100 was received in August 1957. The Jet Provost T.3, as the production version was designated, thus became the first jet trainer to be standardized by any air force.

RAF Service

The first T.3 entered service in June 1959 and the RAF received 201 between 1959 and 1961. Two of the RAF's production T.3s, XN467 and XN468, were modified during construction to take a Viper 11 turbojet of 2,500lb thrust, a 40 per cent increase; the company's T.2 demonstrator, G-AOUS, was similarly re-engined. The benefit of additional power was soon realized and the T.3 was superseded on the Luton production line by the T.4 with

the Viper 11. The extra power enabled the T.4 to climb nearly twice as fast as its predecessor, and the RAF went ahead to order 185 of them. First deliveries of the T.4 were in November 1961 and they soon started to displace the T.3s. However, the T.3 remained in service well into the 1970s and approximately seventy received an avionics upgrade from BAC. The T.4's superior performance with the bigger engine caused fatigue problems for the airframe, and by the mid-1970s the greater majority of the 190 built had been withdrawn from service.

Export Jet Provosts

Hunting also won twenty-two international orders for the Jet Provost T.51, an armed version of the T.3 for weapon

G-PROV was built by BAC Warton as a Jet Provost T.4 for the RAF, but was held in reserve and was bought back by BAC for refurbishment and re-sale. It was converted into a T.52 for the South Yemen Air Force and entered active service as aircraft 104. Sold to the Republic of Singapore Air Force in 1975, it served until it was replaced by a Strikemaster in 1980. It is now privately owned in the UK. Author

XW324 is a former RAF Jet Provost T.5 now in private ownership. Adrian Pingstone

training. This could carry two 0.303in machine guns in the fuselage just behind the engine intakes and, variously, eight 25lb bombs or between four and twelve rockets under the wings. The T.51's customers were the Air Force of Ceylon which ordered twelve, Sudan which received four and Kuwait having six. The T.51 was superseded on the Luton production line by the T.52 version of the T.4. Iraq ordered twenty, Venezuela bought fifteen and Sudan, eight. Yemen also received eight refurbished RAF T.4s, redesignated as T52.

Developing the Jet Provost T.5 and the Strikemaster

Under BAC the Jet Provost's development continued apace. On 16 March 1965 the private-venture BAC 166 made its first three flights at Luton at the hands of BAC test pilot 'Dizzy' Addicott. This was the final Jet Provost T.4, XS231, which had been converted during production to have the Viper 522 of 3,410lb thrust in place of the Viper 11 of the production aircraft.

The BAC 166 was a development machine for the unpressurized 164 and

pressurized 167, both destined for export markets. Both projects were related to the BAC 145, a pressurized Jet Provost being developed for a Ministry of Aviation contract and for the RAF as the Jet Provost T.5. While the T.5 would retain the 2,500lb Viper 11 of the earlier RAF versions, the 164 and 167 were aimed at export sales where nearly 1,000lb more thrust would be a considerable performance advantage, enhancing the weapons-carrying ability for its dual trainer and counter-insurgency role. In the event, the unpressurized export version was not proceeded with while the BAC 167 design became the basis for the Strikemaster

Closure of Luton and Transfer to Warton

Owing to the huge difficulties caused by the TSR2 cancellation in April 1965, the Corporation had no alternative other than to make swingeing cuts in plant and workforce. More than 5,000 employees had to leave Weybridge and the Preston Division plants at Warton, Samlesbury and Preston. At the end of 1965 the closure of the Luton factory was announced. Assembly and flight test

of the Jet Provost was sent north to the Warton while wing assembly went south to Hurn. (All the One-Eleven wing work from Luton went to Weybridge.)

Jet Provost T.5

The T.5 was a logical development of the previous marks with more power, a redesigned wing with greater fuel capacity (allowing the deletion of the tip tanks used up to then) and with a longer fatigue life. The wing was also fitted with strongpoints for carrying underwing stores. The most important alteration was the introduction of pressurization, which resulted in the total redesign of the cockpit, windscreen and canopy. Pressurization offered a more extensive utilization of both aircraft and instructors, and a possible shortening of the training period, for pilots were limited physiologically in the frequency of sorties they could make above 25,000ft in the unpressurized T.3 and T.4.

The T.5 programme was delayed by the transfer of work from Luton to Warton. The two prototypes were rebuilds of the final two T.4s, XS230 and XS231 (the latter had flown with the Strikemaster development engine as the BAC 166), and were moved mid-conversion to Warton. On 28 February 1967 XS230 took to the air at Warton piloted by Reg Stock and Jimmy Dell.

The pressurized cockpit was a major structural change, giving the aircraft a rather bulbous look at the front. This changed the airflow and altered the handling characteristics to such an extent that a flight-test programme was required to re-examine the stalling and spinning characteristics of the aircraft.

On 4 September 1969 XW287, the first of 110 Jet Provost T.5s ordered for the RAF was handed over to the Central Flying School at Little Rissington by Peter Ginger, senior production test pilot of the Corporation's Preston Division. The T.5 continued in service until September 1988 when it was replaced by the Shorts Tucano. BAC built 115 T.5s, the final machine being completed in 1971. Even though production of Jet Provosts then ended, 177 T.3/T.5s were returned to Warton for the installation of updated and revised avionics between 1973 and 1975, and were redesignated as T.3As/T.5As.

Specification: Jet Provost T.5	
Length:	33ft 8in (10.26m)
Wingspan:	35ft 4in (10.77m)
Height:	10in 2in (3.10m)
MTOW:	7,200lb (3,265kg)
Max speed:	326mph (525km/h)
Range:	565 miles (909km)
Crew:	2
Powerplant:	2,500lb Rolls-Royce Viper Mk 11
Jet Provosts built:	600 (Hunting/BAC Luton 480, BAC Warton 120)

Strikemaster

Recognizing the potential of its pressurized BAC 167 and building on the reputation of the earlier exported Jet Provosts, BAC decided to offer an inexpensive weapons trainer or counter-insurgency type. The private-venture Strikemaster proved very profitable for the Corporation and remained in production from 1967 until 1989, twelve years after BAC had become part of British Aerospace.

The prototype BAC 167's maiden flight took place at Warton on 26 October 1967 piloted by Reg Stock. Temporarily registered G27-8, it was destined to be the first of forty-seven Mk 80s for the Royal Saudi Air Force as part of the huge contract to also supply Lightnings and Thunderbird missiles, all BAC products. In October 1968 the BAC 167 was given the name Strikemaster.

The Strikemaster was armed with two guns and had four pylons for up to 3,000lb of bombs or rocket launchers; a pylon-mounted Vinten camera pack could be carried. This triple role trainer/attack/reconnaissance capability was attractive to many air forces. The aircraft was cleared to 6g at an all-up weight of 11,500lb and was a potent ground-attack weapon as well as a trainer capable of taking the student pilot right through to combat. A major selling point for the Strikemaster was its side-by-side seating, which was generally favoured for training, weapon training and in the close-support combat role.

The Strikemaster's 910lb extra thrust conferred a greatly improved rate of climb, with flight time to 30,000ft cut by half. Radius of action with a 3,000lb load of weapons was 250 nautical miles, increasing to 500 nautical miles with 1,000lb. Basic equipped weight was about 6,000lb, increasing to about 8,000lb with full internal tanks (250gal) and to 11,500lb with under-wing stores, including tip-tanks totalling 370gal, making a total fuel capacity of 620gal. To cater for the higher weights the airframe and undercarriage were strengthened

The Strikemaster's sales success persuaded the manufacturers and its suppliers and subcontractors to build aircraft for stock to maintain a competitive fourteen-month delivery period from receipt of order. In the late 1960s the Strikemaster and Jet Provost T.5 production rate was approximately six aircraft per month, rising to eight a month in 1970.

Specification: Strikemaster	
Length:	33ft 8in (10.26m)
Wingspan:	36ft 11in (11.25m) (with tip tanks)
Height:	10in 2in (3.10m)
MTOW:	11,500lb (5,215kg)
Max speed:	481mph (774km/h)
Range:	300 miles (500km) (combat radius)
Crew:	2
Powerplant:	3,140lb Rolls-Royce Viper Mk 535
Strikemasters built	156 (BAC/BAe Warton 150, BAe Hurn 6)

Strikemaster Customers

The Royal Saudi Air Force (RSAF) was the largest customer for the Strikemaster, using forty-seven Mk 80s. Their last flight was on 4 January 1997, when they were phased out and replaced by the Pilatus PC-9. One of the RSAF Strikemasters was returned to Warton, refurbished and presented to the Imperial War Museum at Duxford in 2000.

Other Strikemaster operators were South Yemen, which had previously received four Jet Provost T.52s, Oman, Kuwait (whose aircraft were later sold

The second BAC Strikemaster, registered 902 for the RSAF but also bearing temporary British markings as G27-9. It appeared at the Farnborough Show in September 1968.

BAE Systems via Warton Heritage

Three of the seven BAC aircraft at the 1976 Farnborough Air Show, the last before nationalization. RSAF Strikemaster 1124 is displayed – temporarily registered as G-BECI – with a huge array of its weaponry. Behind it, Jaguar International XZ362 and Concorde G-BBDG. BAE Systems

The same aircraft, 1124, now actually in service with the Royal Saudi Air Force.
BAE Systems via Warton Heritage

Strikemaster Mk 83 registered 115 for the Kuwait Air Force, on a test flight from Warton over Fleetwood. BAE Systems via Warton Heritage

Strikemaster 304, a Mk 84 for the Singapore Armed Forces, bids farewell to Warton flying over the BAC hangars. BAE Systems via Warton Heritage

The Strikemaster production line at the Hurn plant. In the foreground are the first four aircraft; beyond are fuselages for the next six. At the far end of the hanger are three One-Elevens. Of the ten Strikemasters sent to Hurn, six were completed there and four returned to Warton at the closure of the plant for completion. BAE Systems

The second of the six Strikemaster Mk 90s completed at Hurn making its maiden flight piloted by Roy Radford, Chief Test Pilot of BAe Filton, in 1980 as G-16-27. It was eventually delivered to the Ecuador Air Force as FAE260 in November 1987.
BAE Systems

to Botswana), Singapore, Kenya, New Zealand, Ecuador and Sudan. The Omani Strikemasters had a far from quiet life and, according to some sources, each one of them received battle damage fighting insurgents.

Five Jet Provost T.55s were delivered to Sudan in 1969, and it later received three of the last Strikemasters built. The T.55s were essentially T.5s with the addition of machine guns. In 1973 the Greek Air Force wanted to order thirty-five to forty T.55s, but this contract was embargoed by the Labour Government, which refused to support the Greek military junta. In September 1976 at the Farnborough Air Show, BAC stated that of its then nine Strikemaster overseas operators, five had re-ordered on ten occasions and that the total value of export orders exceeded £55m.

The Last Ten Strikemasters

The delivery of the 146th Strikemaster took place at Warton in 1978 with the handing over of a single replacement aircraft to the Royal Saudi Air Force. By then BAC had become part of the nationalized British Aerospace. As English Electric had done with the Canberra, BAe decided to build ten Strikemasters for stock. The final assembly work was redirected to the Hurn plant, which already manufactured the wings and was short of other work now that One-Eleven production was virtually at an end.

The first of this batch flew from Hurn factory in late August 1980 registered as G-16-26. As G-BIDB and in company with Hurn's second Strikemaster, G-BIHZ (previously G-16-27), it embarked on a 4,700-mile demonstration tour of Africa in September 1981. Sales were slow to materialize, but eventually Sudan ordered the whole batch, which were to be designated as Mk 90s. The first three were delivered from Hurn in late 1983, but the others were stymied by an arms embargo. The next three Strikemasters made their maiden flights from Hurn, but when the site closed in May 1984 they flew back to Warton while the four uncompleted aircraft were returned by road. Of these seven remaining Strikemasters, one went to Oman and six were sold to Ecuador, with the delivery of the last three from Warton in October 1989.

In the meantime the Kuwait Air Force traded back its nine remaining Strikemasters to British Aerospace and these flew into Warton, using UK military serials (ZG805–813) and were placed in store. Following a complete refurbishment they were sold to the Botswana Defense Force in 1987; they were delivered in 1987–88 and remained in service until 1997.

Conclusion

Consideration was given to a further development tentatively named the Eaglet, aimed at the USAF requirement for a trainer to replace the Cessna T-37. It was to be re-engined with the Garrett TFE731 engine, with modern systems and avionics and a new rear fuselage. However, this development was not proceeded with.

A grand total of 480 Jet Provosts were built by Hunting/BAC at Luton and Warton, succeeded on the production line by 156 very profitable Strikemaster sales of which the majority was manufactured by BAC before nationalization. The purchase by BAC of Hunting in 1960 had been a very sound investment.

CHAPTER TEN

The Mach 2 Lightning

'No sweat, I was with it all the way ... until I let the wheel brakes off.' This comment, by a fighter pilot after his first flight in an English Electric Lightning, encapsulates the excitement of a pilot's conversion training on the first British Mach 2 aircraft.

This brilliant design followed the Canberra on English Electric's production lines and demonstrated again how the fledgling English Electric design team, only formed at the end of the Second World War, had outshone their more established and illustrious rivals.

When BAC's three founding companies apportioned how the profits and losses of their existing products would be borne by the Corporation, the initial marks of the Lightning – the F.1, F.2, F.3 and T.4 – were deemed to be 'old account', so the profit or loss fell to English Electric. The succeeding marks, the T.5 and F.6 for the RAF and F.53 and

T.55 export variants were 'new account', so all earnings or losses were BAC's. BAC profited well from this arrangement, especially when the sales of Lightnings to Saudi Arabia and Kuwait are factored in, but at the time of the Corporation's founding, none of these developments was planned.

P.1A

Having launched the outstanding Canberra bomber, English Electric's Chief Designer, Teddy Petter, turned his attention to a fighter design that became a classic: a quantum leap to produce Britain's first and only supersonic fighter to go into series production. It grew from a Ministry of Supply specification issued in 1947 for a supersonic research aircraft (ER.103) capable of Mach 1.2–1.3. Both Fairey and English Electric submit-

ted proposals, which led to the Fairey Delta 2 and the much larger P.1A, a very different proposal to Fairey's.

Petter decided to use two engines to provide the performance that a supersonic interceptor must have at altitude for acceleration and manoeuvring. His inspired design had a unique staggered engine configuration with both engines on the aircraft centre line, giving a frontal area only one and a half times that with a single engine. This configuration minimized drag and asymmetric thrust problems in engine-failure situations, and simplified the functioning of systems.

The wing was a notched delta 60-degree swept wing, with the notch in effect moved rearwards as a low-set tailplane. The ailerons were set on the end of the wing, perpendicular to the fuselage. English Electric decided that the best place for the tailplane was low down, away from the wing wake, because high tails had been responsible for pitch-ups and deep stall problems for many aircraft.

The Royal Aircraft Establishment at Farnborough was sceptical about this young design team proceeding with the project, but in 1947 they issued a study contract, followed in April 1950 by a contract for two flying prototypes and a static test airframe. Owing to the RAE's doubts about the wing's 60-degree sweepback and the low tailplane, Shorts was contracted to design and build a research aircraft, the SB5, whose adjustable wing could test the sweep at 50, 60 and 69 degrees, and test the tailplane positioning in the low-speed envelope; its tests vindicated English Electric's decisions. By this time Petter had parted company with English Electric to join Folland: the design of what became the Lightning passed into the hands of Freddie Page,

Lightning T.4 prototype XL628 taken up close to the photographic aircraft for Farnborough 1959 by Roland Beamont. BAE Systems via Warton Heritage

WG760 landing at Boscombe Down after its maiden flight. Note the different intake design to the later Lightning and the drooped leading edge, which was soon dispensed with.
BAE Systems via Warton Heritage

Roland Beamont flying the second P.1A, WG763, in a fast, low pass along the Warton runway. It was trialling the ventral fuel tank introduced to increase range, which became a standard fit on the aircraft albeit with a fin to maintain stability.
BAE Systems via Warton Heritage

who is credited as the engineer behind this superlative machine and its success.

The first flight of the P.1A WG760, at Boscombe Down on 4 August 1954, was made by English Electric's Chief Test Pilot, Roland Beamont, and was remarkably successful. Mach 1 was exceeded on the third flight even though its Armstrong Siddeley Sapphire engines were not fitted with reheat at that stage. A rudimentary fixed-nozzle reheat system was fitted to WG760's Sapphires in November 1955, offering 10,310lb thrust. The effect on performance was noteworthy: the P.1A could reach 40,000ft in just 3½ minutes from take-off and a top speed of Mach 1.53. The second P.1A, WG763, flew on 18 July 1955 and was fitted with reheat and Aden cannon. WG763 was later used in testing the Lightning's belly fuel tank, and

both P.1As flew later in their careers with the cambered leading edge that the RAF belatedly adopted for their Lightnings.

The two prototypes were flown by a range of pilots from the Services and elsewhere, who found them very straightforward flying machines presenting no special conversion problems. The P.1A had excellent control qualities throughout the entire speed range, but tests revealed that the fin area was marginal and would be insufficient when external stores were carried. Testing went well but was not without incident: on several occasions the canopy parted company with the cockpit when Beamont was flying at high speed. Even after repair and modification it happened twice more to Beamont's colleague Johnny Squier, once at supersonic speeds.

By mid-1957 the two P.1As had flown over 500 missions, recording far more than half the total manned supersonic time logged by British aircraft at that time. The two P.1As laid a solid foundation of knowledge for the much more powerful P.1Bs, which were ordered in February 1952.

P.1B

The conversion of the P.1A research aircraft into a fighter was a major undertaking. To accelerate delivery of the RAF's first Mach 2 fighter, twenty pre-production P.1B development aircraft were ordered, each of which was intended to prove some facet of the aircraft, for example powerplant,

THE MACH 2 LIGHTNING

The second P.1B, XA853, which first flew in September 1957 and was used on a variety of trials. The P.1B was noticeably different from the P.1A: it had a redesigned nose, nose radome, higher cockpit and fuselage spine. The Armstrong Siddeley Sapphire engines were replaced by Rolls-Royce Avons.
BAE Systems via Warton Heritage

Three Development Batch P.1Bs including XG309 and XG310 at Warton with four test pilots: (from the left) Desmond De Villiers, Peter Hillwood, Jimmy Dell and Roland Beamont.
BAE Systems via Warton Heritage

handling, guns, Firestreak missiles, radar and autopilot.

The P.1B was planned from the outset as the first British complete weapon system, in which there was a specially designed armament, radar fire-control, electronics, navigational aids, autopilot and autostabilizer, and a host of other equipment. Externally, the P.1B differed substantially from its predecessor, with scarcely any part of the original P.1A remaining unaltered. Most strikingly, a redesigned nose with a centre-body in the air intake accommodating the radar, a raised cockpit, a fuselage spine, repositioned airbrakes and a larger fin. Rolls-Royce Avons replaced the Sapphires, and their higher thrust was further increased by the incorporation of full reheat with a variable-area nozzle.

The first P.1B, XA847, flew from Warton on 4 April 1957 piloted by Roland Beamont, and during its twenty-five minute flight exceeded Mach 1.2. XA847 was soon joined by two more P.1Bs, XA853 and XA856, to perform the main handling, aerodynamic assessment and engine installation trials for what was to be Britain's first supersonic fighter. In a ceremony at RAE Farnborough on 23 October 1958, XA847 was formally named the Lightning by the Chief of Air Staff and on 25 November 1958, with Beamont again at the controls, XA847 became the first British aircraft to fly at Mach 2.0 in level flight.

The Lightning F.1 and F.2

Production orders were placed in November 1956 so that no break would occur between the P.1B development aircraft and the production machines. The first production Lightning F.1, XM134, took to the air in October 1959 and the first Lightning squadron was formed when F.1s joined 74 Squadron at Coltishall in July 1960. They were soon on public display and appeared daily at the Farnborough Air Show, making a powerful impression.

The F.1 was essentially a production version of the P.1B fitted with a Ferranti Airpass air-interception radar and armed with twin 30mm Aden cannon, with the option of a pack carrying two de Havilland (later Hawker Siddeley Dynamics) Firestreak missiles, or forty-eight 2in rockets, or additional Aden cannon. The F.1 only served with 74 Squadron and was quickly superseded on the Samlesbury production line by the F.1A, which had UHF and radio provision

for inflight refuelling. The remaining F.1s in production of the fifty on order were completed to F.1A standard and served with Nos 51 and 111 Squadrons.

The next Lightning mark was the F.2; this was an interim model between the F.1 and the later F.3, which had a more sophisticated weapons fit. The F.2 was indistinguishable from the F.1 except for a small intake at the base of the fin. The main improvement over the preceding mark was fully variable reheat Avon 210 engines offering 14,140lb thrust with reheat. To avoid a gap in production following the completion of the F.1 contract, an order was received in December 1959 from the RAF for forty-four F.2s. The first F.2, XN723, made its first flight in July 1961 and deliveries to Nos 19 and 92 Squadrons in Germany started on 17 December 1962.

Lightnings for Two

As the Lightning came into service it was evident that there was a need for an operational conversion trainer. English Electric set to work and, having rejected a tandem cockpit layout, settled for a side-by-side arrangement. The prototype Lightning T.4, XL628, flew for the first time on 6 May 1959 piloted from Warton by Roland Beamont; it flew for thirty minutes, and went supersonic fifteen minutes after take-off. Though it had a slightly lower top speed than the single-seat variants, the T.4 could carry out all its operational roles as it had the Airpass radar and a twin-Firestreak missile pack, but no Aden cannon.

XL628 had a short but eventful life. It wowed the crowds at the September 1959 Farnborough Air Show, though there was an incident at the end of Beamont's display on the Monday that caused some embarrassment. When landing in a light drizzle, the braking parachute failed and the T.4 ran off the end of the wet runway at about 40kt, into the rough overshoot area; steering through the approach-lighting poles, Beamont eventually made it back to the perimeter track and dispersal with little damage other than some cuts to the tyres.

Production of the Lightning Development Batch and F.1s at Samlesbury in 1959; XG326 is leading the right-hand line. BAE Systems via Warton Heritage

Lightning F.1 XM145 undergoing pre-delivery engine runs at Warton in March 1960 wearing No. 74 Squadron markings.
BAE Systems via Warton Heritage

Five No. 74 Squadron Lightning F.1s.
BAE Systems via Warton Heritage

Piloted here by Roland Beamont, XG310 was one of the Development Batch aircraft converted to Lightning F.3 aerodynamic configuration by BAC sub-contractor Boulton Paul with the larger, square-topped fin, more powerful engines and other improvements. It returned to Warton in January 1962.
BAE Systems via Warton Heritage

A far more critical incident occurred on 1 October when the Chief Production Test Pilot, Johnny Squier, was flying XL628 on its ninety-fourth flight on high-speed rolling trials. The fin failed at Mach 1.7: Squier ejected and survived after spending an exceedingly uncomfortable twenty-four hours in a dinghy in the Irish Sea. This catastrophic fin failure led to modifications to the fins of all the Lightning F.1s, F.1As and T.4s already built or under construction.

Filton's Lightning Trainer Work

Well before this accident the problems related to fin size had seemingly been addressed on the P.1B and pre-production aircraft, and the XL628 already had this larger fin. The designers now had to examine the strength and size of the fin once more. With the advent of the Lightning F.3, the T.4 was superseded by a suitably developed trainer, the T.5, which had the F.3's square-topped fin, Rolls-Royce Avon 302 with variable reheat and Hawker Siddeley Dynamics *Red Top* missiles.

As part of BAC's programme to relocate work to Filton – which was lacking

work at the time of the formation of the Corporation – XM967, although built as a T.4 at Samlesbury, was roaded to Filton for completion as the first prototype T.5; it flew on 29 March 1962. Its predecessor, XM966, made its maiden flight as a T.4 from Samlesbury to Filton and was converted to a T.5, flying in December 1962. Filton's connection with the Lightning continued with the building of twenty T.5 noses and modifications to single-seaters. Filton later built the noses for the Saudi T.55 trainers, as Samlesbury was overloaded with work.

Fin Failure on the Lightning T.5

Both of the T.5 prototypes then engaged in test flying. On 22 July 1965, while trialling roll clearance with the forward rocket pack extended at Mach 1.8, XM966's fin failed and the aircraft went into spin. The flight observer immediately ejected but Preston Division's Chief Test Pilot, Jimmy Dell, had difficulty in ejecting, though he finally managed to activate the system. This structural failure of the fin was an almost exact replica of the T.4's with Johnny Squier

six years earlier, and the engineers had to re-examine their calculations and modify them accordingly.

The first T.4s only entered service in 1963, more than three years after the RAF received its first single-seaters. A total of forty-two Lighting trainers were built for the RAF, of which eighteen were T.4s. Generally each Lightning squadron had a single T.4 or T.5 attached to it while the Lightning Operational Conversion Unit had a far greater number at its disposal.

F.3 and F.6

Only a few months after the F.2 was ordered, negotiations took place with regard to the more advanced F.3, an initial forty-seven of which were ordered in June 1960. The F.2s and F.3s could together equip only six squadrons, so a further forty-five F.3s were contracted for in January 1962.

The F.3 represented a great advance on the earlier marks. It was readily distinguishable from them with its square-topped fin, which was 45 per cent greater in area than the F.2's. It also had the more reliable and more powerful Avon 301 engines and the improved Airpass A123B radar. The F.3 could carry the *Red Top*

XP697 made its maiden flight as an F.3 in July 1963, and on its second flight flew to Filton for conversion to become an F.6. As an F.6, XP697 was fitted with the drag-reducing cambered leading-edge and much larger ventral tank.
BAE Systems via Warton Heritage

No.11 Squadron Lightnings F.6s including XR723, XR724 and XR763. BAE Systems via Warton Heritage

missile which, unlike Firestreak, offered head-on interception. The twin Aden cannon were removed, which was later regarded as a retrograde step.

As an aerodynamic prototype for the F.3, one of the Development Batch aircraft, XG310, was converted and flew in January 1962. Several other Development Batch aircraft and F.2s were converted to F.3 configuration for trials purposes. The first production F.3, XP693, was brought forward in the production sequence to expedite testing and flew without all its equipment

on 16 June 1962. Deliveries to the RAF commenced in April 1964, equipping 23, 29, 56, 74 and 111 Squadrons.

The RAF now developed a requirement to increase the F.3's range. Fortunately, while the F.3 was entering service BAC had considered and trialled three further improvements:

- Fuel tanks carried on pylons above the wing, which carried 2,160lb fuel each and which could be jettisoned in the event of combat

- Arrestor hook
- Twin 30mm Aden cannon in the front section of the newly extended ventral tank

The reintroduction of the 30mm cannon was a sensible step following their deletion from the F.3. Interception is not always concerned with destruction, and in RAF service Lightnings were frequently used for investigating inquisitive trespassing aircraft and escorting them away. It was an advantage to have the option of a

RAF Lightning F.6s in their element.
BAE Systems via Warton Heritage

life of the airframes became an issue. A wing-root strengthening programme was instigated in 1979, and in 1985 some thirty-five F.6s were returned to Warton to extend their lives by another 400 hours. In 1987 the Lightning Training Flight and No. 5 Squadron were disbanded, leaving just No. 11 Squadron active with the Lightning at RAF Binbrook until 30 April 1988 when the Squadron re-equipped with the Tornado F.3 (built at the same factories as its Lightnings).

non-lethal warning shot, which could now be provided by a gun pack containing two 30mm Aden cannon with 120 rounds of ammunition each, in place of the forward portion of the large ventral fuel tank.

XP697 was flown to Filton on its second flight in August 1963 and had these features installed. In April 1964 it flew back to Warton and was informally designated the Lightning F.3A. So marked were all of the changes that these aircraft were redesignated as F.6s. BAC proposed retro-fitting these improvements to the T.5, but the Ministry never sanctioned such modifications and the T.5 trainer fleet essentially remained as trainer versions of the F.3, not the F.6.

Of the seventy Lightning F.3s and sixteen F.3As started by BAC, thirty-eight were completed to F.6 standard on the production line while twenty-five were returned to the factory to be modified to F.6 standard. The first production F.6 flew on 16 June 1965 and entered RAF service in December 1965. The final new-build Lightning for the RAF was handed over on 28 August 1967. The Lightning F.6 served with 5, 11, 23 and 74 Squadrons.

F.2A

In a parallel upgrade, thirty Lightning F.2s were modified for the RAF to a new configuration as F.2As, starting in 1967 and completing in September 1970. They were similar to the F.6, incorporating the cambered leading edge, F.3 fin, arrestor hook and enlarged fuel tank or, alternatively, the twin Aden cannon/fuel tank. As the F.2s were originally fitted with twin integral Aden cannon, which were retained, the latter arrangement provided an advantage over the F.6. The weapons system remained unchanged. The remaining unmodified F.2s were used in training or for supersonic target training.

RAF Lightning Service

In the late 1970 the number of Lightnings in service reached a peak of approximately 150, equipping nine front-line squadrons and a large Operational Conversion Unit. The first reduction in numbers came in 1971 with the disbandment of 74 Squadron from RAF Tengah in Singapore; the 74 Squadron F.6s were then passed to 56 Squadron at RAF Akrotiri in Cyprus.

Between 1974 and 1977 Nos 19, 23, 29, 56, 92 and 111 Squadrons lost their Lightnings, which were replaced by the slower, but longer-legged, twin-seater Phantom FGR2. However, the rundown was then suspended when it was realized that the RAF had a shortage of fighters and that the new Tornado F.2 would enter service later than planned. As a result, a shortage of spares and diminishing fatigue

Exporting the Lightning

Both English Electric and BAC sought to sell the Lightning to overseas air forces, but were faced with a lack of support from the British Government that sharply contrasted with the high level of French and American government support provided to the Dassault Mirage and the Lockheed F-104 Starfighter, respectively. The Lightning might have ideally suited a number of NATO air forces, most notably Germany's, but Germany adopted the F-104 even though it had been rejected by the USAF. In German service the F-104 received the unfortunate epithet 'the flying coffin' owing to the large number of pilots who were killed flying it.

The Saudi Arabian Contract

Following considerable efforts over more than two years by BAC and their agent in Saudi Arabia, Geoffrey Edwards, the Lightning's lack of export sales came to an end with the announcement in December 1965 of the supply to Saudi Arabia of a complete air-defence system. BAC's part of this contract was the supply of thirty-four Lightning F.53s, six F.55 twin-seat trainers and twenty to twenty-five (later increased to forty-seven) Strikemasters and thirty-seven Thunderbird missile systems. The value of the order in terms of British equipment and services was about £100 million (approximately £1 billion in 2010 prices).

Geoffrey Edwards had long cultivated a close relationship with Prince Sultan, who had recently been appointed defence minister, and was on good terms with others

Specification – Lightning F.3	
Length:	55ft 3in (16.84m)
Wingspan:	34ft 10in (10.62m)
Height:	17ft 3in (5.26m)
MTOW:	35,500lb (16,000kg)
Max speed:	Mach 2
Range:	855 miles (1,375km) subsonic; 150 miles (240km) supersonic
Powerplant:	Rolls-Royce Avon 301; 35,500lb with reheat
Armament:	2 × *Red Top* or Firestreak missiles

Former RAF Lightning T.4 XM989 at Warton, awaiting delivery to the Royal Saudi Air Force as a T.54 registered 54-650 in May 1966. Before delivery, the RSAF roundel was repositioned to the nose. The RSAF received four Lighting F.52s and two T.54s as an interim measure, before the delivery of their F.53s and T.55s. BAE Systems via Warton Heritage

RAF Lightning F.6 XR770 appeared at the September 1966 Farnborough Air Show painted in RSAF colours to promote the aircraft's export potential.
BAE Systems via Warton Heritage

RSAF Lightning F.53 53-666 (temporarily G27-2) with 30mm cannon on the front portion of the ventral tank, a camera pod in front of the cannon and underwing Matra rocket pods. This aircraft was originally built for the RAF and flew in January 1965, but was never delivered. Rebuilt as an F.53 and first flying as such in November 1966, it became the trials aircraft for the F.53 weapons fit.
BAE Systems via Warton Heritage

in the Saudi royal circle. To clinch the deal it was necessary to demonstrate the Lightning to King Saud. Despite initial misgivings by the Government in selling Lightnings to the Middle East, Edwards persuaded the Government to loan three RAF Lightning F.2s to BAC. These were flown to Bahrain with the assistance of a Vickers Valiant providing in-flight refuelling. At Bahrain the aircraft's RAF markings and registration were removed and BAC Warton's Chief Test Pilot, Jimmy Dell, flew and assessed each aircraft; he chose XN730 for the demonstration flights, on 4 July 1964 at the Saudi capital, Riyadh. These flights included a supersonic bang and a near-supersonic 'beat up' of Riyadh's main street.

This demonstration was followed up in August 1964 by the visit of a Saudi Arabian evaluation team to the UK. During a visit to Warton the RSAF's senior test pilot, Lt Hamdan, made several training flights on a T.4 with Jimmy Dell but then announced that he was required to make a solo flight at Mach 2 and report to his Government. After considerable deliberation it was agreed that he could make such a flight in an F.2, escorted by Jimmy Dell in a more powerful F.3. Hamdan set off with Dell behind on the supersonic test track up the Irish Sea, but as they approached Mach 2 Dell lost sight of Hamdan who had accelerated ahead. At the end of the Mach 2 run Dell ordered

Hamdan to cut power, and was able to cut the corner and catch up with him as they returned to Warton. However, the drama was not all over, for Hamdan decided to first do an overshoot and only then a landing, with his Lightning very low on fuel. During the flight Hamdan may have actually flown XN723 at Mach 2.1, beyond its RAF design limits.

The RSAF had an immediate requirement for Lightnings, so four F.2 fighters (XN767, XN770, XN796 and XN797) and two T.4 trainers (XM989 and XM992) were withdrawn from storage and prepared at Warton for service in Saudi Arabia. They were redesignated as F.52s (registered as 52-655 to 52-658) and T.54s (54-650 and 54-651), and were delivered to Saudi Arabia in three waves of two under Operation *Magic Palm* by BAC test pilots Don Ferguson and Tim Knight. Four Hunter F.60s and six Hunter T.7s were also delivered, and pre-production Lightning XG313 was supplied for ground instruction. One of the F.52s was soon lost in a take-off accident through over-rotation, and replaced by another former RAF F.2, XN729, which became 52-651.

Multi-Role Lightning

The Warton design team had long been convinced of the Lightning's wider potential; the Lightning was easy to handle

throughout its speed range from 130kt to Mach 2, and inherently stable, a first-class platform for the precision-delivery of weapons either from high altitude or low down beneath the radar. BAC had made definite proposals to the RAF in 1960 for a ground-attack version, but no interest had been shown in it. For the Saudi contract, however, the Lightning had to be turned into a multi-role aircraft with interceptor, ground-attack and reconnaissance capability. The cost of this huge extension to its role was covered entirely at BAC's own expense; there was no help from Government or the Air Staff, which had only countenanced the Lightning as a fighter.

The Lightning F.53 was created for this multi-mission, export role. It had many features in common with the RAF's F.6: the cambered leading edge, large ventral fuel tank, provision for an inflight-refuelling probe and two 260gal drop-tanks mounted on overwing pylons. Specially adapted Rolls-Royce Avon 302C turbojets were installed, each developing 11,100lb thrust 'dry' and 16,300lb at maximum reheat.

The sturdy airframe took engine developments in its stride, and made possible the carriage of external wing stores with very little beefing-up of the original structure. To allow for the carriage of underwing store on pylons outboard of the undercarriage there was some local strengthening, and for the Middle East and other markets better air conditioning was installed. For interception and destruction of supersonic targets, the Lightning was fitted with a Ferranti Airpass radar fire-control and bomb-aiming system, Elliott autopilot and flight-data computers, allowing it to lock onto its target and track it automatically, and deliver its homing missiles, under computer-controlled guidance, with great accuracy. The Lightning could carry two Firestreak or *Red Top* missiles in a pack in the forward fuselage weapons bay.

The forward fuselage pack could instead be used to carry forty-four 2in spin-stabilized rockets housed in twin retractable launchers. These high-explosive rockets were designed for air-to-

RSAF Lightning T.55 trainer delivery from Warton with some of the BAC Warton test pilot team: Jimmy Dell, Peter Ginger, Roland Beamont, Derek Ferguson and Paul Millett.
BAE Systems via Warton Heritage

air or air-to-ground attack, giving a large spread, and were useful against dispersed targets. They fired two rockets at a time, in ripple salvos every 25 milliseconds.

The Aden cannon pack in the front portion of the ventral tank was available in addition to the missile or rocket packs. While the Aden guns were usable for air-to-air combat as in the interceptor role, on the F.53 they were envisioned for ground-strafing of troops and light targets. In a pylon under the wing the F.53 could carry a 1,000lb bomb or a Matra 155 launcher housing eighteen SNEB 68mm rockets to be fired individually or in a pre-arranged firing pattern. These would deliver a heavier punch against concentrations of troops or against armed strong points on the ground. For reconnaissance missions, the fuselage missile/rocket pack could be replaced by a camera pack containing five Vinten cameras, giving vertical, oblique and forward coverage at supersonic speeds and at all altitudes.

Specification – Lightning F.53	
Length:	55ft 3in (16.84m)
Wingspan:	34ft 10in (10.62m)
Height:	17ft 3in (5.26m)
MTOW:	42,000lb (19,000kg)
Max speed:	Mach 2
Range:	1,000 miles (1,600km) subsonic; 150 miles (240km) supersonic
Powerplant:	Rolls-Royce Avon 392C; 42,000lb with reheat
Armament:	2 × 30mm cannon, 2 × *Red Top* or Firestreak missiles, Matra rocket pods, 2 × 1,000lb bombs, 44 × 2in unguided rockets

RSAF Production

One of the RAF contract Lightning F.3s, XR722, which had already flown, was converted to become the prototype F.53 and first flew in this configuration on 1 November 1966, registered with Class B marking as G27-2. A substantial period of flight testing began to confirm the results of the wind tunnel tests and flight simulator studies, to assess the aircraft's characteristics with external stores and to determine the effect of weapon release. Flight trials showed that the weapons pylons were entirely satisfactory throughout the full speed range, with or without stores. The aircraft was inherently stable and still fine to fly when carrying

underwing or overwing weapons, even asymmetrically. Minor troubles with the Aden guns were soon cured.

As with the prototype F.53, an RAF T.5, XS460, was converted to become the prototype T.55 and flew as RSAF 55-710 on January 1967. It was never delivered, as on a training flight on 7 March it skidded off the runway while landing at Warton in very strong crosswind. Both mainwheel tyres deflated just after touchdown making differential braking very difficult, and the Lightning's lack of nosewheel steering meant it was impossible for Jimmy Dell to keep the Lightning on the runway. It collided with an arrestor hook base and was written off, seriously injuring both Jimmy Dell and Peter Williams, an Airwork pilot who was training on the aircraft. A new T.55, 55-716, was built to replace it.

Production of the single-seaters and trainers ensued and deliveries of the forty ordered to Saudi Arabia started on 1 July 1968 when two F.53s flew from Warton to Jeddah under Operation *Magic Palm*. By September 1969 all bar one had been delivered, but owing to the loss of one of the single-seaters, 53-690, on a test flight from Warton in September 1968, a replacement F.53 had to be built, which was the last Lightning constructed. It flew on 29 June 1972 serialled 53-700 and left Warton on delivery on 4 September 1972, bringing to an end Lightning production, but not Warton's connection with it.

Saudi Service

The Saudi Lightnings had the distinction of being used in anger, unlike the Lightnings with the RAF and Kuwait Air Force. Though intended for training, the 'stop-gap' F.52 and T.54 Lightnings were soon brought into service flying attack missions against Yemeni insurgents, even though their ground-attack capabilities were very limited in contrast to the F.53 and T.55. They were employed firing 2in rockets against Yemenis involved in border incursions in 1969–70; and one was lost to ground fire, but the pilot ejected safely and was rescued.

The RSAF Lightnings flew in both the fighter and ground-attack roles until late 1981, when they were replaced in the ground-attack role by the Northrop F-5; though they continued in the reconnaissance role for some time after, they were soon used only as interceptors.

With the purchase of F-15s by the RSAF, the Lightnings were retired from service in January 1986. As part of the subsequent contract to supply seventy-two Tornadoes, British Aerospace bought back twenty-two of the surviving Lightnings. Of the forty F.53s/T.55s and seven F.52s/T.54s delivered, eighteen were lost in Saudi service. The former Saudi Lightnings had their Saudi markings removed and were painted in RAF colours with military registrations and were flown back to Warton by pilots from Binbrook immediately following retirement from Saudi service. They languished at Warton, unsatisfactorily stored in the open, exposed to the elements. British Aerospace had hopes of possibly selling them to Austria but no such deal materialized. It might have made sense to have transferred the four T.55s to the RAF, with their larger ventral tanks and cambered leading edges giving them greater range and endurance. In the end, many of these aircraft wound up in museums.

Kuwaiti Lightnings

Following on from the large Saudi order, BAC was rewarded a year later with a second export contract in December 1966 for fourteen aircraft from Kuwait. This order consisted of twelve F.53K single-seaters and two T.55K trainers, of very similar standard to the Saudi aircraft. Deliveries to Kuwait began on 18 December 1968 and were completed in December 1969.

Disappointingly, the Kuwait Air

The first of two Lightning T.55Ks for the Kuwait Air Force. It first flew in May 1968 carrying British 'B' registration G27-78 and later became 410 in service in Kuwait. The T.55 had all the benefits of the F.53, including the cambered leading edge and extended ventral tank. The RAF T.5s never received these modifications. BAE Systems via Warton Heritage

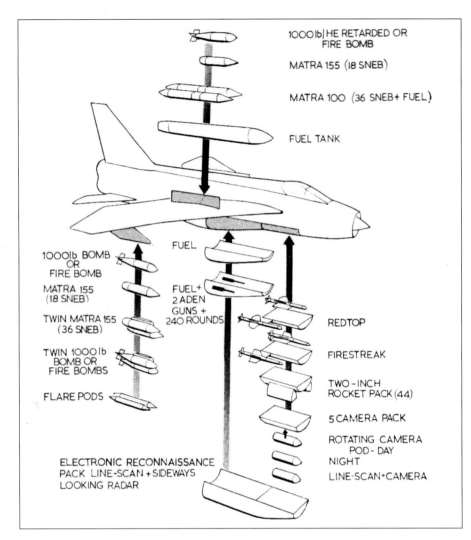

1000lb| HE RETARDED OR FIRE BOMB

MATRA 155 (18 SNEB)

MATRA 100 (36 SNEB + FUEL)

FUEL TANK

1000lb BOMB OR FIRE BOMB

MATRA 155 (18 SNEB)

TWIN MATRA 155 (36 SNEB)

TWIN 1000lb BOMB OR FIRE BOMBS

FLARE PODS

FUEL

FUEL + 2 ADEN GUNS + 240 ROUNDS

ELECTRONIC RECONNAISSANCE PACK LINE-SCAN + SIDEWAYS LOOKING RADAR

REDTOP

FIRESTREAK

TWO - INCH ROCKET PACK (44)

5 CAMERA PACK

ROTATING CAMERA POD - DAY NIGHT

LINE-SCAN + CAMERA

A diagram showing all the possible weapons loads of the multi-mission Lighting development. Unfortunately, none was ever ordered. Author

Lightning's life but few came to fruition. Britain had been at the forefront of variable-geometry ('swing-wing') research from just after the end of the Second World War, but no actual aircraft had flown. The most remarkable Lightning project was a naval version proposed by BAC in 1962 with variable geometry. It was based on the T.5 with an even larger ventral tank, an arrestor hook and a swing wing that could sweep from 25 to 60 degrees – in the fully swept mode it had almost the same sweep as the conventional aircraft. The undercarriage configuration was re-arranged, mounted further outboard to retract inwards.

A further BAC proposal, in 1963, was a far more radical transformation with the swing-wing, a redesigned nose with twin forward engine intakes at the side of the radome and, instead of the Avon engines, either Speys and a deepened fuselage or the smaller RB153, which could have been fitted into a fuselage of the normal girth of the Lightning.

The Final Lightnings

Even though Lightning flying with the RAF ended in 1988 after twenty-eight years' service, the aircraft continued to be seen in British skies. Owing to continuing problems with the Tornado's Foxhunter radar, four Lightnings – XR724, XR773, XS904 and XS928 – were fitted with overwing tanks and continued in use flying as high-speed targets against Buccaneer trials aircraft specially fitted with Foxhunter. The first F.6, XP693, was also at Warton as a chase aircraft on the Tornado programme. The final Lightning flight from Warton was on 21 January 1993, when XS904 departed for Bruntingthorpe and preservation.

Force's employment of the Lightning was far less distinguished than Saudi Arabia's. The Lightning's maintenance had proved quite a challenge even for the RAF, and had initially equated to twenty hours' maintenance for each hour of flying. The Kuwait Air Force never mastered the complexities of the Lightning and utilization soon became poor. Kuwait endeavoured unsuccessfully to dispose of them, and they were eventually replaced by Mirage F.1s in 1977.

Multi-Mission Developments

In 1968 BAC offered a developed F.53 with an even heavier ground-attack punch and a comprehensive electronic reconnaissance pack with both Linescan and sideways-looking radar. This developed F.53 could carry a total of two cannon, forty-four 2in rockets, 144

SNEB 68mm rockets or six 1,000lb bombs, or various combinations of these loads. Such a load would have incurred considerable drag, but the Lightning was still able to make high subsonic speed at low level, and when the weapons had been released it could have sped away to optimum height at supersonic speed. This refinement appeared to open up the possibility of more Lightning sales in the Middle East and South America; Jordan at one point seemed a very likely purchaser, but despite an intensive sales campaign no further orders were forthcoming.

Variable-Geometry Lightning Proposals

As with most aircraft, plenty of developments were proposed during the

Conclusion

A total of 339 Lightning was built; 337 by English Electric/BAC at Preston, Accrington, Samlesbury and Warton, and two by BAC at Filton.

The Lightning was rightfully named and impressed many with its performance

Lightning F.6s XP693, XS904 and XR773 make their farewell flight over Warton on 16 December 1992. BAE Systems via Warton Heritage

Malay Peninsula reached an incredible 88,000ft.

The Government's penny-pinching attitude towards Lightning development and improvement meant that the cambered leading edge and enlarged ventral tank – which bestowed better range and had first been proposed by English Electric in 1958 – were not fitted to the earlier Lightnings during production. When it was finally decided to fit these improvements, they had to be retro-fitted at substantially greater expense than if they had been installed during production. This late development to the aircraft's range greatly widened the subsonic scope of the Lightning, and greatly assisted its export market potential.

The manufacturers offered the RAF plenty of opportunities to improve the aircraft with increased weapon load and greater fuel capacity. Features such as a much improved auto-attack system, look-down radar and inertial navigation would have created a very useful multi-role fighter/bomber/reconnaissance aircraft. Greater development would have given the RAF a better aircraft, and if these improvements had been made in the early years could well have resulted in far greater export sales.

and its delightful handling. However, the early versions had poor combat range and limited armament while its maintenance was challenging. According to Roland Beamont the RAF applied too few resources to Lightning maintenance following its entry into service, which resulted in poor serviceability. The opinion was gained in the higher echelons of the RAF that the fault lay with the aircraft, which resulted in a lack of approval for further development. Though these matters were rectified in part in the later marks, the Lightning's maximum endurance without flight refuelling was still only two hours.

The sight of a Lightning's almost vertical climb-out until invisible remains in many people's memories. Unlike many interceptors it could achieve Mach 1 without reheat at all altitudes. Below 25,000ft it could cruise on one engine. Without wing stores it could climb to its operational height of 36,000ft and a speed of Mach 0.9 in 2½ minutes, and accelerate from Mach 1 to over Mach 2 in thee minutes. There are even reports that an RAF F.6 flying over the

CHAPTER ELEVEN

TSR2 – From Inception to Cancellation

Replacing the Canberra

From its maiden flight in 1949 the Canberra, which TSR2 was designed to replace, had been progressively developed to enable it to stay in the front line of air forces all over the world as a tactical bomber, strike and reconnaissance aircraft. But by the mid-1950s the Air Staff were of the view that the Canberra could not go on beyond 1968 in strategic roles (though it actually served in some roles until 2006!). Indeed Freddie Page, one of Britain's most distinguished aeronautical engineers, who at English Electric played a key role in the design and development of the Canberra and Lightning, stated in 1953 that English Electric had already begun considering Canberra replacements.

Operational Requirement 339 was issued to a select number of firms in September 1957. It called for a two-seat bomber capable of supersonic speed at high and low altitudes, which could penetrate enemy territory to a distance of 1,000 miles at low level, 'beneath the radar', both in the European theatre and east of Suez in support of British strategic commitments.

As manufacturers of the Canberra, English Electric had been designing projects for its replacement prior to the issue of OR339. Working in conjunction with Shorts, English Electric proposed the P17A together with the Shorts PD17 lifting platform, which would take off vertically with the P17A on board, then accelerate forwards to allow the P17A to take off. The PD17 had sixty lift jets, of which sixteen could also tilt, and ten additional jets for forward propulsion. The design appears rather fanciful nowadays, but was much less so at the time, when vertical take-off was considered a significant tactical advantage, allowing dispersal of aircraft away from airfields. Shorts already had appreciable experience of VTOL aircraft with the Shorts SC1 research aircraft.

As the designers of the Spitfire, Vickers-Supermarine was a famous name although its more recent types such as the Swift had not replicated the Spitfire's success. Vickers-Supermarine functioned with considerable autonomy, even though wholly owned by Vickers-Armstrongs. For OR339 Vickers-Supermarine proposed the Type 571 in both single-engined and twin-engined arrangements. With the gradual closure of the Vickers-Supermarine design office at Hursley Park between 1956 and 1958 a large number of their designers relocated to Weybridge, and their proposal became the Vickers entry for OR339.

In March 1958 the Ministry short-listed Avro, English Electric, Hawker and Vickers to bid for OR339, and indicated that the eventual contract would be placed with a consortium of these firms. As Avro and Hawker were loosely grouped as members of Hawker Siddeley, they agreed to work together on a joint proposal. Since Shorts was not included in the shortlist it was obvious that English Electric and Vickers would have to collaborate. In June the Ministry of Supply selected English Electric and Vickers for the project, somewhat surprisingly as no joint proposal had been forthcoming from them and they had only undertaken some preparatory meetings. The Ministry preferred English Electric as project leader according to Freddie Page, Chief Executive of English Electric's Aircraft Division, but Sir George Edwards lobbied hard for Vickers-Armstrongs to be given the leading position on the TSR2 contract; Sir George foresaw that Vickers would lose money on the Vanguard and VC10, so it needed to profit from TSR2.

The first solid meetings to examine their individual approaches did not begin until November 1958 and on 1 January 1959 the Ministry announced that the new aircraft would be called TSR2. The prime contract would be placed with

Vickers-Armstrongs with English Electric as the main sub-contractor and work shared on a 50/50 basis. English Electric was exceedingly unhappy about this decision and believed that their firm should have been granted design leadership with their supersonic experience from the Lightning. They felt that Vickers lacked the facilities and knowledge for the design and testing of supersonic aircraft and was preoccupied with civil aircraft.

During the early part of 1959 a combined Vickers–English Electric team met at Weybridge, under the leadership of Vickers' Technical Director, H.H. Gardner, and Freddie Page. Meetings were convened to hammer out the basic design of the optimum weapon system to meet the requirements of OR339 for the RAF. When the Government granted the TSR2 contract to Vickers-Armstrongs and English Electric, it was with the condition that these two firms would merge their aircraft and guided weapons interests to form a major new manufacturer – BAC. This duly took place in the middle of the following year.

BAC was faced with the immense task of merging its forerunners' different working practices while simultaneously designing, developing and building the most advanced aircraft of its kind, the TSR2. Intended to be a 'complete weapon system', where the operational systems are designed in as an integral part of the aircraft from the first, rather than being added on later, it was a huge technological advance for a company that had been handicapped by the lack of similar projects in the preceding years, so had to bear the cost of development of materials, structures, electronics, computing, systems and propulsion. As no such similar project had ever been previously undertaken there was no benchmark for costs, which caused major difficulties in assessing the budget for the project.

In the meantime OR339 grew steadily more ambitious and developed into

OR343, demanding increased range, payload and shorter take-off and landing distances from rough strips. This requirement asked for an aircraft capable of striking against any surface target with nuclear or conventional weapons and carrying out reconnaissance by day or by night in all weather conditions. Radius of action remained at 1,000 miles, of which 240 miles had to be flown at Mach 0.9 to and from the target at sea level. The specification demanded Mach 1.1 at 200ft and Mach 2 at altitude – against the previous requirement of Mach 1.7 – with a take-off run from rough strips of no more than 1,800ft and the ferry range increased from 2,000 to 2,750 miles. In his memoirs Freddie Page expressed the view that Vickers should have made clear that these additional performance increases might well prove to be prohibitively expensive to achieve and possibly unrealistic.

By the summer of 1959 TSR2 had taken shape, an amalgam of the best features of the separate submissions by Vickers and English Electric. It was agreed that Vickers would be responsible for the design and development of the front fuselage, undercarriage and the electronics and armament installations, while English Electric would be responsible for the wings, rear fuselage, engine installation, fuel system, powered flying controls and autostabilization. Manufacturing was divided cleanly at the trailing edge of the wing box, Vickers building everything in front of the wing box and English Electric everything behind.

On 7 October 1960 a contract was placed for the construction of nine development aircraft; a contract for a pre-production batch for eleven aircraft was placed in June 1963 and one for materials for thirty production aircraft in March 1964. First flight was planned for autumn 1963 with delivery of the first pre-production aircraft in 1965. (All contracts were cancelled on 6 July 1965.)

Design

TSR2's configuration was determined by the Operational Requirement's main factors: low-level high speed penetration, STOL capability from rudimentary airfields and in cross-winds, and the operational and ferry range requirements, including the carriage of external stores. To achieve the low-level demands TSR2

had a 60-degree delta wing of minimum span and area to minimize gust response. For flight at Mach 2 at altitude the wing had to be very thin; this militated against the STOL requirement, so to counteract this, large blown flaps were employed over the full span of the wing. Short take-off performance was ably assisted by the excellent thrust/weight ratio while the landing roll was short owing to the enormous braking parachute and powerful brakes. Although the wing was mainly straight, to provide anhedral and avoid Dutch roll at low speed the outermost portions tilted sharply downwards. The wing was unencumbered with fences, sawcuts or vortex generators. There were no ailerons on the wing, control being effected by an all-moving vertical tail and elevons. Fuel was carried in integral tanks and there was provision for inflight refuelling.

The undercarriage, with its demanding short-field requirement, was the responsibility of Vickers, who typically designed and built landing gear for their own aircraft. Each main undercarriage unit had tandem wheels with low-pressure tyres on a long-stroke leg. On retraction the tandem wheels folded up by 90 degrees and folded forward. The steerable nose unit retracted backwards into the fuselage, and could be lengthened to increase both lift and drag and to reduce the field-length required. Although the TSR2 only achieved a few flights prior to cancellation it was decided that this sophistication would be unnecessary in service use, owing to the better-than-predicted take-off performance.

Weapons System and Avionics

The UK electronics industry was responsible for equipping TSR2 with all of what was at that time the most advanced navigation, reconnaissance and weapon-aiming system in the world. Vickers-Armstrongs' guided weapons section under John Clemow took responsibility for the integrated weapons system – now a common feature in combat aircraft but in the 1960s an innovation in the UK. The usual practice up to then had been to build an airframe and engine combination before adding navigational and operational systems; for TSR2, however, these would be designed in from the start.

For all-weather navigation the inertial system outputs were calculated against the planned path and fed into a central computing system to manage the track of the aircraft via the autopilot and control system. Both pilot and navigator had moving-map displays, and for low-level flight the pilot had a head-up display that presented attitude information on the windscreen. TSR2's nose radar was for terrain clearance, enabling the pilot (and the autopilot) to fly the aircraft at 200ft (below enemy radar) at near-supersonic speeds.

Reconnaissance was provided by cameras, sideways-looking radar and Linescan, an optical scanning system that scanned the ground beneath the aircraft and transmitted real-time data to soldiers on the ground. For attack purposes, weapon-delivery computers used the nose radar for information on the proximity of the target and optimum launch point.

However, the key to effectively controlling aircraft projects rests upon the use of previously developed component systems. The integration of nav/attack systems is a difficult developmental task, but a manageable one. In the case of TSR2, the attempt was made to develop and integrate a number of new electronic systems simultaneously, making the disastrous cost escalations that affected TSR2 inevitable.

Powerplant

As the TSR2 contract was the catalyst to set the merger of Vickers and English Electric in train, so too was the engine contract the catalyst for the merger of Bristol Aero-Engines and Armstrong Siddeley Motors. BAC had wanted to use the Rolls-Royce RB131 Medway for the TSR2, but the Government overruled them and awarded the contract to Bristol for its Olympus engine on the condition that they merged with Armstrong Siddeley, which they did to form Bristol Siddeley Engines.

The Olympus had shown its mettle by enabling specially converted Canberras to achieve altitudes greater than 60,000ft and to create World Altitude Records. Olympuses also powered the Avro Vulcan bomber. But these were both subsonic aircraft built to far less demanding requirements than the supersonic TSR2. To fulfil

the demands of OR343, huge and costly development was necessary. Sir Stanley Hooker, then Chief Engineer of Bristol Siddeley, wrote in his autobiography *Not Much of an Engineer* that the Olympus would have been suitable without too great a development for the Mach 1.8 of the original English Electric P17A proposal; for the very ambitious OR343, however, it had to be redesigned for the higher weights and temperatures of the Mach 2+, STOL TSR2 specification. The resulting Bristol Siddeley Olympus 320 was designed with full reheat and infinitely variable nozzles providing 19,600lb thrust, boosted by reheat to 30,610lb with a development potential of 33,000lb static thrust.

Testing development Olympuses had led to major failures on static test beds at Filton, which required expensive redesigns. For airborne trials Vulcan B.1 XA894 was fitted with an Olympus 320 in a custom-built nacelle on the underside of the aircraft, giving it a grand total of five Olympus engines – its own four standard Olympuses and the Olympus 320 trial engine. It commenced its test programme in February 1962 and made impressive appearances at the Farnborough Air Show in September 1962. However, on December 1962 during a full-power run on the ground, the low-pressure shaft failed and the turbine disc was ejected, cutting through fuel lines and causing a huge fire at Filton. All the crew escaped but the Vulcan and a brand new fire engine were totally burnt out, so no further airborne trials of the Olympus 320 could take place until the first flight of the TSR2 – when it became evident that serious problems remained unsolved.

Project Management and Budgeting

Although BAC was the prime contractor and carried overall responsibility for the project, the Government awarded 'Category One' contracts for major items such as the engines. This practice served two political ends: greater Government control and – thanks to the opportunity to force a merger on the strength of a lucrative contract for the engine – a more streamlined aviation industry. Category One suppliers such as Bristol Siddeley treated the Government rather than the aircraft's manufacturers as the customer. 'Category Two' suppliers, for items such as the sideways-looking radar, were selected by BAC but needed Government approval. BAC could purchase 'Category Three' items directly, provided that the product fulfilled the Government's specification. In such an environment the strict control of costs was very difficult, and matters were exacerbated by the Government's insistence, against all previous experience, that costs for the development of all the equipment to be installed in TSR2 were placed on its budget. This was obdurate and unhelpful in the extreme.

Not only were Vickers and English Electric having to learn to work together, but so too were Bristol Engines and Armstrong Siddeley, major ancillary suppliers, the RAF and the Ministries of Defence and Aviation. BAC's Deputy Chief Test Pilot Roland Beamont, in his book *Phoenix into Ashes*, reported attending a progress meeting where fifty-two people were in the room; the chairman asked that for future meetings fewer should attend, yet at the next meeting the headcount was sixty-one. Under such conditions, effective project management was impossible.

In December 1959 the TSR2 research and development costs up to Controller (Air), or CA, release (at which stage the TSR2 would be ready for RAF service) were estimated at £90m, but in March 1962 the MoD called for a new review of the project, because estimates of the development costs had risen to £137m; by December 1962 the cost estimates were up to £175–200 million, with a rather large margin of error. The estimated cost of each TSR2 had risen to £2.1m and the predicted service entry of the TSR2 had slipped from 1965 to 1967.

The MoD Management Board was highly dissatisfied and suggested that BAC should improve its management of the programme. One suggestion from the MoD, that the number of TSR2s on order be reduced from 138 to fifty or sixty, was rejected by the RAF and Air Ministry. By the beginning of 1964, costs had increased to £240–270m. Equivalent engine costs for the same time period had increased from £7.3m to £32.5m.

The TSR2 production line at Weybridge on 10 July 1963. BAE Systems via Warton Heritage

RAAF Decision to Order the F-111 Instead of the TSR2

BAC was courting the Royal Australian Air Force in the hope of an order for TSR2. The RAAF had been early adopters of the Canberra and continued to use them for many years. BAC's Military Sales Manager, Jeffrey Quill, regularly visited Australia to make presentations about the progress of the project, as an order from the RAAF would have hindered any Government attempt at cancellation. However, a purchasing decision of such magnitude for a country's major strike aircraft carried great political implications, and by the early 1960s the bonds of the Commonwealth were loosening, making it possible for Australia to look to the USA for its strategic alliances.

According to Phil Strickland in *TSR2 with Hindsight*, Chief of the Defence Staff Lord Mountbatten expressed his doubts about TSR2 ever going into production to his opposite number, the Chairman of the Australian Chiefs of Staff Committee, Air Chief Marshal Scherger, in April 1963; Scherger had previously been strongly inclined towards it. These doubts influenced Scherger's view and may well have given rise to Australian suspicions the project might be cancelled and that US aircraft were a safer choice. Once the

seeds of doubt had been planted they were not easy to dispel, even when the British Government pressed the Australians hard to buy British.

Whereas the United States had licence-built English Electric Canberras, they were now developing the General Dynamic TFX (Tactical Fighter Experimental), not only to fulfil a USAF fighter-bomber requirement but also US Navy fighter specification. The TFX, which later became the F-111, had an operational requirement similar to TSR2's but was of a markedly different appearance, with side-by-side seating for the two crew and variable-geometry wings.

An Australian evaluation team visited the USA and concluded that the F-111 was superior in some aspects to TSR2. However, the TSR2 was far nearer to flight than its American competitor and so estimates of its actual performance were reasonably accurate while the F-111's performance estimates were more in the nature of predictions.

According to Phil Strickland, in mid-1963 the Australians were quoted £A81m for twenty-four TSR2s with delivery for entry into squadron service in mid-1969. It would appear that General Dynamics were eager for an order for their F-111 and offered the same number of aircraft with an initial delivery in 1967 for £A56m.

The Australians should have been cautious about accepting this figure at face value, as the US Department of Defense had told them that these figures were unreliable. The Australians did not inform the British of this lower price offer from the Americans and did not employ it as a bargaining tool. On 24 October 1964 the Australian Government went ahead and ordered twenty-four F-111s. When the Labour Minister of Aviation, Roy Jenkins, heard this he described the news as a nearly fatal blow for TSR2.

The F-111 had severe developmental problems and, owing to flaws in the design, a number crashed during development and in initial service. It only entered RAAF service in 1973, six years late and cost $A344m – more than 200 per cent greater than the original quote of £A56m ($A112). The F-111s served for thirty-seven years and were withdrawn from service in 2010.

Assembly, First Flight and Test Programme

Assembly of the nine development aircraft commenced in the West Side hangers at Weybridge, mating Weybridge-fabricated front fuselages and wings to the Samlesbury-built tail sections. The original programme had called for a first flight in March 1963; this was an amazingly tight schedule for such an innovative design, and it is not surprising that this over-optimistic schedule was unachievable.

As prime contractor, Vickers (by 1964 BAC Weybridge Division) saw the venue for flight test as within their remit and regarded the flight test centre at Wisley with its 6,900ft runway to be the appropriate site. However, BAC's Deputy Chief Test Pilot Roland Beamont turned this down as the Ministry demanded sufficient room to stop in the event of braking chute or brake failure. Wisley's runway could prove too short in the event of such a failure, and landing in the westerly direction could have resulted in an overrun onto the A3 London to Portsmouth road. Beamont proposed Warton in Lancashire as the obvious choice, being a BAC plant with flight test facilities, staff and

The first TSR2, XR219, in primer in the final assembly hangar at Weybridge in October 1963. In the background is the second aircraft, XR220. These hangars on the south side of the BAC site had originally been built for Viscount production.
BAE Systems via Warton Heritage

Engine runs for XR219's troublesome Bristol Siddeley Olympuses at Boscombe Down. The possibility of a cataclysmic low-pressure shaft failure was possible with the initial engines installed in XR219.
BAE Systems via Warton Heritage

The first TSR2 during taxi tests with the drogue chute deployed and the main braking parachute (the large bundle) about to unfurl. During one of these runs the parachute did not unfurl and Beamont had to brake sharply to avoid running off the end of the Boscombe Down runway. BAE Systems via Warton Heritage

a 7,900ft runway. However, the Ministry insisted on the Aeroplane & Armament Experimental Establishment at Boscombe Down in Wiltshire, which had a 10,500ft main runway. On completion of initial trials the aircraft would relocate to Warton, which begs the question why not fly from Warton in the first place? Though Boscombe Down had often been used by Vickers-Supermarine for maiden flights in the 1950s, it was a major inconvenience for all concerned owing to its distance from all of the BAC plants. BAC was obliged to set up a substantial base there and rent a hanger, office and staff accommodation.

On 4 March 1964 the first development TSR2, XR219, was transported from Weybridge to Boscombe Down where it was re-assembled so that engine runs and

system tests could begin. However, there were ongoing problems with the Olympus engines fitted to the aircraft. Worse was to follow in July 1964 when another failure in a test cell, replicating that in the Vulcan, caused substantial damage to the test cell's structure. Such a failure would be catastrophic to TSR2 either in the air or on the ground.

The manufacturers were concerned that the project was running late, and with a General Election in the offing an incoming Labour Government might well seek to cancel the project. Despite

the attendant risk of another low-pressure shaft failure it was decided to fly XR219 as soon as possible. Bristol Siddeley engineers gauged that if the engines were only opened up to 97 per cent power and warning lights indicating likely failure were installed, then the crew might have sufficient time to eject.

Against this backdrop, taxiing tests started in early September. Roland Beamont was soon vindicated in his rejection of Wisley, as during a high-speed taxi run the braking parachute failed to inflate and he had to brake hard to stop running

Beamont and his navigator/flight test observer, Don Bowen, boarding XR219 prior to its maiden flight from Boscombe Down on the afternoon of 27 September 1964. BAE Systems via Warton Heritage

XR219 taking off on its maiden flight.
BAE Systems via Warton Heritage

Successful completion of its first flight: XR219 lands safely with its huge braking parachute deployed. Overhead is one of the two 'chase' aircraft, Canberra B.2 WD937.
BAE Systems via Warton Heritage

From the third until the ninth flight the progress of flight testing was held up by problems with undercarriage retraction and extension. On the fifth flight there was an extremely dangerous situation when, on extension, the tandem wheels on the main legs did not rotate into the landing position. Eventually Beamont had to land with the wheels in this position. BAE Systems via Warton Heritage

off the end of the runway – had the trials been based at Wisley, the TSR2 would have run off the runway.

At 3:15pm on 27 September 1964, following two high-speed taxi runs in the morning, XR219 made its first flight with Roland Beamont as pilot accompanied by Donald Bowen, senior navigator of BAC Weybridge Division. As the undercarriage was not cleared for retraction the Olympus engines had to be run at 100 per cent power during climb-out, which put them into the danger zone for catastrophic low-pressure shaft failure. The TSR2 was accompanied throughout its brief fifteen-minute flight by Canberra WD937 and Lightning XM968. The TSR2 performed well inside its flight envelope despite the severely limited engine restrictions of a total thrust of only 40,000lb (rather than the specification 58,000lb) and the undercarriage remaining extended. The excellent control, stability and manoeuvrability were evident, although items for concern were severe engine resonance at certain power settings, strong mainwheel vibration and front fuselage oscillation on landing.

The installation of partly modified engines to counteract the low pressure shaft problems for the second flight on 31 December failed to ameliorate the vibration and during a subsequent flight on 2 January 1965 the engine resonance was so severe that Beamont landed after only eight minutes airborne. In fact, the fault was not caused by the engine but a fuel pump.

From flight three until flight nine progress was blighted by undercarriage retraction problems. Flight five on 14 January 1965 proved especially challenging to Beamont when one mainwheel undercarriage leg refused to retract; extension of the undercarriage brought all the wheels down but the mainwheel beams failed to rotate into a horizontal position, remaining vertical. After considering recycling the landing gear it was agreed that it was best to leave it and attempt a landing. There was the very real danger of a crash on landing so Beamont offered Don Bowen the chance to eject, but Bowen decided to remain onboard. Beamont then had to land the TSR2 very gently at Boscombe Down with the incipient danger that either of the wheels might collapse and the aircraft crash. However, with his great piloting skill coupled with the excellent control capabilities of TSR2 Beamont was able to execute a safe landing.

XR220's Mishap

Boscombe Down was also planned as the venue for the first flight of the second TSR2, XR220, so on 9 September 1964 the fuselage was transported from Weybridge to Boscombe Down. Unfortunately, when endeavouring to negotiate a sharp reverse turn into the hanger the trailer tipped and the fully

XR219 (left) and XR220 in the hangar at Boscombe Down. XR220 was being repaired after its accident on arrival at Boscombe Down.
BAE Systems via Warton Heritage

swathed fuselage was dumped unceremoniously onto the Boscombe Down apron. Most of the damage was borne by the left tailplane spigot, and several panels were damaged.

On 11 September a complicated series of procedures using lifting bags and five cranes proved sufficient to right the fuselage. In the event the damage was not as great as feared, and XR220 was thoroughly inspected, repaired and mated with its wings, rudder and tailplane.

Opposition to TSR2

The Treasury and politicians of all parties were naturally concerned at what the TSR2 might cost. Amongst these powerful forces lobbying against the programme was Admiral of the Fleet Lord Louis Mountbatten, the Chief of Defence Staff (1959–65), who was wrongly convinced that the Blackburn Buccaneer could perform OR343, frequently pointing out that five Buccaneers could be purchased for the price of one TSR2. He was strongly supported by Sir Solly Zukermann, Chief Scientific Adviser to the UK Government (1964–1971) and an influential confidant of Mountbatten. Partly owing to inter-service rivalry and partly because their requirement was far more demanding, the RAF had not given serious consideration to the Buccaneer, which had been designed for a far less demanding specification to operate as a strike aircraft from Royal Navy aircraft carriers.

On 15 October 1964 the British General Election resulted in Labour winning power, but with an exceedingly slim majority of just four parliamentary seats. The new Government inherited a poor economic situation and sought to carry out their election promises and seriously trim expenditure. In late October the new Government announced that owing to the country's worsening economic situation, prestige projects including TSR2 and Concorde might be scrapped.

Lack of Confidence at the Air Ministry

According to senior MoD civil servant Sir Frank Cooper in *TSR2 with Hindsight*, in the early part of 1964 senior RAF officers were raising concerns about TSR2's cost and whether it could fulfil its intended role. Prior to the General Election the Chief of Air Staff, Sir Charles Elworthy, had actually written to the Conservative Minister for Aviation, Hugh Fraser, recommending cancellation.

In December 1964 an Air Ministry team travelled to the USA to examine the F-111. In January the House of Commons Defence and Overseas Policy Committee concluded that the F-111 was cheaper, available at a fixed price with fixed delivery dates and on favourable financial terms. According to Edward Pearce in his biography of Denis Healey, then Minister of Defence, Sir Charles Elworthy believed the F-111 was a better

aircraft on military grounds. It became evident by the beginning of 1965 that the performance of the British aircraft would be below specification in a number of areas. It was overweight, while range and airfield performance were well below requirements. Roy Jenkins wrote that by early 1965 TSR2 had few supporters: the Ministry of Defence, RAF chiefs and Ministers all wanted to cancel the aircraft.

BAC, aware of the vulnerability of the TSR2 to cancellation, met the new Minister of Aviation, Roy Jenkins, who arranged for Sir George Edwards and Sir Reginald Verdon-Smith to meet the Prime Minister, Harold Wilson, at Chequers on 15 January 1965. Wilson was keen to establish a fixed price for TSR2. Following meetings of the BAC board a fixed price contract of £430m was offered to the Government for the supply of twenty development and pre-production aircraft and one hundred production TSR2s.

Cancellation Looms and the Workers Protest

On 14 January 1965, several thousand aircraft BAC workers from Weybridge, Hurn, Preston, Stevenage, Luton and Bristol were joined by others from Hawker Siddeley at Kingston and Coventry and from a number of TSR2 subcontractors to demonstrate in London. The workers, justifiably alarmed at the rumours emanating from the newly elected Labour Government calling for cancellation of TSR2 and the Hawker Siddeley P1154 and HS681, marched from Waterloo Station to Parliament to present a petition. Thousands of aircraft workers took part in the protest march bringing much of central London to a halt. Leaving Parliament Square the workers marched to Speakers Corner, Hyde Park to further voice their protests. Following the Hyde Park demonstration, deputations to the Ministry of Aviation also called at No 10. Downing Street and left a message for the Prime Minister Mr Wilson.

BAC and Hawker Siddeley aircraft workers gathering by the south side of Hungerford Bridge (also known as Charing Cross Railway Bridge) on 14 January 1965 to protest outside Parliament against the expected cuts to aircraft programmes.
Richard Hitchins

Discarded placards after the march, including one from BAC Weybridge's Dept 37 protesting that the Government was selling out the industry to the USA. Richard Hitchins

XR219 in the air from Boscombe Down on its thirteenth flight, on 16 February 1965. BAE Systems via Warton Heritage

But the workers' protests were to no avail, and on 2 February 1965 the Labour Government announced the cancellation of two Hawker Siddeley projects: the HS681 jet STOL transport aircraft, to be replaced by the Lockheed C-130 Hercules, and the P.1154 supersonic V/STOL strike aircraft, which was replaced by the subsonic Harrier. TSR2 was given a reprieve; no final decision was to be made until June 1965. The Government further announced that Nimrod maritime reconnaissance aircraft would be ordered to replace the Shackleton, and that McDonnell Douglas Phantoms would be ordered for the RAF to replace the Lightning.

The American aircraft industry was the main beneficiary of these decisions with the Hercules and Phantom orders, though there was offset work contracted to British firms. For example, BAC Preston Division manufactured tails for British Phantoms which, uniquely, were to be powered by Rolls-Royce Speys; Hawker Siddeley at Brough became the British-based design organization qualified to clear modifications and technical instructions without reference to the manufacturers for the Phantom. Marshall of Cambridge became the UK completion centre for the Hercules.

On the same day Hawker Siddeley announced:

On the basis of our knowledge today the redundancies in Hawker Siddeley Aviation Ltd will be in the region of 14,000 to take effect during 1965. The process will start immediately. There will be a serious diminution of design capability during this process.

A few days later the announcement came that Hawker Siddeley's Coventry factory was to close. On 4 February 1965, Sir George Edwards, BAC Managing Director, sent a memo to BAC staff:

Since last summer we have had to fight for the future of the VC10, Concorde and TSR2. Today, the VC10 is doing all the things that you, who worked on it, knew it could do. Concorde is now going ahead and on Tuesday, the Prime Minister said of TSR2 that a decision would not be taken 'for some months'. It is clear that the Government has put it squarely on us to show we can do the job. We have to satisfy them about our aeroplane's performance, its cost and the deliveries. This we can do, but only if we all go to it. If we do that, then not only will TSR2 be saved and the team which has worked so hard will be kept together, but the future of BAC will be assured.

XR219 Departs Boscombe Down for Warton

Undercarriage retraction and extension problems continued until finally, on flight ten, Beamont was able to retract the landing gear cleanly and re-cycle it without failure. Immediately the test regime was expanded and he took TSR2 up to 500kt, where he found its handling to be akin to a fighter's. The following flight explored single-engine handling and on flight twelve Don Knight piloted it for the first time, though he had the misfortune to make a rather rough landing, which required repair work to the landing gear.

On 22 February XR219 was airborne with Beamont heading for Warton and Jimmy Dell as chase in a Lightning T.4. Beamont took TSR2 out over the Irish Sea to use the company's supersonic test track. Igniting the reheat on just one Olympus was enough to send it supersonic, far ahead of the Lightning, itself no slouch. Then to Warton for a low, fast pass and landing on the main apron.

With the arrival of XR219 at Warton the pace of flying increased, and by the end of February main initial test parameters had been successfully accomplished.

XR219 arriving at Warton on 22 February 1965, after its first supersonic flight. Beamont wrote in his biography of how glad he was the aircraft was now based at Warton, so that concerted flight testing could commence on home ground.
BAE Systems via Warton Heritage

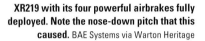

XR219 with its four powerful airbrakes fully deployed. Note the nose-down pitch that this caused. BAE Systems via Warton Heritage

As flight testing continued, TSR2 production was building up at the Preston Division's Samlesbury factory. Here, the Weybridge-built forward fuselage of the first pre-production aircraft, XS660, is being off-loaded so that it may be joined to the Samlesbury-built rear fuselage. In the background are Samlesbury-built rear sections. (It had now been settled that from XS660 onwards TSR2s would be assembled and first flown from Warton.)
BAE Systems via Warton Heritage

A temporary strut was fitted to XR219's mainwheels to see if this could cure the main undercarriage vibration; this was successful and, while this temporary device did not allow undercarriage retraction, flights continued examining the low-speed envelope. Freddie Page held the view that the problem of the severe front fuselage oscillation caused by the nose undercarriage leg still remained.

On 31 March TSR2 made its last ever flight when Jimmy Dell, with Brian McCann as navigator/observer, made a thirty-two minute sojourn. XR219 was then laid up for modification and the fitting of a strut that could allow under-carriage retraction. It had made twenty-four flights totalling thirteen hours and nine minutes.

Cancellation

Although the Government had stated that no decision would be made on TSR2 until June, Minister of Aviation Roy Jenkins wrote in his memoirs that the decision to cancel was made at a Cabinet meeting on 1 April 1965; it was a unanimous decision by the Ministers with agreement by some to take an option on F-111s. The decision was made public during the Budget speech on 6 April and Chancellor of the Exchequer James Callaghan's reason for cancellation was the cost. Later that day, Minister of Defence Denis Healey announced that an option had been taken out on fifty F-111Ks at a cost of £2.1m per aircraft; if this option was taken up then the cost saving over TSR2 would be £300m.

Meanwhile at Boscombe Down, Jimmy Dell and Peter Moneypenny had been preparing to fly XR220 and were to have made taxi runs that morning followed by its first flight, but were prevented by minor faults. By the afternoon the air-craft was ready to go, but owing to the

The second aircraft, XR220, at Boscombe Down. It was ready to fly on the day the programme was cancelled, but never did. It was retained at Boscombe Down for Concorde engine trials and then passed to the RAF Henlow and finally to the RAF Museum, Cosford, where it is on public display.
BAE Systems via Warton Heritage

BAC aircrew who flew the aircraft. From left: Jimmy Dell, Don Knight, Roland Beamont (all pilots) and Don Bowen, the only one of the three navigators/flight test observers present that day.
BAE Systems via Warton Heritage

XR219's destiny was to be roaded from Warton to the Proof & Experimental Establishment, Shoeburyness, for destruction by gunfire.
BAE Systems via Warton Heritage

The front fuselage of XS660 awaiting the scrap men at Samlesbury. BAE Systems via Warton Heritage

XR226 part-scrapped at Weybridge in September 1965. In the background to the right are the hangars in which the TSR2s were constructed.
BAE Systems via Warton Heritage

While fuselage sections are driven away at Weybridge, the partly built XR226 is on the ground in the foreground with XR227 behind, waiting to suffer a similar fate. BAE Systems via Warton Heritage

cancellation any movement was prohibited. XR220 never even taxied under its own power, let alone flew.

All work on the project ceased and in June BAC approached the Government to propose a limited flight programme for the first three aircraft to check the functioning of the design at a cost of £2m. Roy Jenkins rejected this proposal, but said that BAC was at liberty to fund this testing if it so wished. The Corporation was in no position to finance this, and the aircraft never flew again. Sir Freddie Page wrote:

> Such was the determination to stamp TSR2 out of existence that immediate orders were received to scrap all the components on the assembly lines, all jigs and tools and any other work in progress. Even the low cost scheme to save something for the country by using the three completed aircraft for a minimal research project was refused and these aircraft were either destroyed or made useless.

Denis Healey strongly denies that he ever gave such an order, so its source remains a mystery.

The first TSR2 XR219 lingered at Warton until 14 August 1965, when it was transported to Proof & Experimental Establishment Shoeburyness to test the vulnerability of a contemporary airframe to gunfire. BAC asked if they could fly it to the nearest airport at Southend, but this was strictly forbidden. The cancellation was still a matter of huge controversy and the authorities did not want attention drawn to the aircraft. It remained at Shoeburyness until left a wreck after trials, and was scrapped in 1977.

None of the other TSR2s ever flew. XR220 was used on Olympus engine trials at Boscombe Down. On 20 June 1967 it was moved to RAF Henlow, where all equipment was removed. Fortunately in September 1975 it was presented to the RAF Museum at Cosford, where it is now on display.

At cancellation XR221, tasked with testing nav/attack systems, was complete at Weybridge, undergoing final systems checks and due to move to Wisley on 11 April to fly from there in mid-May. XR221 had already proved by means of ground tests and simulated flights that the nav/attack system functioned. It had demonstrated that no electrical cross-talk existed either within the avionics system,

or between it and the extensive instrumentation. But this was not to be further tested and, together with the structurally complete XR223, it was despatched to Shoeburyness in September 1965.

XR222 was essentially complete, although some panels were missing and only 20 per cent of its systems were installed. It was taken by road from Weybridge to the College of Aeronautics at Cranfield at the end of October 1965. After thirteen years at Cranfield XR222 was delivered to the Imperial War Museum at Duxford on 21 March 1978; in due course a team from British Aerospace made and fitted the missing panels to give the TSR2 the appearance of being complete, and it is now on display at Duxford. The other aircraft were cut up at Weybridge or Samlesbury.

Reasons for Cancellation

1. Originally designated as a Canberra replacement, the specification for TSR2 was a mighty challenge and exceedingly ambitious to achieve in a short timescale. The manufacturers, the RAF or the Air Ministry should have recognized that costs would rise steeply, and lobbied to temper the specification and contain costs.

2. The merger between Vickers-Armstrongs and English Electric with TSR2 as the catalyst took time to achieve real synergy. It was unrealistic to attempt a very ambitious project and a company merger simultaneously.

3. Owing to the lack of recent development of high-specification military aircraft in the UK, OR343 called for new materials, new manufacturing techniques, new avionics and a huge amount of new equipment, all of which were loaded onto the TSR2 programme causing a disproportionate weighting of costs.

4. Although the airframe appears to have been successfully developed, the advanced avionics systems were each in the hands of a different contractor. Elliot Automation was responsible for the flight-control system, Ferranti the terrain-following radar and navigation/attack system, EMI the sideways-looking radar and Marconi the general avionics.

5. The serious problems and delays caused by developing the Olympus engine. The Government's choice of the Olympus was against the wishes of the manufacturers, who wanted the Rolls-Royce Medway.

6. Decision making was extremely slow and difficult owing to the large number of civil servants, RAF staff and company representatives involved.

7. The UK's economic situation and the weakness of sterling, coupled with the Labour Government's belief that TSR2 could not be afforded in that economic climate.

8. Opposition from the Chief of Defence Staff, Lord Louis Mountbatten, who actively lobbied for the Buccaneer to be bought as the Canberra replacement instead.

9. Lack of support from the Air Ministry, who came to believe that the F-111 was superior.

10. The failure to win an order from the RAAF. A firm order from Australia would have been a substantial obstacle to cancellation.

11. The mistaken belief in Britain and Australia in the supremacy of American technology. As things turned out, the F-111 had a large number of development problems, entered service very late and cost far, far more than originally estimated.

12. The unrealistic timescale for TSR2's development. Though it was considered slow, when compared with today's Eurofighter Typhoon it was exceedingly quick. TSR2 development started in January 1959 and it flew in September 1964.

13. Constant criticism in the British media of the project. Compare this with the similar criticism of Concorde, where the constant barrage of media criticism eventually receded, to turn to adulation.

Redundancies and Closure of BAC Luton

At the time of the aircraft's first flight in 1964 over 6,000 BAC employees (15 per cent of the workforce) were working on the production of TSR2, and throughout Britain over 1,000 manufacturers were involved in the supply of materials, components and equipment for it.

Many small firms supplied one particular component in which they had specialized skills, while large subcontractors supplied, for instance, the engines, electronics, crew ejection systems and powered flying controls.

The loss of BAC's principal military programme, for which the Corporation had been formed, was a mighty blow, with major ramifications for the actual ability of BAC to continue to function as a going concern. Within a fortnight of cancellation BAC announced the dismissal of 1,700 workers: 1,200 from Preston and 500 from Weybridge. Eventually, approximately 5,000 BAC staff lost their jobs, along with many others in the ancillary suppliers.

In order for BAC to function as a going concern the Board had to contemplate major surgery in their relatively newly formed firm. At the beginning of December 1965 the unexpected decision to close the former Hunting factory at Luton was announced. Described by Sir George Edwards as 'well-run', it was producing the Jet Provost in its entirety and One-Eleven wings. Fortunately Vauxhall Motors acquired the premises and many staff were redeployed with them. Jet Provost fuselage manufacture, development and test flying was transferred to Preston, but wing production passed to Hurn and its first set of wings were delivered to Warton in March 1967. Luton's One-Eleven wing manufacture was passed to Weybridge.

TSR2 Compensation

BAC and the Labour Government negotiated from 1965 through to 1967 to settle the issue of compensation for the cancellation of TSR2. BAC threatened the Government with an eventual rundown of the business owing to its poor financial position if it did not receive the sum it believed it was due, but the Labour Government was eager to force a merger of BAC with Hawker Siddeley by prevaricating over BAC's claim. BAC also had severe problems with its civil programmes, but in time, with improving income from One-Eleven airliner sales, Government support for the stretched One-Eleven 500, the commencement of Jaguar, Saudi Arabian Lightning and Strikemaster production, by 1967 BAC's fortunes had reversed. In September 1967

the Government agreed a final settlement of £13.25m compensation for TSR2 cancellation and abandoned its merger plans.

Aftermath – Co-Operation with France on New Military Projects

On 17 May 1965, in the immediate aftermath of the TSR2 debacle, the Government entered into a Memorandum of Understanding with France to jointly develop an advanced trainer – which later became Jaguar and is described in the next chapter – and the Anglo-French Variable-Geometry aircraft (AFVG). The trainer was to be based on an existing design by Breguet, so the French firm had design leadership for the airframe with BAC in the subordinate role and Rolls-Royce leadership on the engine. However, BAC would hold design leadership on the new AFVG design with Dassault while SNECMA would have the powerplant lead. Whereas the Jaguar proved a success, the French withdrew from the AFVG in July 1967.

Aftermath – BAC/Dassault Spey-Mirage 4

Following TSR2's cancellation BAC acted speedily and, together with Rolls-Royce, approached Dassault with a request for a proposal for a new version of the Dassault Mirage 4A nuclear strike bomber then in service with the French air force; this version was to be fitted with Rolls-Royce Spey engines in place of the French-built Atars of the existing Mirage 4. BAC and Rolls-Royce presented the project, designated Mirage 4 Spey (commonly referred to as the Spey-Mirage), to the British Government on 16 July 1965. There were some substantial changes from the Mirage 4A already in service: a new nose with a radome, a relocated in-flight refuelling probe, larger intakes and air ducts to cope with the Spey's higher airflow, a redesigned rear fuselage to accommodate the larger engines, modifications for low-altitude missions and a new navigation/attack avionics package including much British equipment inherited from the TSR2 programme. The

Spey's higher thrust and superior fuel consumption meant that predicted range and payload performance were superior to those of the Atar-powered version.

BAC claimed the Spey-Mirage could fulfil the entire OR343 requirement except for the short-field performance. The division of work between Dassault and BAC was never finalized, but BAC might have carried out as much as 75 per cent of the total value, dependent on the quantity ordered. Initial deliveries would have been in late 1969 and BAC offered a unit price of £2m based on an order for seventy-five.

According to Charles Gardner of Vickers, Denis Healey reacted violently to the Spey-Mirage proposal, which he saw as a threat to his F-111 deal and to the AFVG, and it was never seriously considered; the RAF likewise were determined to have the F-111.

Aftermath – F-111 Cancellation

The February 1966 Defence Review recommended that the Government take up the option for fifty American General Dynamics F-111K long-range strike aircraft that had been arranged in 1965. All manner of spurious reasons were promoted as to why the Buccaneer or Spey-Mirage would not do. One was entirely British and the other predominantly so, so much of the expenditure on either would return to the UK Treasury in the form of taxation on those building it – not so the case with the F-111. In January 1966 in the House of Commons, Minister of Aviation Roy Jenkins stated that the Spey-Mirage's 'performance did not match that of the F-111; that it might (I do not say more than might) be a barrier to the Anglo-French VG aircraft; and that it would not be in service until 1972.'

Although the F-111K order was placed, the whole sorry saga was brought to a close in January 1968 when the Government cancelled it, incurring sizeable cancellation charges. The Government cited rising costs and a significant degradation in performance estimates as justification for this cancellation.

The AFVG and F-111 were supposed to take over the role left vacant after the TSR2 cancellation. The TSR2 was to cost £270m in launch costs and £3.4m per aircraft based on 100 aircraft, fifty F-111s

A French air force Dassault Mirage 4P at Cazaux in June 2005. The Mirage 4 served with the French air force in the bombing role from 1964 until 2005. A version with Rolls-Royce Spey engines and TSR2 avionics was proposed by BAC to the RAF following the TSR2's cancellation, but was rejected. Jean-Pierre Touzeau

Hawker Siddeley Buccaneer S.2B XW525 at the Farnborough Air Show in September 1972. Though originally rejected by the RAF in favour of the TSR2, in the end the Buccaneer had a long career with the RAF. BAE Systems

were to cost £125m (this escalated to £425 million by the time of cancellation). The UK share of AFVG launch costs was £150m and each AFVG would have cost £1.7m. So with the final price escalation the two competing programmes would have cost approximately the same amount.

Along with a great deal of money wasted, more serious was the loss of expertise, craftsmanship and cutting-edge technology, doing untold damage to the British aircraft industry in the longer term. The Canberras would remain in service, and in July 1968 the MoD announced that the RAF, which had rejected the Buccaneer as a candidate for OR339, would now inherit seventy from the Fleet Air Arm along with twenty-six newly built aircraft. This was an interim measure to reduce the gap in Britain's strike/reconnaissance capability following the F-111 cancellation; this 'interim measure' continued until 1994, when the last Buccaneers were replaced by the Tornado.

Let Sir Freddie Page have the last word:

The early death of TSR2 was assured in the circumstances of its birth. If the contract had been given to the experienced Warton team and based on their proposals [the P17A] to meet the original OR339, the aircraft would have been in production with development flying much more advanced at the critical moment when Labour came to power.

Specification – TSR2	
Length:	89ft (27.13m)
Wingspan:	37ft 2in (11.33m)
Height:	23ft 8in (7.21m)
MTOW:	103,500lb (47,000kg)
Max speed:	Mach 2 (high altitude), Mach 1 (low altitude)
Range (combat):	750 miles (1,200km)
Crew:	2
Powerplant:	Bristol Siddeley Olympus Mk 320, 30,610lb with reheat
Armament:	4 × 10-kiloton WE.177 tactical nuclear bombs

CHAPTER TWELVE

Jaguar – the Anglo-French Strike Trainer

The Jaguar arose from a British and French requirement to replace their strike and trainer aircraft. The French Air Force (Armée de l'Air) wanted to replace its obsolete Dassault Mystére 4s, North American F-100 Super Sabres and Republic F-84 Thunderchiefs in the strike role and Lockheed T-33 Shooting Stars in the training role with one aircraft. In January 1964 the French issued a requirement for the ECAT (*Ecole de Combat et d'Appui Tactique* – 'School of Combat and Support Tactics') to replace these four; it received submissions from French manufacturers Breguet, Dassault, Nord, Potez and Sud. The requirement called for the trainer to be ready for service in 1970 and the strike aircraft two years later.

In January 1965 the Breguet 121 was chosen for the ECAT role, much to the chagrin of its competitors, especially Dassault. It was also foreseen that a version of the Breguet 121 could be built to fulfil a French Navy requirement for a strike aircraft.

Similarly, in 1962 the RAF issued Air Staff Target 362, specifying a replacement for the Folland Gnat advanced trainer and the Hawker Hunter tactical strike aircraft. The RAF wanted a more sophisticated aircraft than the French, supersonic and with superior ground-attack capability. Hawker Siddeley offered two designs – the variable-geometry Folland Fo.147 and the Hawker P1173 – while BAC countered with the Luton Division's H.155 and Preston's supersonic, variable-geometry P45. In the event, none of these went ahead as the Labour Government that came to power in 1964 was anxious to promote collaboration with France, and both countries were keen to reduce costs and benefit from a larger order book.

Anglo-French Memorandum of Understanding

On 17 May 1965 the British and French Governments signed a Memorandum of Understanding (MoU) on the development of two aircraft – an advanced trainer/ strike aircraft and the Anglo-French Variable-Geometry aircraft – for which all costs were to be shared equally. Roy Jenkins, Minister of Aviation, stated in his autobiography that the Government chose BAC over Hawker Siddeley for the contract to compensate for the TSR2 cancellation.

As it was agreed that the strike/trainer was to be based on the Breguet 121 the French firm was granted design leadership for the airframe, putting BAC in a subordinate role. Both countries initially agreed to receive 150 aircraft, each with a 50/50 workshare. BAC and Breguet, who had not worked together before, set to work with a will, eager to have half share of an order for 300 aircraft. In February 1965 Rolls-Royce and Turbomeca had already agreed to collaborate on their respective submissions for the Breguet 121, and would jointly produce the RB172T/T260 Adour. This agreement over the powerplant was also announced as part of the MoU.

On 10 June, less than a month after the MoU was signed, and with the British car manufacturer's blessing but without prior consultation of the respective air forces, the new aircraft was named 'Jaguar'.

BAC was happy with the overall Jaguar/AFVG agreement, because though Breguet had design leadership on Jaguar, BAC did on the potentially far more significant AFVG, in collaboration with Dassault. However, the AFVG was to prove a short-lived project, as related in Chapter 13.

SEPECAT

The Memorandum of Understanding called for the establishment of a joint Anglo-French firm to develop, design, co-ordinate manufacture, finance and sell the new aircraft. In May 1966 this was registered in France as SEPECAT (Societé Européene de Production de l'Avion Ecole de Combat et d'Appui Tactique). In a similar fashion a British-registered company, Rolls-Royce Turbomeca Ltd, was formed to manage the Adour engine. Chairmanship of SEPECAT alternated annually between BAC's Sir Freddie Page, as Managing Director of BAC's Preston Division, and Breguet's Chairman, M. Vallieres. In the early years relations between the two partner firms were extremely amicable.

Breguet was to build the front and centre fuselage, with BAC manufacturing the remainder at its Preston plant. There were to be final assembly lines and flight testing in both countries. BAC's final assembly and flight test would be at Warton and, following Breguet's takeover by Dassault in 1971, its activities were centred at Toulouse.

Developing the Design

The French and British requirements were initially quite different, but soon became reconciled. The agreed requirement was for good handling, Mach 1.7 at high altitude, Mach 1.1 at low altitude, short take-off from rough surfaces with a tactical weapons load, long-range capability using internal fuel only and ease of maintenance – for example, an engine change within thirty minutes. Even though it was more costly, twin engines were settled upon as they offered the ability to return home following engine failure.

To achieve these requirements, BAC took a major role in improving the design from its Breguet 121 origins. Besides many internal changes, the fuselage was lengthened, a new, thinner 40-degree wing and tailplane were designed, the vertical tail was made taller and the cockpit was raised to enhance the pilot's rearward view. Control was by wing spoilers to provide roll control, an all-flying tailplane, airbrakes and rudder. To provide short-field performance in and out of rough runways, the wing had leading edge slats and full-span, double-slotted wing flaps. As weight increased the engine thrust requirements were increased. With this growth in the weight and complexity, both France and Britain altered their requirements and initiated completely new trainer projects. These later emerged as the Hawker Siddeley (later BAe) Hawk and the Dassault/Dornier Alpha Jet.

Different Versions

The British and French Jaguars shared common airframes from aft of the rear seat bulkhead. Differences were confined to the cockpit arrangement, ejector seats, fixed guns, refuelling probe, navigation and attack system. The two air forces adopted very different nav/attack systems, using widely different philosophies. The RAF regarded their twin-seat trainers as aircraft that could fly alongside the single-seaters in combat, while the French did not equip their Jaguar E for such a role. The Jaguar was initially developed into five versions for the two countries, as follows:

- Jaguar A – single-seat strike aircraft for the French air force with twin DEFA 30mm canon, five external stores points, provision for flight refuelling and nav/attack system similar to the Mirage 4 bomber.
- Jaguar E – advanced trainer for the French air force with twin DEFA 30mm cannon, five external stores points, no provision for flight refuelling, and a basic nav/attack system.
- Jaguar M – single seat strike aircraft for the French navy, equipped for aircraft carrier operations and fitted with twin DEFA 30mm cannon, flight-refuelling and a nav/attack system similar to the Jaguar E.
- Jaguar S – single-seat strike aircraft for the RAF with twin Aden 30mm cannon, five external stores points, provision for flight refuelling and sophisticated nav/attack system.
- Jaguar B – two-seat trainer for the RAF with one Aden 30mm cannon, five external stores points, no provision for flight refuelling and the same nav/attack system as the Jaguar S.

The Jaguar M (Marine) for the French navy's air arm, the Aeronavale, differed from all of the other versions in having a strengthened airframe and undercarriage. It had single mainwheels and a twin nosewheel on an extendable nose leg for aircraft carrier catapult launching, and was designed for the higher descent rates needed for deck landing. The Jaguar M, like all the other versions, was equipped with an arrester hook, though it was stressed for the higher loads associated with deck landings. With the passage of time, the Jaguar M was not proceeded with, and the other variants received much additional and different equipment.

The Prototypes

It was decided to build eight prototypes for the Jaguar programme. As the Armée

The first three Jaguar prototypes, all assembled in France: two-seaters E01 and E02 and single-seater A03. All have the original short fin.
BAE Systems via Warton Heritage

The first British-assembled Jaguar prototypes, S06/XW560 and S07/XW563, both fitted with the extended tail. XW560 appeared at the Farnborough Air Show in September 1970, the first appearance of the Jaguar there. BAE Systems via Warton Heritage

de l'Air had a pressing need for Jaguars, the first four prototypes were all French-assembled. These were two-seaters E01 and E02 and single-seaters A03 and A04, which flew in numerical order. M05 was the French-assembled prototype for the Aeronavale, and then came three British-built prototypes: single-seaters, S06 and S07 and finally the two-seater B08. Each prototype was allotted specific roles in the test programme.

The first prototype, E01, was rolled out at Breguet's plant at Villacoublay, near Paris, on 19 April 1968; with typical French flair, it made a fast taxi down the runway to impress the invited dignitaries. The prototype's maiden flight was then much delayed, owing partly to the civil unrest that hit France that summer and partly to the need to dismantle it and transport it to French flight test centre at Istres, near Marseilles.

The first flight of E01 finally took place on 8 September 1968 with Breguet's Chief Test Pilot, Bernard Witt, at the controls. Even though the flying was meant to be shared with BAC's Chief Test Pilot, Jimmy Dell, Witt continued to hog the flying until Dell finally made his first flight in the Jaguar over a month later, on 15 October. E02 made a supersonic maiden flight, again piloted by Witt, on 11 February 1969 and reached 30,000ft during its first sortie. A03 soon followed, with Witt again at the controls, in March, but it was Jimmy Dell who took A04 into the air for its first flight in May. The test programme suffered its first loss on 26 March 1970 when E01 crashed on approach to Istres; it appeared that an engine had failed and the pilot shut down the other engine in error.

The first British prototype, S06/XW560, first flew on 12 October 1969 piloted by Jimmy Dell, and S07/XW563 flew on 12 June 1970. XW560 made the type's first appearance at the Farnborough Air Show in September. The final and

The Jaguar M05 prototype on take-off trials on the RAE Bedford catapult. The Jaguar M was planned for the French navy but never went into production. It had an undercarriage noticeably different to that of the ground-based versions, which was necessary for the far heavier loads involved in carrier landing. BAE Systems via Warton Heritage

eighth prototype, B08/XW566, which was built to production standard, flew on 30 August 1971 with Paul Millett at the controls.

During the test programme various external refinements were made to the design including revised nosewheel doors, engine air intakes and spine contours (to house an improved air-conditioning system), cambered tailplane and a dorsal fin of increased area. The ventral fins were added early in the test programme to improve stability, while the airbrakes were enlarged and perforated during development flying.

Flight testing took time to gain momentum owing to problems with the Adour engine, which had never been flown before and had not had the benefit of a flying test bed. Rolls-Royce and Turbomeca had claimed that ground-based rig testing obviated the need for a flying test bed, but this did not prove to be the case and during the early years of flight testing there were frequent hold-ups to flying, a very high engine failure rate – it was fortunate indeed that the partners had decided on a twin-engined aircraft! – and the concomitant need to constantly replace them.

From September 1971 prototype E02 was based at Warton for three years, during which time it was used by Rolls-Royce/Turbomeca for Adour development – the Adour was still a poor and erratic performer even after two years and 1,000 flying hours. At Warton the concentration on Adour performance proved very successful. The thrust gap between the maximum dry and minimum reheat throttle settings had been problem-atic for single-engined or heavy-weight approaches, and the introduction of part-throttle reheat solved this. At the end of E02's Warton programme most of the performance requirements for Adour had been achieved.

Once the first Adour variant for Jaguar was thoroughly sorted out, the way was clear to develop an uprated version. The Mk 804 Adour was flight-tested on development aircraft XX108 and proved to be an enhancement in every area, especially at take-off and during acceleration at high speed and low level, offering 27 per cent more thrust at low level and 10 per cent more at take-off.

Aside from the ongoing issues with the Adour engines, very few serious development problems arose during the test programme, although some delay resulted from the loss of three of the five prototypes: E01, as mentioned above, after an engine failure, A03 after a heavy landing in February 1972 and S06 after an engine fire during ground running at A&AEE Boscombe Down in August 1972. By the end of 1973, with production aircraft entering service, the development programme was declining in intensity and trials shifted on to more esoteric items such as spinning, which required a considerable amount of analysis, dangerous test-flying and subsequent modification.

Rejection of the Jaguar M

Jaguar M05, the prototype for the Aeronavale, first flew on 14 November 1969 from Melun-Villaroche. M05 embarked on trials pertinent to its naval role, twice visiting RAE Bedford for catapult trials and twice performing catapult launching and deck landing trials on the French navy carrier *Clemenceau* in 1970 and 1971. During one of these landing trials M05's arrestor hook missed the arrestor cables; with the need to accelerate sharply to make a circuit and land again, the lack of part-throttle reheat resulted in only marginal power being available and the Jaguar sank very close to the sea before climbing away. Though part-throttle reheat was being developed, the Aeronavale decided the Jaguar M's performance was inadequate for carrier operations and rejected it outright, including any proposed developments such as a larger-winged version that had been projected.

Dassault benefited from the Jaguar M's cancellation as its Super Etendard took the Jaguar's place for the French Navy order. Despite rejection, the Jaguar M05 continued in use on the test programme, most notably on spinning trials, until December 1975 when it made its final flight. It is now preserved at the Musée de Tradition de l'Aeronautique Navale at Rochefort-Soubise, France.

Changing Requirements

On 9 January 1968 the British and French governments had signed a further MoU on the Jaguar, providing for the manufacture of 400 aircraft, both countries increasing their order to 200 aircraft each. The RAF was now to receive 110 Jaguar B trainers and ninety Jaguar S single-seat strike fighters, with the Armée de l'Air receiving seventy-five Jaguar E trainers and seventy-five Jaguar A strike variants. The Aeronavale would obtain ten Jaguar E land-based trainers and forty Jaguar M single-seat, carrier-born strike variants. But in 1970, after six prototypes had flown, Britain changed its requirement again and dropped the Jaguar from the training role, reducing its order for trainers to thirty-five and increasing its single-seater order to 165. Henceforth the trainers would be dedicated to conversion training for prospective Jaguar

The first production Jaguar E1 for the French air force, which flew in November 1971 at Toulouse.
BAE Systems via Warton Heritage

The first production Jaguar GR.1 single-seater for the RAF, XX108. This aircraft remained with the manufacturers and is now preserved at the Imperial War Museum, Duxford.
BAE Systems via Warton Heritage

To demonstrate the Jaguar's ability to operate from improvised runways, BAC used the virtually complete M55 Preston–Blackpool motorway, only a few miles north of Warton, as an example of the aircraft's flexibility. On 26 April 1975, Tim Ferguson landed the second production Jaguar GR.1, XX109, on 1,350ft of the road, refuelled, bombed-up and departed to Warton, demonstrating how this could be done in a combat setting. BAE Systems via Warton Heritage

RAF Jaguars in production in Warton's no. 4 hangar in September 1974. An early production Jaguar GR.1 in the foreground with a display of its offensive weapon capabilities. BAE Systems via Warton Heritage

Specification – Jaguar GR.1A	
Length:	55ft 2½in (16.83m)
Wingspan:	28ft 6in (8.69m)
Height:	16ft ½in (4.89m)
MTOW:	34,612lb (15,697kg)
Max speed:	Mach 1.6 (high altitude), Mach 1.1 (low altitude)
Range (combat):	530 miles (850km)
Crew:	1
Powerplant:	Rolls-Royce/Turbomeca Adour Mk 104, 7,305lb with reheat
Armament:	2 × 30mm cannon, 2 × AIM Sidewinder, Martel missiles, bombs etc

pilots. France also changed its order, to 160 Jaguar A strike aircraft and only forty Jaguar E trainers. The forty Jaguars originally intended for the Aeronavale were delivered to the Armée de l'Air as Jaguar As.

Dassault Takes Over Breguet

With the takeover of Breguet by Dassault in 1971 the relationship with BAC became difficult, as Dassault regarded the Jaguar and their 50 per cent share in it unfavourably in contrast to their own new Mirage F.1, which they wholly produced. This conflict of interest would plague Jaguar export sales, as Dassault was not interested in promoting sales of the Jaguar in preference to the Mirage. Eventually, in 1980 British Aerospace obtained full rights from Dassault to export Jaguar, but often this was then in direct opposition to the Mirage.

In Service with the French Air Force

The French Jaguars entered service in May 1973 and the last aircraft, which was the final French-assembled Jaguar, was delivered in December 1981. They were formed into nine squadrons (three of which had a nuclear strike role) plus a tactical navigation unit. They were used offensively on a number of occasions.

The Jaguar seemed to be the poor relation in the Armée de l'Air, possibly because of Dassault's lack of interest in it. Unlike its British counterpart it never received upgraded Adour engines, so its take-off performance from airfields in high temperature zones often proved poor. Nor did the French Jaguars receive the overwing missile pylons retrofitted to the RAF fleet, but they did get nav/attack modifications and other major additions to their weaponry.

Owing to the operational flexibility provided by their inflight-refuelling capability, Jaguars were employed several times against insurgents in former French African colonial possessions, and some were lost to enemy fire. These actions occurred in Senegal and Mauretania in 1977, and in Chad from 1978 to 1987

French A-120 in desert markings, retired at Cazaux 2005. Jean-Pierre Touzeau

E-22 in special markings to celebrate the end of service at Cazaux in 2005. Jean-Pierre Touzeau

In Service with the RAF

The first Jaguar arrived at the OCU at Lossiemouth at the end of May 1973 and others gradually followed, with training courses beginning there in February 1974. The RAF's Jaguars soon took on a distinctively different appearance from their French counterparts, acquiring a chisel-nose window for a laser rangefinder and marked target seeker (LRMTS), which was an aid to automatic weapon release. It was tested on the first production aircraft, XX108, in early 1974 and all except the early production Jaguar GR.1s had LRMTS fitted during production. Over time, the Jaguars received a number of improvements to the engine, better chaff dispensers and overwing missile pylons as fitted to the Jaguar International (*see* below).

At its peak the Jaguar equipped eight units in Britain and Germany, playing an important NATO strike and reconnaissance role. Paradoxically, it was only after the end of the Cold War that the Jaguar was used in a conflict when it was employed in 1991 as part Operation *Desert Storm* to drive Iraqi forces out of Kuwait. Jaguars remained in this theatre after the cessation of hostilities, as part of Operation *Northern Watch* to contain Iraqi activities against the Kurds. Jaguars flew similar operations over the former Yugoslavia in 1996.

After its successful use in these operations, the aircraft received an avionics upgrade including Thermal Imaging Airborne Laser Designation (TIALD) pod for self-designation of targets and the uprated and more economical Adour 106 engines. With these modifications the GR.1 became a GR.3A and the T.2 the T.4.

Despite its obvious value, in 2004 the RAF announced it would be withdrawn from service in 2007 – two years earlier than planned – as an economy measure.

against a Libyan-backed insurgency. They were also deployed as an indicator of continuing French influence to deter further insurgency. In 1991 twenty-eight French Jaguars were sent to the Gulf as part of Operation *Desert Storm* to counter the Iraqi invasion of Kuwait. Cuts were made to the size of the Jaguar force after the Gulf operation, but they were still a valuable asset for the French forces, flying bombing missions over Bosnia in 1993 and Kosovo in 1999. After a thirty-two-year career they were withdrawn from service in July 2005.

Two RAF single-seaters and three two-seaters.
BAE Systems via Warton Heritage

Jaguar single-seater XZ358 making a sizzling take-off at the 1976 Farnborough Air Show. BAE Systems

Jaguar International

The Jaguar International was announced at the 1974 Farnborough Air Show, a month after orders were received from Ecuador and Oman. These countries' initial orders were valued at £108m in 1974 prices.

As Dassault were uninterested in Jaguar

export sales, BAC had to be the driving force behind the project. The Jaguar International was based on the RAF version, with BAC carrying out trials at Warton. The first production RAF Jaguar GR.1, XX108, which had been retained by BAC for trials, was presented statically at Farnborough as the prototype of this version with a huge variety of weapons

displayed in front of it, and an Agave radar in the nose, as was later fitted to the Indian Air Force's Jaguar IM variant. Trials of the actual Jaguar International specification on XX108 began the following year, with Adour 804s installed to provide a much improved performance and trials of Magic air-to-air missiles on over-wing mountings, which allowed the full range of attack weapons to be carried on the under-wing positions. The over-wing pylon used the same hardpoint as the normal inboard pylon, and replaced the wing fence. Trials followed with the Agave radar, which offered the potential (soon exploited by BAC) for a maritime strike variant.

In 1975 BAC organized a 15,000 mile Jaguar International sales tour of the Middle East with a twin-seater, but failed to win any additional orders in the region. BAC continued to promote the Jaguar International and offered the even better Adour Mk 811 engines, overwing air-to-air missiles, digital nav/attack systems, and improved head-up and head-down cockpit displays.

Jaguar XX108 on display at the 1981 Paris Air Show with an Agave radar nose. The Indian Air Force fitted the Agave radar to some of its Jaguars.
BAE Systems via Warton Heritage

Two Ecuadorian Air Force Jaguars fitted with underwing fuel tanks taking off from Warton.
BAE Systems via Warton Heritage

Orders From Ecuador, Oman and Nigeria

Ecuador ordered ten Jaguar ES single-seaters and two EB trainers for delivery in 1977. Oman ordered the same quantity, designated as Jaguar OS and OB respectively, for delivery in 1977–78 and re-ordered the same number in 1980, which were all delivered by the end of 1983.

The first production Jaguar Inter-national was two-seater FAE283 for Ecuador, the 168th Jaguar assembled at BAC Warton; temporarily registered as G27-266, it first flew in August 1976. After steady usage, by 1991 the Ecuadorian Air Force only had nine Jaguars flying and so topped up its fleet with three former RAF GR.1s, which were refurbished by BAe at Warton. However, in 2004 Ecuador withdrew its aircraft from service. In a similar fashion Oman added to its Jaguar fleet with a former RAF T.2 and a GR.1, and contracted BAe Warton to carry out a nav/attack upgrade on all its remaining fleet between 1986 and 1989. At the time of writing in 2012 the Omani Jaguars remain in service and may be replaced by Eurofighter Typhoons.

After lengthy negotiations, Nigeria became the final customer for the Jaguar International with an order for eighteen and an option on a further eighteen; five of the initial order were trainers. All of these Nigerian aircraft were built to the final Jaguar International standard with Adour 811 engines. Unfortunately the option to purchase further aircraft was not taken up, and these Jaguars were the final ones manufactured by SEPECAT. The Nigerian aircraft had a short life, serving only from 1984 until 1991 when they were withdrawn from use. Apparently BAe endeavoured to repurchase them, but was unable to do so.

Ecuadorian Jaguar FAE302 in service in Ecuador. BAE Systems via Warton Heritage

An Omani Jaguar International two-seater taking off from Warton. BAE Systems via Warton Heritage

Four Omani Jaguars on patrol. BAE Systems via Warton Heritage

NAF700, the first of eighteen Jaguars for the Nigerian Air Force, at Warton. It first flew in October 1983 and was delivered in September 1984. The Nigerians received five two-seaters and thirteen single-seaters.
BAE Systems via Warton Heritage

Nigerian Air Force Jaguar NAF703 in service in Nigeria immediately after delivery in August 1984. BAE Systems via Warton Heritage

Specification – Jaguar International	
Length:	55ft 2½in (16.83m)
Wingspan:	28ft 6in (8.69m)
Height:	16ft ½in (4.89m)
MTOW:	34,612lb (15,697kg)
Max speed:	Mach 1.6 (high altitude), Mach 1.1 (low altitude)
Range(combat):	875 miles (1,400km)
Crew:	1
Powerplant:	Rolls-Royce/Turbomeca Adour Mk 811, 8,400lb with reheat
Armament:	2 × 30mm cannon, 2 × AIM Sidewinder, Martel missiles, Sea Eagle missiles, bombs etc

Indian Air Force Order

As early as 1968 the SEPECAT Sales Director, Jeffrey Quill (the well-known former Spitfire test pilot) and Paul Jaillard of Breguet had made a presentation on the Jaguar to the Indian Air Force (IAF). This presentation evinced little

apparent interest, though the manufacturer had identified India as a possible Jaguar customer owing to its need to replace its Canberras and Hunters in their strike role. Quill and Jimmy Dell made another presentation in 1970, but at this time the Indians were hopeful that their indigenous Hindustan Marut might prove able to carry out the strike role. However, at the end of 1970 the Marut was abandoned and the possibility of a Jaguar sale became more likely.

India was seeking to become more self-reliant and would only consider those aircraft where licence production in India was possible. This automatically ruled out some manufacturers, but though SEPECAT could satisfy this requirement so too could the Dassault Mirage F.1 and the SAAB Viggen. The IAF sought a twin-engined aircraft, which appeared to sway matters in the Jaguar's favour since the Mirage and Viggen were single-engined, but India's concerns over the poor performance of the Adour engine

clouded the Jaguar's prospects. However, in March 1978 an Indian evaluation team visited France, Sweden and Britain and on 6 October 1978 a contract for the Jaguar was announced. The Indian Government stated that Jaguar was chosen for four reasons: it fulfilled the IAF's requirements, it was the most economical, it could be delivered ahead of its two competitors and it was the only twin-engined aircraft in the field.

In April 1979 a Memorandum of Understanding detailed the purchase of 130 aircraft, licence production and technology transfer to India. Thirty-five single-seaters and three two-seaters were to be built at Warton, then forty-five would be assembled by Hindustan Aircraft Ltd (HAL) at Bangalore from kits provided by SEPECAT. Thereafter an increasing proportion of Indian components would be employed and from about 1984 the Jaguars would be entirely built in India. To provide for the Indian Air Force's immediate needs the RAF loaned

The final ten of thirty-five Jaguar single-seaters for India assembled at Warton awaiting delivery; later Indian Jaguars were assembled by Hindustan Aircraft Ltd at Bangalore. The nearest Jaguar, with B-class registration G27-367, is still in primer and also bears the marks S(I)35, indicating that it is the thirty-fifth IAF strike Jaguar; it was later registered JS135. Also visible is an Indian Air Force Antonov An-12 L647, and in the distance a Tornado in primer. BAE Systems via Warton Heritage

Indian Air Force J1004 in flight in the UK. This aircraft was an early production RAF GR.1, XX117; it was upgraded to Jaguar International standard at Warton and delivered to India in October 1979. It returned to the UK in February 1984 to be upgraded to GR.1A standard at Warton and re-enter service with the RAF, and was only withdrawn from service in 2005. BAE Systems via Warton Heritage

eighteen Jaguars, including two trainers, and also embarked on training some of the pilots and ground crew. The value of the contract was in the order of £1bn in 1979 prices. According to some sources, the French Government and Dassault were angered at this turn of events; even though 50 per cent of the work would be French, the French Ambassador appealed in person to the Indian authorities to purchase the Mirage despite the Jaguar contract having been announced.

Although the contract was only finalized after BAC had become part of the nationalized British Aerospace, the Corporation can essentially be credited with the achievement of this sale. The first handover of two loaned, refurbished RAF Jaguars, a single and a twin-seater, occurred on 19 July 1979 when they left Warton, the trainer piloted by Tom Ferguson, Deputy Chief Test Pilot, with Wing Commander Nadkarni of the IAF and designated commanding officer of the first Indian Jaguar squadron in the rear seat; the single-seater was flown by test pilot Chris Yeo. Only one more delivery involved BAe pilots, as all subsequent flights were made with IAF pilots.

The loaned RAF Jaguars were fitted with uprated Rolls-Royce/Turbomeca Adour 804 engines producing 27 per cent more combat thrust than the standard Adour. However, the new-build aircraft received the even more powerful Adour 811.

Five IAF squadrons were equipped with Jaguars. The IAF received twenty Jaguar IB two-seaters, 136 Jaguar IS single-seaters and twelve Jaguar IM ('India Maritime') single-seat anti-shipping strike aircraft fitted with the Agave radar and Sea Eagle missile. During their years of service the IAF's Jaguars have been in minor actions including peace-keeping in Sri Lanka in 1987–90 and against insurgents in 1999. The Indian Air Force Jaguars are a potent force that remain in service today, and may yet receive further avionics and engine upgrades.

Conclusion

BAC's half share in Jaguar proved a blessing to the firm after the travails of TSR2. As a collaborative project it was shielded from cancellation, even though there were French rumblings about cost escalation in the 1970s. BAC had not chosen to join the programme but was nominated by the Labour Government to take on the role instead of Hawker Siddeley. It provided steady work at the Preston Division's plants from 1965 until 1984, supplemented by upgrade work that continued until the end of the 20th century. Whereas BAC's own P45 was an ambitious project at the time when variable geometry was fashionable, the Jaguar proved a very capable performer without the complexity and added weight of wing sweep.

The Jaguar was held back in the early years by the engine problems and then in later years beset by Dassault's pernicious influence following its takeover of Breguet. This especially manifested itself in Dassault competing against Jaguar with its Mirage for many overseas contracts, which on some occasions had the opposite effect of allowing American aircraft to win the order. In the end, at least 623 Jaguars were built – 295 by BAC, 205 by Breguet/Dassault and 123+ by HAL. Although Jaguar operations have ceased with the original customers, it remains in operation in India in substantial numbers.

CHAPTER THIRTEEN

MRCA to Tornado

With the demise of TSR2 in April 1965 and the rejection of BAC's speedily prepared Spey-Mirage proposal, it appeared that the RAF was to have a mixed fleet of American-built F-111Ks and the smaller Anglo-French Variable Geometry (AFVG) aircraft built in collaboration with Dassault. BAC was to take design leadership on the AFVG because of the company's superior variable-geometry know-how. The AFVG, with a top speed of Mach 2+, was to replace the RAF's Lightning and the French Mirage III in the air defence role, and Canberras, Buccaneers and Phantoms operated by the British in the strike role.

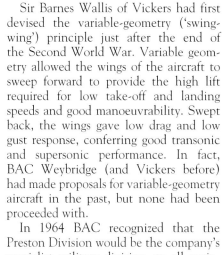

Sir Barnes Wallis of Vickers had first devised the variable-geometry ('swing-wing') principle just after the end of the Second World War. Variable geometry allowed the wings of the aircraft to sweep forward to provide the high lift required for low take-off and landing speeds and good manoeuvrability. Swept back, the wings gave low drag and low gust response, conferring good transonic and supersonic performance. In fact, BAC Weybridge (and Vickers before) had made proposals for variable-geometry aircraft in the past, but none had been proceeded with.

In 1964 BAC recognized that the Preston Division would be the company's specialist military division, so all variable-geometry work was transferred from Weybridge to Warton. This research was employed on the Gnat/Hunter trainer/light fighter proposal for the RAF, work on which had started in the previous year. Warton designed the variable-geometry, supersonic BAC P45 in the hope that this research would lead to some real hardware. However, Government talks were already in progress with France over a collaborative project: this became the BAC/Breguet Jaguar, was based on Breguet's 121 submission and superseded the P45.

Collapse of F-111K / AFVG Strategy

The Government's F-111K/AFVG scheme was short-lived. Although a Memorandum of Understanding was signed with the French in May 1965, it was only in January 1967 that the

AFVG mock-up at Warton. This mock-up only has one wing, but it does bear some similarity to the MRCA design. However, the engine intake design on the MRCA was very different.
BAE Systems via Warton Heritage

decision was formally made to proceed. Yet only six months later the French withdrew from the AFVG: Dassault had already been developing its own experimental VG aircraft, the Mirage G, and on 18 October 1965 the French Defence Ministry placed an order for the Mirage G, which flew in October 1967. (Despite this considerable investment, the French did not develop its VG programme further, and there was no production beyond the three prototypes constructed.)

At the end of 1967, owing to escalating costs, the Labour Government cancelled the F-111K order, but in the meantime funded BAC to continue work on a 'UKVG' project for eighteen months until June 1969. This work provided continuity of design, wind tunnel and materials testing for BAC and strengthened the basis for the huge UK input into the MRCA (Multi-Role Combat Aircraft), which became the Tornado, was produced alongside the Jaguar, and in turn led to Eurofighter Typhoon.

Sir George Edwards made a speech in Oxford in July 1970, quoted in *Flight*, describing the problems of working with Dassault and France on the AFVG:

The MRCA follows an international concept that goes back to the AFVG. After years of painful negotiation between the two Governments the French withdrew. At the meeting between British and French ministers in May 1965 there was a clear understanding that Jaguar and AFVG constituted a package deal, with the French leading on the Jaguar and the British on the variable-geometry aircraft. It was specifically on this understanding that we embarked on Jaguar. During the following months British officials and BAC made strenuous efforts to try to work out an industrial arrangement for the VG aircraft that would be acceptable to the French. Many concessions were made, including giving the French firm SNECMA the leadership on the engine with Rolls-Royce/Bristol Siddeley playing a secondary role, and it must be said that at this stage many French Government officials worked very hard to try to find an acceptable compromise.

The French subsequently withdrew, officially for reasons of finance. The emergence of their own VG project prompted us to our own conclusions as to their real reasons for not going for the joint programme. They have, however, managed to find the resources necessary to continue with their own VG project, which they have lately tried to persuade the

Germans and Italians to adopt in preference to the MRCA.

This kind of history underlines my warning that we must be careful of the defence and industrial implications of what we are doing or, more accurately, of what may be done to us.

Joint Working Group

Within a month of France's withdrawal from the AFVG the West German Government indicated its willingness to replace France in the joint partnership. There was some feeling that a new project might evolve with the Joint Working Group that had been formed by Belgium, Italy, the Netherlands and West Germany (and later Canada) in 1967, which was seeking to replace the Lockheed F-104 Starfighters that they all operated. Despite some pressure to buy an 'off-the-shelf' American aircraft, there was also a drive for a European collaborative project. Within this disparate group, a wide spread of requirements needed to be met.

In July 1968 Britain joined the group to examine whether there was common ground between them and the British specification. Britain's presence was significant as it had the greatest experience in advanced combat aircraft design. As Belgium and Canada primarily required an interceptor they dropped out of the group, as later did the Netherlands, leaving Britain, Germany and Italy. Britain offered a VG design similar to the final one selected for the MRCA. Messerschmitt-Bolkow-Blohm (MBB) also proposed a VG design, but with a low wing, conventional ailerons and elevators, with the wing pivots sited outside the fuselage.

Eventually a compromise design was achieved using most of the BAC offering; that is, a high wing with elevons, but using the wing pivot positioning favoured by MBB. Remarkably the different partners wanted different control forces – Britain wanted lighter controls, the other countries sought a heavier option. The final result was a compromise, heavier than the British pilots were accustomed to but lighter than German and Italian pilots had experienced. Owing to its size the design could not contain a weapons bay, so BAC proposed a fuselage with flat underside for the easy carriage of weapons or stores.

Panavia

The MRCA programme was launched in December 1968 and in March 1969 a tripartite-owned company called Panavia was formed, with its headquarters in Munich. As it was initially understood that Germany's requirement would be the largest, MBB held 50 per cent of the shares, BAC had 33 per cent and Fiat just 17 per cent. Fiat participated as it wanted the experience of this high-technology programme, even though it doubted that its Government could afford Tornado.

Although BAC had no choice in its partners, they worked well together. Both MBB and Fiat looked to BAC as Germany and, to an even greater extent, Italy, had never mounted an aircraft programme of anywhere near comparable magnitude. Their industries did not have the experience of designing and building many of the very advanced systems that were essential for the MRCA.

BAC was able to apply its unique experience with the recent research, design, development and curtailed flight test of TSR2 to the design. For instance, though MBB had initially decided on placing the tailplane higher on the rear of the fuselage, BAC's view prevailed and its preference for low-set elevons were agreed. In a similar fashion the Corporation's experience with full-span flaps, intake positioning and control systems was applied to MRCA. BAC engineers had also learned from engine accessibility challenges on TSR2, and were insistent that the engine panels should swing down to allow the engines to be removed downwards, rather than having to slide backwards out of the aircraft.

Go Ahead

On 14 May 1969 a Memorandum of Understanding was signed by representatives of the British, West German and Italian Governments to develop a joint development and production programme for an MRCA. Finally Britain was to build a VG aircraft – or at least part of one.

Another variable-geometry BAC collaborative project might have occurred, for in 1969 BAC and the Australian Commonwealth Aircraft Corporation projected the AA107, a variable-geometry light twin-seat strike trainer to satisfy a market for up to 1,000 aircraft. Unfortunately in July 1970 the Australians withdrew from the project and the AA107 was abandoned, so MRCA was to be the only BAC (and part-British) variable-geometry aircraft.

At the same time as the AA107 was abandoned the MRCA workshare agreement was established. Even though final assembly would take place in each of the participating countries, BAC was to build all the noses and tails, Germany each centre-section and Italy the wings. English was chosen as the project language.

Panavia has proved to be a successful organization, based on BAC's experience of collaborative working successfully with Concorde and Jaguar, but less successfully with the AFVG. Panavia was and is a separate company charged with providing the customer NAMMA (NA(TO) M(RCA) Management Agency) with the MRCA. NAMMA was situated in Munich, alongside Panavia in the same building.

In contrast to the TSR2 experience, strict budgetary control was maintained on the project. Initially there was a separate avionics consortium, but this was soon dispensed with and control was passed to Panavia, which assigned design, development, integration and management of the avionics to Easams, a GEC-Marconi Electronics subsidiary, in Camberley, Surrey, which in turn placed work-sharing contracts with ESG in Germany and SIA in Italy.

When the actual German order diminished from 700 to 320 the shareholdings were adjusted to better represent expected production: BAC (now BAE Systems) and MBB (now DASA) each held 42½ per cent while Fiat Aviazone (now Aeritalia) had 15 per cent. At the same time the distinct MRCA design emerged, albeit in two versions: the single-seater Panavia PA100 and the two-seat PA200. Britain in particular wanted the two-seater, and in March 1970 all three parties accepted the PA200 design as the basis for the MRCA.

The Design

The aircraft that had evolved was much more than a Canberra replacement, yet was only about half the size of the TSR2. It was approximately the size the British had wanted, yet larger than that originally desired by the other partners.

Standardizing on a two-crew cockpit allowed for a navigator, or a trainee pilot operating dual flying controls in the rear cockpit. The aircraft's compactness is a great advantage, making it a far more difficult target for air or ground interception. Its multi-role specification required it to carry out close air-to-ground support, air superiority, interdiction, reconnaissance and maritime strike.

The MRCA succeeded in being very appreciably smaller than TSR2 because of the adoption of efficient VG wings and state-of-the-art engines that were light, compact and powerful, and had excellent fuel-consumption characteristics. But it must not be thought that the range of MRCA was drastically reduced: in fact, it was practically that of the larger UKVG, which had represented British views before the quasi-imperial 'East of Suez' defence role was discontinued in 1971.

The MRCA benefited from compactness, but because of the size of its radar dish, the nose cone (which housed the radar) could not be significantly scaled down, and it is large in proportion to the remainder of the aircraft. This is an advantage to the crew, who benefit from ergonomically good cockpit characteristics.

The MRCA, or Tornado as it is now better known, is controlled by a triplex fly-by-wire system with a fully powered rudder and all-flying elevons. The elevons operate in harmony for longitudinal control and differentially for roll control, augmented in the latter task by spoilers on the upper wing that operate together as lift dumpers after touchdown. In addition, large air brakes are positioned either side of the fin.

The wing has full length leading-edge slats, double-slotted flaps, spoilers and Krueger flaps under the leading edges of the fixed inboard wing. The wing is swept fully forward for take-off and landing, providing the best low-speed handling; mid-sweep offers best agility while fully swept is the configuration for high speeds. The undercarriage has single-wheel main gear and a twin-wheel nose assembly, all of which retracts forwards into the airframe.

The Rolls-Royce RB199

Rolls-Royce was determined it should to win a contract to supply its new RB199

engine for MRCA, and not have Pratt & Whitney supplying the TF-30. The one disadvantage they were up against was that the RB199 existed only on paper while the TF-30 was already in service. The Germans were favourably inclined to an American bid, so to ensure it won Rolls-Royce made a keenly competitive offer that neither Germany nor Italy could refuse. A tripartite engine company, Turbo-Union, was formed on 1 June 1969 with its headquarters in Bristol. Rolls-Royce and Motoren-Turbinen-Union (MTU) each had a 40 per cent holding in Turbo-Union and Fiat Aviazone a 20 per cent share. This arrangement guaranteed MTU and Fiat technology transfer from Rolls-Royce and shared production: this obviously appealed and the American firm could not match it. Sir Freddie Page wrote that as a result Pratt & Whitney did not make a serious bid for the MRCA engine supply contract, as they realized that Turbo-Union would be certain to receive the contract. (As it transpired, the TF-30 ran into severe technical problems.)

The RB199 was selected as the powerplant for the MRCA in September 1969. BAC was uneasy about the challenge of flying the combination of a new airframe and a new engine, and would have preferred to have been able to use an existing, tried and tested powerplant.

The RB199 had to be created in a very short timescale. The timing proved most unfortunate, as problems developed with the RB199 engine that coincided with Rolls-Royce's going into receivership, resulting in nationalization in 1971 and serious worker unrest. The first complete engine test took place in September 1971, but problems soon developed and a shortfall in engine deliveries held up the maiden flight for several months; even then, the maiden flight took place with derated engines. Subsequently there was a shortfall in the number of engines available for flight test work, especially as some of the earlier engines had to be returned to Turbo-Union. At one point there were only six flight-cleared engines available at the three flight test bases at Warton, Manching and Caselle. An 80 per cent thrust limitation on initial standard engines also greatly restricted performance, which caused obvious obstacles to flight test work and the RB199 was the pacing factor in development flying. In the opinion of Dr Gordon Lewis of Rolls-Royce:

Avro Vulcan XA903, with a Rolls-Royce RB199 fitted in a replica half-MRCA fuselage, carrying out Mauser gun trials. It was the only Vulcan ever to carry and fire a gun. This same aircraft had flown trials with the Concorde Olympus engine.
Rolls-Royce Historical Trust

Mature engines cannot be made available at the start of flight testing unless the full engine development programme is started at least two years ahead of airframe development.

Vulcan RB199 Testbed

The RB199 prototype engine made its first flight, from Filton in April 1973, in test bed Vulcan XA903, which had previously been used to test the Olympus engine for Concorde. XA903 was unique amongst Vulcans in carrying a gun, as the ventral nacelle was equipped with an accurately positioned Mauser 27mm cannon, as installed on the Tornado, so that gun gas ingestion trials could be carried out. The firing trials were carried out on the ground and, contrary to some sources, also in the air. A total of 285 engine test flight hours were accumulated with the RB199 on XA903. However, according to Paul Millett, BAC Military Aircraft Division's Chief Test Pilot, the installation of the RB199 in the Vulcan was so seriously delayed that it added little to the experience of the engine prior to the maiden flight.

Flight Test

As the management and the production were tripartite, so too was the flight testing: each country flew an allotted number of prototypes and tested them from their bases, BAC at Warton, MBB at Manching and Fiat Aviazone at Caselle. Nine prototypes (P01–09) were provided for in the tripartite Memorandum of Understanding, plus one non-flying example (P10) assembled at Warton for static testing. Six pre-production machines were also built (P11–16). The first flight was scheduled for December 1973, which seemed easy to achieve as the first prototype D-9591 (98+04) was completed at Ottobrunn in February 1973 and moved by road to Manching. The Germans had insisted on this honour of hosting the first flight as at the time they were buying the largest number of aircraft, but Sir Freddie Page cleverly ensured in return that a British pilot, Paul Millett, would fly it with his German opposite number, Neils Meister, in the back seat.

Following reassembly at Manching a large number of trials ensued to check all the systems, the engines and the telemetry. Non-flight cleared RB199s were used for initial ground running and taxiing tests. However, when flight-cleared engines arrived and were installed, the compressor of the left engine exploded during its first full-power run. Four months later, on 14 August 1974, D-9591 finally made its first flight, climbing to 10,000ft and performing well. On the second flight the wings were swept for the first time without any problems in trim or aerodynamics. On the subsequent flight the pilots reversed positions and then the German test pilots took over the testing of the P01. The first aircraft's initial role was to expand and confirm the flight envelope and general handling. Later in the test programme P01 took on other roles, including engine and thrust reverser development.

The first prototype MRCA landing after its maiden flight from Manching, piloted by BAC's Chief Test Pilot, Paul Millett, on 14 August 1974. The MBB Chief Test Pilot, Neils Meister, occupied the rear seat and piloted the second flight. It was accompanied by a Fiat G91 chase aircraft.
BAE Systems via Warton Heritage

The first MRCA, D-9591, flying with its wings swept fully back. BAE Systems

XX946, the first BAC-assembled Tornado and the second aircraft to fly, landing at Warton at the end of its maiden flight. It was piloted by Paul Millett and wore the colourful Panavia livery. BAE Systems

XX947, the second British Tornado and the first with dual controls. It was an essential tool in the development programme at this early stage, and was used to train pilots involved in the development programme. This aircraft was the first painted in camouflage.
BAE Systems via Warton Heritage

A rear view of XX947 with its wings swept fully back. BAE Systems via Warton Heritage

Tornado P08/XX950 at the Farnborough Air Show in 1976 with an array of the weapons that the interdictor/strike variant could carry. In the background are two other BAC aircraft, One-Eleven N111NA and Concorde G-BBDG. BAE Systems

In September the MRCA was formally named the Tornado, and on 30 October 1974 Tornado P02, registered XX946, made its maiden flight from Warton. At the controls for the sixty-minute flight was Paul Millett, with Aeritalia's MRCA project pilot Pietro Trevisan in the navigator's seat. The flight covered the flight envelope cleared by the first prototype, including a short supersonic run, and concluding with low-level swept-wing passes and a full roll over the airfield for the benefit of the watching workforce. P02 had an eventful life, tasked with flight-refuelling trials, external stores carriage, and high incidence and spinning trials. The clearance of Tornado for airborne refuelling in July 1975 allowed test flights to be prolonged, with sorties of nearly two hours rather than one hour.

XX947, the third Tornado prototype and first with dual controls, made a supersonic first flight on 5 August, from BAC Military Aircraft Division's airfield at Warton. The pilots were David Eagles, the division's project test pilot, with Tim Ferguson, deputy chief test pilot, in the rear seat.

Tornado P04, registered D-9592 (98+05), flew from Manching; P.05 X-586 (MM586) was the first Italian machine, first flying at Caselle in December 1975. Unfortunately, on only its fifth flight P05 was badly damaged on landing and was taken out of the flight test programme for more than two years. Its test roles of flutter and load measurement were taken over by BAC's P02 – fortunately the Tornado programme provided a back-up for all aircraft, and P02 was already suitably instrumented.

The sixth prototype, XX948, was another British machine and was the first to incorporate a slimmer rear fuselage and the twin Mauser cannon. (Tornados carried one or two Mauser 27mm cannon, located on the lower front fuselage.) P06 tested performance and drag, stores handling, rapid rolling and gun firing. The seventh and eighth prototypes, 98+06 and XX950, flew from Manching and Warton, respectively, and engaged in weapons trials. The final prototype, P09 X-587(MM587), flew from Caselle on the same day, in February 1977 as P11, the first dual-control German aircraft and the first of six pre-production machines. The pre-production aircraft were typically employed at military test centres undertaking trials as a prelude to squadron service. Of these, the last four were later refurbished and issued to the services.

By February 1978 the unladen aircraft had achieved over Mach 1.9 at altitude, and Mach 1 plus at low level. Acceleration was impressive: it could reach 30,000ft in two minutes from a standing start. Owing to continuing engine problems, however, it was not until March 1979 that P02 achieved Mach 2.

During the test programme telemetry was extensively used and virtually any parameter could be recorded, instantaneously processed and displayed to the test engineers working in the telemetry room. Trials were also supported by two Buccaneers fitted for avionics development and a Lightning F.2A, XN795, mounted with a 27mm Mauser gun.

Specification – Tornado GR.1A	
Length:	54ft 10in (16.71m)
Wingspan:	45ft 7½in (13.9m) extended
	28ft 2½in (8.6m) fully swept
Height:	18ft 8½in (5.7m)
MTOW:	60,000lb (27,000kg)
Max speed:	Mach 2.2 (high altitude)
Mach 1.1	(low altitude)
Range:	810 miles (1,300km) combat
Crew:	2
Powerplant:	2 × Turbo-Union RB199 Mk 104,
	16,920lb with reheat
Armament:	1×27mm Mauser Cannon, Storm
	Shadow, Brimstone, ALARM, AIM-9
	Sidewinder, Paveway, bombs

Production

Critics of the Tornado existed in each of the producing countries, but by the time the first prototype flew there was a general realization that the Tornado project's costs had been kept under control and no other aircraft existed that could fulfil the role. Accordingly, in 1976 the Batch 1 production order was placed for forty aircraft, twenty-three for Britain and seventeen for Germany, followed in May 1977 by the Batch 2 order for 110 more. Further batches followed until the completion of production in 1999. Two new hangers were constructed at Warton for the Tornado production lines. The British, German and Italian aircraft and aero-engine industries and approximately 500 ancillary firms now had the advantage of projected orders for over 800 aircraft, providing employment for 70,000 people throughout Europe.

On 29 April 1977 the British Aircraft Corporation ceased to exist, becoming part of the nationalized British Aerospace (BAe), along with Hawker Siddeley and Scottish Aviation. BAe did not include Shorts, Westland or Rolls-Royce.

Initially West Germany had expected to order 700 aircraft, the UK 385 and Italy just 100. However, the final production, including attrition replacements, was: UK, 228 IDS (Interdictor/Strike) and 173 ADV (Air Defence Variant); Germany, 357 IDS; and Italy, 99 IDS. In addition, Saudi Arabia received 96 IDS and 24 ADV, all of which were assembled at Warton. Of the 977 Tornadoes built, BAC and its successor firms at Warton assembled 527.

The first production Tornado, ZA319, was ceremonially rolled out at Warton on 5 June 1979 and flew on 10 July. A week later it was followed into the air by the first German production aircraft; the first Italian production machine did not fly until September 1981. After initial trials ZA319 went to the Aircraft & Armament Experimental Establishment at Boscombe Down for six months of flight-testing.

TTTE

On 1 July 1980, two Royal Air Force Tornado GR.1s – as the IDS was designated in RAF service – flew into RAF Cottesmore, the first arrivals at the new Trinational Tornado Training Establishment (TTTE). Just as the aircraft, engines and avionics were tripartite, so to was the training. Until 1999 British, German and Italian crews were based at Cottesmore to complete a common operational conversion course. However, the three air forces were unable to agree on a common weapons portfolio, so the IDS Tornados have been equipped with an extremely wide range of weaponry.

Service with the German Air Force and Navy

The German air force (Luftwaffe) and Navy (Marineflieger) received a total of 357 IDS Tornados including four pre-production machines. Of these all but thirty-five were IDS variants; the others were the Electronic Combat and Reconnaissance (ECR) variant. Germany ordered these in May 1986, which were designed for Suppression of Enemy Air Defences (SEAD) missions; however, most of the IDS's original radar and navigation systems remained intact. The ECR prototype was a converted production model IDS and first flew in August 1988, production deliveries starting in 1990.

German Tornados began weapons training in February 1982 and the first squadron, which had previously flown F-104s, was formed by the navy as Marinefliegergeschwader 1 (MFG1, Naval Flying Wing 1) in July that year, becoming fully operational at the beginning of 1984; eventually a second wing, MFG2, was also formed. However, as part of the post-Cold War fleet reductions, MFG1

Tornado P16 98+03 in German Navy livery.
This Tornado first flew in March 1979 and
in 1988 became the Electronic Combat and
Reconnaissance prototype. BAE Systems

Luftwaffe Tornado Electronic Combat and
Reconnaissance variant taxiing out to take off at
Fairford in July 2010. Author

was disbanded in 1993 and MFG2 in 2005. Fifty-one of the navy's Tornados then became part of the Luftwaffe as a dedicated Reconnaissance Wing, and the anti-shipping strike role was passed to the Luftwaffe.

When the Tornados first entered service with the Luftwaffe they formed five strike wings. In August 1995 these Tornados had the distinction of flying the Luftwaffe's first offensive action since the close of the Second World War when ECR Tornados were tasked to track hostile anti-aircraft radars and destroy them with HARM missiles during the Balkan Conflict. Tornados have continued to be deployed in offensive operations, and since 2007 six aircraft have operated in Afghanistan.

By 2010, with the passage of time and changing strategic priorities, only two strike wings and one reconnaissance wing remained. The number of Tornados is to be reduced to just eighty-five ECR and RECCE variants (the latter is an IDS with the ability to carry a reconnaissance pod) as the IDS aircraft are not being upgraded and are gradually being phased out with the delivery of Eurofighter Typhoons. Those being withdrawn are being cannabilized for spares usage.

The eighty-five aircraft remaining in service will receive life extension and comprehensive modernization programmes, weapons improvements plus a software update called ASSTA 2 (Avionic System Software Tornado in Ada). In 2010 the Luftwaffe received the first of these to be upgraded to ASSTA 2 standard; these aircraft are also due to receive ASSTA 3 upgrades starting in 2012. Currently, the Tornado's planned out-of-service date is 2025–2030.

Italian Air Force

The Aeronautica Militare Italiana received ninety-nine new-build Tornado IDS plus one refurbished pre-production aircraft, P.14. Of these 100 aircraft, twelve were dual-stick. The first Italian Tornado, registered MM50000, flew in September 1981 and deliveries began in May of the following year; they were completed in

1986. Italian Tornados initially served in four squadrons and had nuclear capability under ultimate US control within NATO. Following delivery, twelve were rebuilt as Electronic Combat and Reconnaissance (ECR) variants, similar to the German ECR versions.

Italian Tornados have been employed in the 1991 Gulf War, over Bosnia and Kosovo, and currently in Afghanistan. In order to maintain their capabilities, thirty-three of the Italian IDS fleet are in the process of receiving a mid-life update due for completion in 2011.

In addition to its own IDS fleet, to fill a gap in its air defence capability prior to Typhoon entering service, from 1994 until 2004 the Italian Air Force leased twenty-four Tornado F.3s from the RAF.

The RAF's IDS Tornados

The RAF's Tornado GR.1s entered service in 1981 and eventually formed eleven squadrons. The first three squadrons to receive the Tornado were

UK-based, and converted from the aging Vulcan. The other eight squadrons were based in Germany, part of the front-line defence against the Warsaw Pact nations, and could carry both conventional and nuclear weapons. The low-level attack capability of the Tornado was particularly important in this role.

Ten years later after they entered service, and after the end of the Cold War, the Tornado GR.1s were used in anger for the first time in a very different theatre, as part of the RAF contingent in the 1991 Gulf War. Almost sixty Tornados were employed of which six were lost. The Tornado GR.1 proved itself not only in the Gulf War but also over Kosovo, Iraq and Afghanistan as an exceedingly capable ground-attack aircraft.

Between 1997 and 2003, 142 Tornado GR.1s were upgraded to GR.4 standard by BAE Systems at Warton. Since entering service in 1981 the GR.1 had developed into a number of sub-fleets with varying equipment standards. One of the main objectives of the conversion was to

ZG750, one of the two Tornado GR.4 development aircraft, taking off. 142 Tornados were upgraded to GR.4s or GR.4As at Warton from 1997 to 2003.
BAE Systems via Warton Heritage

The Tornado GR.4 production line at Warton. The primer areas on the aircraft in the foreground indicate where modification work was carried out.
BAE Systems via Warton Heritage

The first Tornado GR.4 returned to front-line service in May 1998, the type becoming fully operational by 2001; the final example was delivered from Warton in 2003. The GR.4 will ensure that the RAF Tornados remain a formidable ground-attack aircraft for the foreseeable future. In 2011 RAF Tornados were involved in strike operations to help protect the rebels against Government forces in Libya.

All the Tornados are currently due to be retired from RAF service in 2020, with a gradual running down from 2017–18. As with the other nations' Tornados, BAE Systems is working to extend the lifespan to an eventual 8,000 hours to enable it to reach this out-of-service date.

The RAF's ADV Tornados

The Tornado ADV (Air Defence Variant) was developed for the RAF as a long-range interceptor fighter to replace the Lightning and the Phantom. The RAF evaluated American types including the F-14 Tomcat, F-15 Eagle and F-16, of which the F-15 was deemed the most suitable. However, the final decision by the RAF was to seek a development of the Tornado. Although the Tornado IDS could fulfil aspects of the requirement, its existing twin radar fit of one attack and one terrain-following radar would need replacement with intercept radar, and it would also need provision for air-to-air missiles.

The Tornado ADV embodies aerodynamic refinements and can easily be distinguished from the IDS owing to its longer nose radome for the AI24 radar and 4ft front fuselage extension, which increased internal fuel capacity and reduced drag. The lengthened fuselage provides space for four semi-recessed

have a common standard of equipment throughout the fleet with the exception of the Tornado GR.1As, which kept their sideways-looking and linescan infra-red systems and become GR.4As. The GR.4 can be distinguished from the GR.1 by the additional fairing under the nose to house the Forward Looking Infra-Red (FLIR) and the removal of one of its two 27mm Mauser cannon. During the conversion major new systems were installed, and the GR.4 and GR.4A became more potent with additional and more powerful weapons.

Tornado F.2 prototype ZA254 taxiing in at Warton on 27 October 1979, following its first flight. The F.2 was longer than the GR.1 as it needed a large radome, and the fuselage was extended 4ft to provide additional fuel capacity. Note how the BAC hangars are now 'British Aerospace'.
BAE Systems via Warton Heritage

A dramatic shot of ZA254 taking off at the Farnborough Air Show in 1982.
BAE Systems via Warton Heritage

Tornado GR.1 ZA449 and F.2 ZD899. The difference in length between the two variants is clearly visible in this view. BAE Systems via Warton Heritage

Tornado F.3 ZE907 in special markings for the 50th Anniversary of the Battle of Britain, photographed from a BAe Hawk. BAE Systems via Warton Heritage

Skyflash air-to-air missile missiles in the underside of the fuselage. The leading edge of the fixed part of the wing was extended forwards, sharpening its angle to the wing, so that when the wings were fully swept back the wings had a concave interface, rather than the convex form on the IDS. The ADV has uprated RB199s producing 17,000lb thrust. Though the ADV was destined only for the RAF, manufacture was shared among all three participating countries, just as with the IDS variant. However, manufacture of the fuselage plug and final assembly of the aircraft was carried out at Warton. Altogether, 165 of the 385 RAF Tornados were ADV interceptors.

The first Tornado ADV prototype A.01, registered ZA254, was rolled out at Warton on 9 August and flew on 27 October 1979 piloted by Warton's Chief Test Pilot, David Eagles. The maiden flight was very successful, with the aircraft airborne for ninety-two minutes and reaching Mach 1.2; by flight 3 it had achieved Mach 1.75. The flight test programme developed very successfully except for the radar, the development of which ran behind schedule. The second prototype A.02/ZA267, the first twin-stick ADV, flew on 18 July and the third and final prototype, A.03/ZA283, tasked with radar trials, on 18 November 1980. By the end of the year the F.2 – as the new version was designated in RAF service – had reached the important psychological goal of Mach

2, and two years later cleared Mach 2.16. Throughout the following year an intensive test programme took place at Warton for all three prototypes.

An improved version of the Tornado's power plant (the RB199-34R Mk 104) was produced by Rolls-Royce, offering a significant increase in thrust and incorporating a 14in-longer jet-pipe. In the winter of 1982–3 Tornado prototype ZA267 had the new engine and enlarged reheat system installed, which entailed a slight lengthening of the rear fuselage. ZA267 flew with the new engine in April 1983 and effectively became the prototype for the next version, the F.3. The first eighteen ADVs were completed as F.2s with the lower-powered RB199, of which the first six F.2s were dual-stick trainers. All subsequent aircraft had the higher-powered Mk 104 and were designated as Tornado F.3. The F.3 entered service with the RAF in 1986 and deliveries were completed seven years later. The only other customer for the F.3 was the Royal Saudi Air Force, which ordered twenty-four.

The RAF's F.2s entered service without a functioning radar, but with the advent of the F.3 these problems were solved. Seven squadrons were formed, later reduced to five by the 'peace dividend' of 1990. With the introduction into service of the Eurofighter Typhoon in 2010 the number of Tornado F.3 units fell to just one, No. 111 Squadron at Leuchars. In March 2011 the Tornado F.3 was retired from active service in the RAF.

Specification – Tornado F.3	
Length:	61ft 3½in (18.68m)
Wingspan:	45ft 7½in (13.9m) extended
	28ft 2½in (8.6m) fully swept
Height:	19ft 6½in (5.96m)
MTOW:	61,700lb (28,000kg)
Max speed:	Mach 2.2 (high altitude)
	Mach 1.1 (low altitude)
Range:	460 miles (740km) combat air
	patrol
Crew:	2
Powerplant:	2 × Turbo-Union RB199 Mk 104,
	17,000lb with reheat
Armament:	1 × 27mm Mauser cannon, 4 ×
	AIM-9L Sidewinder, ALARM,
	AMRAAM, ASRAAM

Tornado Export

Canada, as an original partner of the 'Starfighter replacement consortium', made a serious examination of the aircraft in 1977–78 with visits to Tornado sites including Warton, but chose to buy the McDonnell Douglas (now Boeing) F-18. In 1985 Panavia seemed to have broken the barrier to export sales with a small order from Oman for eight ADVs. However, five years later the order was cancelled and the only export sale has been to Saudi Arabia.

Building on BAC's export success in 1965, when it won a large order from Saudi Arabia to supply Lightnings and Strikemasters, in 1985 the RSAF ordered forty-eight IDS and twenty-four ADV Tornados. This contract also included the delivery of British Aerospace (formerly Hawker Siddeley) Hawks and Pilatus PC-9 trainers. In order to expedite deliveries to Saudi Arabia, eighteen RAF and two Luftwaffe IDS Tornados were diverted to the RSAF. The Saudi Air Force also received its twenty-four ADV Tornados ahead of schedule, when the RAF agreed to give up delivery positions. Additionally, in 1993 forty-eight more Tornado IDS were ordered by the RSAF.

RSAF Tornados were formed into two IDS and one ADV squadrons. Saudi Arabia employed them in the 1991 Gulf War against Iraq, following

القوات الجوية الملكية السعودية
ROYAL SAUDI AIR FORCE

Four Royal Saudi Air Force Tornado IDS being readied to leave on delivery.
BAE Systems via Warton Heritage

the occupation of Kuwait. Beginning in 2006, RSAF Tornado IDS aircraft were returned to Warton as part of the RSAF Tornado Sustainment Programme (TSP) to upgrade up to eighty of its fleet. The objective of the TSP was to modify Saudi Tornados in a similar fashion to the work carried out on RAF GR.4s. The first part of the work is carried out in the UK, with the completion on return of the aircraft to Saudi Arabia.

Importance to BAC and Warton of Tornado

The Tornado enabled BAC finally to utilize its variable-geometry experience and to produce a fine aircraft in collaboration with others. Although the vogue for VG has now passed, the Tornado is proof of the great advantage the swing-wing can provide to a small but highly effective war machine. BAC and its successors at Warton and Samlesbury gained the advantage of a large production run, with the threat of cancellation diminished by the very nature of an international collaborative programme.

Following their order for Tornado IDS variants the Royal Saudi Air Force ordered seventy-two ADVs. This aircraft, bearing the temporary RAF serial ZE906, was delivered as 2912 in 1989. BAE Systems via Warton Heritage

Conclusion

Vickers and GEC, which owned BAC, would have preferred to continue with their highly profitable organization, which had made a profit after tax in its last full year of £14.1m and which and had tremendous potential in its Military and Guided Weapons divisions. However, the Labour Government forced their hand and on 29 April 1977 nationalized all of the major British aircraft manufacturers: BAC, Hawker Siddeley and Scottish Aviation to form British Aerospace.

BAC was a remarkable success story: in seventeen short years the Corporation melded four firms into one, gainfully employing more than 30,000 people and exporting a large number of aircraft and missiles. In addition, those products that were bought by the RAF or domestic operators prevented substantial imports into the UK, benefiting Britain's balance of trade.

Why was BAC established? Along with its counterpart, Hawker Siddeley, it was established by Government coercion to strengthen the dangerously fragmented British aircraft industry. Government intervention was necessary owing to the powerful figures still controlling these firms, who would never have freely agreed to merge.

The main partners forming BAC joined for differing reasons. As a condition of the TSR2 contract English Electric and Vickers had to merge. The third shareholder, Bristol, was in a parlous financial state with production of the Britannia complete and only Bloodhound missile work to take it forward – failure to join a large grouping would bring it perilously close to collapse. Huntings was in a different position, not being a shareholder as it was purchased by BAC, and proved a sound investment.

Besides working on behalf of the original founding companies to build, sell and support 'old account' products like the VC10, the Corporation developed the 'new account' aircraft such as the later marks of the Lightning, Bloodhound and Thunderbird. Then there were BAC's new programmes: TSR2, which was the catalyst for the formation of BAC, but brutally cancelled causing redundancies at several sites and a factory closure at Luton. The One-Eleven was moderately successful but unable to fulfil its potential, thwarted by the lack of investment.

Forced into international collaborative projects by Government policy, BAC developed the Jaguar with the French and exported it even when its French partner endeavoured to hinder this. The success of the Anglo-German-Italian Tornado is self-evident, as it is still in use today with each of these countries' air arms. Lastly, the unsurpassed technological challenge of the Anglo-French Concorde proved a triumph for BAC. Even though these three programmes were all collaborative projects, that cannot diminish their significance.

In guided weapons BAC sought to exploit the programmes inherited from its founding companies. However, within two years of BAC being established the vagaries of Government decision-making led to the cancellation of the *Blue Water* missile and the closure of the guided weapons works in Luton. The Corporation fought back and in 1963 established the Guided Weapons Division, later developing and exporting the superlative Rapier, Sea Wolf and Sea Skua. The profit-making ability of this division was to prove especially important to the Corporation in its later years.

In its formative years there had been the expectation of continuing civil airliner projects, but when support for the BAC Three-Eleven was denied by the Government and with the understandably greater emphasis on financial return within the organization in the 1970s, the Commercial Aircraft Division at Weybridge could only develop its One-Eleven in a limited way. So by the last years of its existence BAC had predominantly become a defence contractor, with its Military Aircraft Division centred at Warton and guided weapons at Stevenage. This focus was to some extent inherited by British Aerospace and increasingly so by BAE Systems, which has no civil aircraft programmes.

In the south of England only two BAC sites remain: Filton, which is shared by BAE Systems, Airbus and GKN, and Stevenage where one plant is part of MBDA and the other is with Astrium. However, in the north of England the two former BAC plants at Warton and Samlesbury are still producing, developing and testing military aircraft.

The designing, testing and production of BAC's aircraft, guided weapons and space vehicles were the result of the great endeavours by inventive, talented and creative individuals who can take a justifiable pride in what they achieved. The legacy of their fine work at the British Aircraft Corporation was inherited by British Aerospace and BAE Systems.

A production Concorde at BAC's Fairford Flight Test Centre. Note the RAF VC10s in the background.
BAE Systems

Bibliography

Books

Adams, A.R., *Good Company* (BAC, 1996)

Andrews, C.F. and Morgan, Eric, *Vickers Aircraft since 1908* (Putnam, 1995)

Barnes, C.H., *Bristol Aircraft since 1910* (Putnam, 1970)

Barnes, C.H., *Shorts Aircraft since 1900* (Putnam, 1989)

Barnett Jones, Frank, *Tarnish 6* (Old Forge Publishing, 2008)

Barnett Jones, Frank, *TSR2 Phoenix or Folly* (GMS Enterprises, 1998)

Beamont, Roland, *And the years flew past* (Airlife, 2001)

Blake, John and Hooks, Mike, *40 years at Farnborough* (Haynes, 1990)

Bowman, Martin, *English Electric Lightning* (Crowood, 1997)

Bowman, Martin, *Sepecat Jaguar* (Pen & Sword, 2007)

Burke, Damien, *TSR2 – Britain's Lost Bomber* (Crowood, 2010)

Clarke, Bob, *Jet Provost* (Amberley, 2008)

Darling, Kev, *Concorde* (Crowood, 2004)

Delve, Ken, Green, Peter and Clemons, John, *English Electric Canberra* (Midland Publishing, 1992)

Evans, Harold, *Vickers: Against the odds 1956–77* (Hodder & Stoughton, 1978)

Forbat, John, *The Secret World of Vickers Guided Weapons* (Tempus, 2006)

Freschi, Graziano, *BAC Three-Eleven* (Tempus, 2006)

Gardner, Charles, *British Aircraft Corporation* (Batsford, 1981)

Gardner, Richard, *From Bouncing Bomb to Concorde* (Sutton, 2006)

Hunter, Air Vice Marshal (ed.), *TSR2 with Hindsight* (Royal Air Force Historical Society, 1998)

Jenkins, Roy, *A Life at the Centre* (MacMillan, 1991)

Jones, Barry, *British Experimental Turbojet Aircraft* (Crowood, 2003)

Littlefield, David, *Bristol Britannia* (Halsgrove Press, 1992)

Longworth, J., *Triplane to Typhoon* (Lancashire County Developments, 2005)

Page, Sir Frederick, *Memoirs* (1997 unpublished text held at the National Aerospace Library, Farnborough)

Payne, Richard, *Stuck on the Drawing Board* (Tempus, 2004)

Pearce, Edward, *Denis Healey: a Life in Our Times* (Little, Brown, 2002)

Ransom, Stephen and Fairclough, Robert, *English Electric & their Predecessors* (Putnam, 1987)

Reed, Arthur, *Sepecat Jaguar* (Ian Allan, 1982)

Royal Air Force Historical Society, *The Birth of Tornado* (seminar proceedings, 2002)

Scott, Stewart, *English Electric Lightning Vols 1 & 2* (GMS Enterprises, 2000, 2004)

Silvester, John, *Percival & Hunting Aircraft* (Nelson & Saunders, 1987)

Skinner, Stephen, *BAC One-Eleven* (Tempus, 2002)

Skinner, Stephen, *British Airliner Prototypes* (Midland Counties, 2008)

Skinner, Stephen, *Concorde* (Midland Counties, 2009)

Skinner, Stephen, *Wisley – the story of Vickers' own airfield* (GMS, 2005)

Trubshaw, Brian, *Concorde* (Sutton, 2002)

Trubshaw, Brian, *Test Pilot* (Sutton, 2002)

Williams, Geoffrey, Gregory, Frank & Simpson, John, *Crisis in Procurement: a Case Study of the TSR2* (RUSI, 1969)

Wood, Derek, *Project Cancelled* (Tri-Armour Press, 1990)

Zuckerman, Solly, *Monkeys, Men & Missiles* (Collins, 1988)

Brochures

BAC One-Eleven
Concorde
English Electric Canberra
English Electric Lightning
Vickers VC10
Vickers Viscount

Magazines

Aeroplane
Aircraft Engineering
Air International
Air Pictorial
Flight International
Interavia

Index

RELATED TITLES
FROM CROWOOD

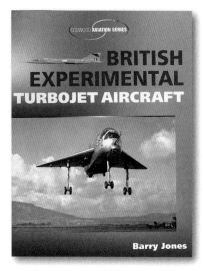

British Experimental Turbojet Aircraft

BARRY JONES
ISBN 978 1 86126 860 0
208pp, 380 illustrations

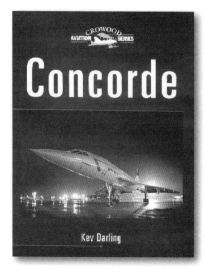

Concorde

KEV DARLING
ISBN 978 1 86126 654 5
200pp, 300 illustrations

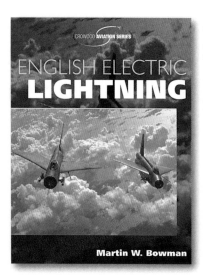

English Electric Lightning

MARTIN BOWMAN
ISBN 978 1 86126 737 5
200pp, 200 illustrations

TSR2

DAMIEN BURKE
ISBN 978 1 84797 211 8
352pp, 450 illustrations

In case of difficulty ordering, contact the Sales Office:

The Crowood Press Ltd
Ramsbury
Wiltshire
SN8 2HR
UK

Tel: 44 (0) 1672 520320
enquiries@crowood.com
www.crowood.com